Moving Mountains

Leon H. Sullivan

Moving Mountains

The Principles and Purposes of Leon Sullivan

Judson Press®
Valley Forge

Moving Mountains: The Principles and Purposes of Leon Sullivan
© 1998 by Judson Press, Valley Forge, PA 19482-0851
All rights reserved.

Cover photo of Rev. Sullivan with the children courtesy of David Barnes, *Philadel-
phia Inquirer.* Other photographs in *Moving Mountains* by and/or courtesy of: Gustave
Assiri, AG; *Business Week;* Carlisle OIC, Pennsylvania; M.Sgt. Joe Fallon, U.S.A.F.;
Jack T. Franklin; International Foundation for Education and Self-Help; Robert E.
Kaiser, Department of State; Karamar Studio; © Leeds Castle Foundation; Bob Mc-
Cartney, Jet Commercial Photographers, Inc.; OIC International; OIC West, Menlo
Park California; Philadelphia OIC, Pennsylvania; Phoenix OIC, Arizona; Ronald Rea-
gan Library; Jules Schick; Rev. Leon Sullivan; Urban Archives, Temple University,
Philadelphia, PA; Official Photograph, The White House, Washington. Specific cita-
tions are noted with the photographs. The cover photograph of Leon Sullivan and
Nelson Mandela (© Arnold Turner) is reprinted with permission of Arnold Turner
for Visual Design.

Library of Congress Cataloging-in-Publication Data

Sullivan, Leon Howard, 1922-
    Moving mountains : the principles and purposes of Leon Sullivan /
Leon H. Sullivan.
      p. cm.
    ISBN 0-8170-1289-3 (hardcover : alk. paper)
    1. Sullivan, Leon Howard, 1922- . 2. Afro-Americans – Biography.
3. Afro-American clergy – Biography. 4. Business consultants – United
States – Biography. 5. Sullivan, Leon Howard, 1922- – Philosophy.
6. Sullivan, Leon Howard, 1922- – Views on Africa.
7. Corporations, American – South Africa. 8. Apartheid – South
Africa. I. Title.
E185.97.S95 1998
973'.0496073'0092–dc21
[b]   98-23790

Printed in the U.S.A.

06   05   04   03   02   01   00   99   98

5   4   3   2   1

To my wife,
"Amazing Grace"

Contents

Foreword

Someone once said, "You cannot teach what you do not know, and you cannot lead where you do not go." There are few, if any, African Americans whose knowledge and experience can surpass Rev. Leon H. Sullivan's.

If I were writing a Freedom Symphony and if that symphony had four movements, the first movement would be the human franchise — the end of slavery, that traumatic period in our nation's history during which Africans subsidized America's development. Harriet Tubman and Dred Scott were overcome by fits of dignity and led our people to emancipation.

The second movement would be the public franchise — the end of legal segregation. A young attorney named Thurgood Marshall, a young seamstress named Rosa Parks, and a young preacher named Martin King changed their minds and changed public policy.

The third movement would be the political franchise — the right to vote. Activists, both black and white, were beaten and bloodied across the Edmund J. Pettus Bridge so that we could fulfill the promise of democracy. Today, America is a Martin Luther King democracy of inclusion, not a Thomas Jefferson democracy of exclusion, because all of our people can be equal participants in the political process.

The fourth movement (the most mature stage of our struggle) would be the economic franchise — the right to our share of the growth, wealth, and prosperity in this country.

Over the last thirty years, both my mission and Leon Sullivan's mission have been to find the notes to finish this Freedom Symphony. We have sought to open doors of opportunity for African Americans and expand the marketplace for everyone. We know that inclusion is the key to economic growth.

Leon Sullivan's story resonates for me, not only because he is a friend but also because we share similar life experiences. Leon was born in Appalachia poverty. I was born in South Carolina poverty. While he was a seminary student in New York, Dr. Sullivan worked with Adam Clayton Powell Sr. and Adam Clayton Powell Jr. He introduced Dr. King to a private-sector economic component, Operation

Breadbasket, which I was privileged to direct. Rev. Leon Sullivan has been and continues to be a selfless visionary who has proved that strong minds break strong chains.

He has made a profound difference in America and Africa as an international bridge builder. In many ways, I feel that we have been partners in this struggle to make Dr. King's dream a reality. Together we have helped tear down walls of apartheid in two nations — both South Africa and the United States. While I was seeking election to the highest political office in the land, Leon was seeking international justice from his seat on one of the highest corporate boards in the world.

Leon Sullivan has been to the mountaintop. He has penetrated the impenetrable halls of corporate America. But he has never forgotten from whence he came. Instead of resting on the mountaintop and relishing all that the power of his personality and his ideas have wrought, Leon Sullivan has time and time again made the long and difficult journey back down the mountain to lead those who have been left behind.

For any serious student of race relations in America, for any serious student of American foreign policy in Africa, for any student of business wanting to break through the glass ceiling that has historically limited African Americans' growth potential, and for any serious student of the American dream, Rev. Leon Sullivan's *Moving Mountains* is a must-read. Whether red, yellow, black, brown, or white, every American ought to read *Moving Mountains*. The Sullivan Principles ought to be as required for every American child as the Pledge of Allegiance and the Bill of Rights.

The requests I receive to contribute to other people's books are as many as the stars in the sky. But rarely is it such a profound pleasure to attach my name and thoughts to a work with as much historical significance as this one. I thank Leon Sullivan for his strength and leadership down through the years.

One hundred years from now, long after Leon and I have departed from this place, African Americans will still point to *Moving Mountains* as a road map to the Promised Land.

Keep Hope Alive!

Rev. Jesse Jackson, Sr.
Founder and President
Rainbow/PUSH Coalition

Preface

NOT LONG AGO I received a call from my longtime secretary, Peaches Love, who suggested that I should see all of the materials in my Philadelphia office regarding my work. She said, "There are thousands and thousands of letters, reports, articles, and pictures here in the files about the Sullivan Principles and your efforts in South Africa." She went on to say, "Reverend, no one will ever know about what you did in South Africa unless you write about the happenings. If you do not write about it, no one else will, and people will never know the great role you played to help end the most reprehensible system of racial discrimination and hate that existed in the world at the time." Through the years many others had asked me to do the same.

I decided that I would take the time to write about the Sullivan Principles, including the problems, the objections, and the successes along with the many series of steps that were required for the Principles to succeed in helping to end injustice and to bring human rights and democracy into South Africa, a process that many have said was the beginning of corporate social responsibility in America and the world. In all, this book will deal with four efforts of faith.

Within these pages, I will write about how I initiated the Sullivan Principles and used the economic strength and clout of corporations from the United States and the world in dismantling and ending apartheid in South Africa. I shall also deal with the organization of the most effective and extensive, nongovernmental, self-help training program in America and, perhaps, the world — the OIC (Opportunities Industrialization Center) — to help school-leavers and dropouts and masses of unemployed persons in cities and towns across America as well as in developing nations, especially Africa, to become self-dependent with better attitudes, skills training, and jobs so that people in need can look in the future to a better way of life. I shall further describe the launching of the African–African American summits, which have become the most important and best-known gathering of people and nations to support sub-Saharan Africa ever attempted. And I shall describe the formulation of ways — devised through a new, growing movement for humanity called IFESH (International Foundation for Education and Self-Help) — to help deal with inadequate education, poverty, disease, child mortality, and tribal and national rivalries and wars in sub-Saharan Africa, which have kept the nations from moving forward and competing equally with the rest of the world. And most of all, I will describe my faith in God, who above all else has made possible these many accomplishments.

For all these efforts, there are many I want to acknowledge for helping me: some living, some dead. Their names are legion, but I can cite only a few whose efforts are intended to represent the hundreds and thousands of others who have worked with me through the years. Among the many whom I would like to thank and acknowledge are Leone Chavet, who first gave me the idea for what later became the OIC program; Thomas Ritter, who more than any other person helped to put the first OIC together in Philadelphia; my longtime friend Clarence Boxdale, who worked with me day by day to get OIC started; and others, such as Fr. Robert E. DuBose Jr.; Judge Allen; Rev. Leonard G. Carr; Bishop Albert Dunston; Sol Feinstone; James Gaither; Rev. Cecil Gallup; Rev. Arthur Johnson; Bishop O. T. Jones III; Rev. Alfred Mallett; Rev. William Shaw; Percy Labohne; Rev. William Glenn Jr., devoted assistant at Zion Baptist Church; our attorneys, Ira J. K. Wells Jr., Herbert R. Cain Jr., and Ron Harper; the loving Utence Hillian and Ruth Talafaro; Joseph Fisher; and many other key supporters at the beginning of OIC — such as John C. Haas of the Haas family of Philadelphia; Richard K. Bennett; John C. Connelly of Crown Cork and Seal; the Philadelphia Foundation; the Samuel S. Fels Fund; the Ford Foundation; Mark Morton; Dick Jackman and Otto Klima of the General Electric Company; Roy Kohler and Luddy Hayden of Chevron; and Ronald Harper — and in the spread of OICs across the United States.

My thanks also goes to the dedicated Elton Jolly, who provided the leadership for the development of OICs across America, and his coworker Kenneth Duffon; Rev. Maurice Dawkins; Rev. Gus Roman; Lawrence Reddrick; the wonderful and ever-supporting vice chairman of OIC of America, Connie Collins; and the able president of OIC of America, Art Taylor, and his staff. In addition, I thank the thousands of dedicated OIC employees and board members throughout the United States who have worked conscientiously and tenaciously to make the OICs of America the most successful self-help movement for the unemployed of all races and creeds. I also thank OIC International: Valo Diallo, the first executive director; the unforgettable Gary Robinson, now deceased, who put OIC International on the world map; Folorunso Salawu of Nigeria, who gave leadership for OIC's development on the African continent; and C. L. Mannings, the wonderful and efficient leader of the OIC worldwide movement, and his staff. My appreciation extends to the thousands of OIC staff members who are training youth in Africa and other parts of the world every day and who have made OIC a household word in many countries, especially Africa.

My special appreciation goes to the African envoys who, in 1991, made possible the beginning of the African–African American summit movement, which is today reaching millions throughout Africa with education, agriculture, economic development, democracy, and peace. Especially I recognize Ambassador Moumouni Djermakoye of the Republic of Niger, with whom I first discussed the idea of the summits, and extend my great thanks to others who helped make the African–African American summits such a successful reality, including Ambassador Charles Gomes, United States envoy from Côte d'Ivoire, who gave special leadership; Ambassador Archibald Mogwe, Embassy of Botswana; Ambassador Jerome Mendouga, Embassy of Cameroon; Ambassador Rufino Mendes, Embassy of Guinea-Bissau; Ambassador Mamadou M. Seck, Embassy of the Republic of Senegal; Ambassador Ibrahima Sy, representative of the Organization of African Unity, who never missed a meeting of the summit planning committee; and to the many other African envoys who helped launch what until now remains as the greatest gathering of African Americans, leaders of African nations, and friends of Africa held on African soil.

I thank the dedicated supporters of IFESH, especially Brooks Mc-Cormick, my friend, who more than any other helped make IFESH possible, and offer my appreciation to Andrew Brimmer, one of the great economic leaders of America, who helped from the beginning with this first private foreign-aid organization in the world. And thanks to others who helped IFESH become such a success, namely, Edward D. Eddy, recently deceased, my longtime co-worker; William E. Simon, former U.S. secretary of the treasury and another great friend; Esther Ferguson, an active helper of youth and lover of Africa; and other great friends, such as Donald Kendall, past chairman and leader of Pepsico; Rev. William Gray; Blenda Wilson; the Honorable Louis Sullivan; Maceo Sloan; the Honorable Lawrence Eagleburger, former U.S. secretary of state; and my special thanks to Lamond Godwin, who has been a friend, councilor, and advisor with OIC, IFESH, and all my other endeavors in the United States and the world. I acknowledge also the existence of so many friends who have helped with special projects, such as the Blacks in Wax Museum and SOS for books and supplies for the schools of Africa, and other summit activities, namely, Isabella Jackson, Jessie A. Woods Jr., Frank Stevens, Clinton Connor, Dr. Mildred Johnson, Anita Chappell, William Downes Jr., Harvey C. Holloway, Hugh Henderson, and a great helper from General Motors, Vivian Rogers Pickard.

I offer my great thanks to those who helped our economic activities in Philadelphia and in other places in America, especially William V. Downes Sr., who gave up everything to work with me, and others, such as Elmer Young, the first economic program manager; Hillary Holloway, the first black legal counsel of the Federal Reserve Bank, who still serves as chair of our economic work in Philadelphia; Allen Harberg, committed developer; and Deacon Jessie Lundy, now deceased, who was one of my closest friends and confidants who provided great leadership to the Progress movement. I acknowledge others, such as Anita Chappell; Wendall Whitlock, the present dedicated chairman of the Progress movement; Mack Washington, the able administrator of Progress Plaza, the largest shopping center built by blacks in America; and all the other members of the board of directors of the Progress Investment Associates.

Thanks especially to all four hundred ministers, many of whom have already been mentioned, who mounted the selective patronage boycotts during the days of the civil rights movement that opened jobs to blacks, women, and other minorities by the thousands and that became the model for the economic development activities of Martin Luther King Jr. And thanks as well to the many, many others, whom I do not have space to name, who helped and sacrificed to make possible the accomplishments of my life's work.

I acknowledge also with appreciation the many from corporate America who diligently strove for the implementation of the Sullivan Principles in South Africa, noting in particular those from 184 U.S. companies who worked with me and supported me in the development of the Principles; D. Reid Weedon Jr. of the Arthur D. Little

Company; Daniel Purnell, my wonderful helper and supporter, about whom more will be written later; also J. A. McCabe, W. Mark Schmitz, and Mark T. Hogan of General Motors; Wayne Fredericks and Robert Copp of Ford; Sal Marzullo of Mobil; Roger Crawford of Johnson & Johnson; Nancy Russell of Pfizer; Gavin Anderson and George Schroll of Colgate-Palmolive; John Groomes of John Deere; and Harold Sims, a longtime friend.

And I particularly acknowledge and thank all the members of Zion Baptist Church of Philadelphia, without whom none of the things written about in this book could have ever been done in Philadelphia, in the United States, in Africa, or around the world. I thank all the deacons, those serving in the early days when I first arrived in Philadelphia, James Gibson and LeRoy Jackson, all the trustees from Eustace Gay and James Buffalo on; and all the thousands of women, men, and children of this great church, who with its unity, its prayers, its financial and other support unequaled by any church I know, helped me with our many endeavors to lift and change the lives of millions in Philadelphia, in America, and throughout the world. In this regard, I also acknowledge the continuing support of the present pastor of Zion, the very highly talented and capable Rev. William Key.

And I extend my greatest appreciation and acknowledgment to the United States government for the help it has given my work, including the State Department for three decades of support and the former Secretaries of State Henry Kissinger, Cyrus Vance, and George Schultz for their encouragement. I thank current Secretary of State Madeleine Albright for her present assistance to my work in Africa. I acknowledge and thank the Agency for International Development (USAID) for assisting OIC and IFESH efforts in Africa, especially Administrator Brian Atwood, for all his support for our work, and the wonderful AID project officer Don Muncy, who has been such a help to us.

Special thanks also to Peaches Love, my ever-faithful and supportive secretary for three decades, for her indispensable experience and assistance in gathering materials for this book and to a truly remarkable man, C. T. Wright, for all his inspiration and continued support. Also, my appreciation and thanks to Samuel Atteh of IFESH, who ably assisted with research and in other valuable ways, to Santry Elmer, who assisted me in the compilation of this manuscript, along with Callie Bonine, William Downes Jr., and others from the Philadelphia and Phoenix staffs, and to the wonderful editorial assistance of Mary Nichols, Tina Edgington, and John Eagleson.

Most of all, my thanks to "Amazing Grace," my wife, to whom this book is dedicated, about whom more will be written, and without whom I perhaps would not be living today. I will never be able to repay her for standing by me and helping me throughout all these years while still accomplishing many significant goals through her work as a trained educator. She developed "The Miniversity," one of the most successful educational programs ever attempted in Philadelphia, and initiated one of the first successful police and community relations programs in that city. Through her efforts hundreds of men and women were prepared to become members of the police force.

These same heartfelt thanks go also to my children, Howard, Julie, and Hope, who even now continue to work with me with the things I attempt to do.

To all of these and many more, I would like to say, "Thank you." And above all else, my thanks to almighty God for giving me the opportunity and the strength and the faith to do whatever I have done to help people to help themselves.

Abbreviations

ACES	Americans for the Competitive Enterprise System
ADB	African Development Bank
AFRICARE	development organization doing important work in Africa with offices in the United States
AKA	Alpha Kappa Alpha Sorority
ANC	African National Congress
ECA	Economic Commission of Africa
ECOWAS	Economic Community of West African States
EEOC	Equal Employment Opportunity Code
FAO	Food and Agriculture Organization
G-7	Group of Seven
G-8	Group of Eight
HBCU	historically black colleges and universities
IFESH	International Foundation for Education and Self-Help
IFP	International Fellows Program
IMF	International Monetary Fund
LINKS	nationwide major women's organization in America and other nations
NAACP	National Association for the Advancement of Colored People
NGO	nongovernmental organization
OAU	Organization of African Unity
OIC	Opportunities Industrialization Centers
PAC	Pan-African Congress
PROSERA	Program of Support to Educational Rehabilitation in Africa
PVO	private voluntary organization

SADC	Southern African Development Community
SAP	Structural Adjustment Program
SHIP	Self-Help Investment Program
SOS	Support of Sub-Saharan Africa
TFA	Teachers for Africa
UN	United Nations
UNESCO	United Nations Educational, Scientific, and Cultural Organization
UNICEF	United Nations International Children's Emergency Fund
USAID	United States Agency for International Development
WHO	World Health Organization

Chapter 1

David Meets Goliath

MY NEW WHITE SHIRT and black suit, freshly cleaned and pressed, went well with my uncharacteristically black-shined shoes as I stood in my room at the Plaza Hotel in New York City. My wife, Grace, reached up to straighten my new light gray tie. Since she is five feet seven inches tall and I am six feet five, it was quite a reach, but one she had made many times before. Applying the finishing touches, she spoke: "David goes forth to meet Goliath." Her words rang profoundly true.

The date was March 1, 1971, and I — a black man born in a back alley in a coal-mining town in West Virginia — was about to attend my first meeting of the board of General Motors (GM). I was about to assume my role as one of twenty-one top decision makers for the largest corporation in the world. It was the stuff of which dreams are made. This particular dream was once thought impossible; now it was about to become reality. But the road ahead would be full of challenges and confrontations. David was indeed venturing forth to meet Goliath.

Across the street from the Plaza Hotel loomed the tall, gleaming-white General Motors Building, the site of my first official confrontation with the white corporate world. This opportunity, forged through years of struggle, suffering, and the tears of many, was now just a short walk away. A new chapter in my life was about to be written, one that would have an impact on the human rights policies of corporations in the United States and in other parts of the world.

Little did I know that my walk across the street would, by God's grace, sow seeds that would grow to help bring down one of history's most unjust and inhumane systems of racial segregation: South African apartheid. Little did I realize that my walk would lead to the building of a bridge between two continents — North America and Africa. This bridge of understanding, support, and interchange would in time make a difference in the lives of millions of Africans —

1

especially youth — through education and business, as well as through the important task of building democratic nations throughout Africa. Nor did I realize the extent to which this bridge between continents would raise aspirations and hopes among black youth in American cities who had labored too long without an identity, whose lives were falling apart, and who were sinking deeper and deeper into poverty, crime, drugs, and unemployment. As David went forth to meet Goliath, God was present. God was about the business both of tearing down the wrong and building up the right.

I put on my overcoat. As I took my hat in hand, I kissed Grace good-bye. It was a brisk Monday morning. Once outside, I pulled my hat firmly down on my head and raised the collar of my coat about my neck. My journey into a world I had not known before — and toward a new kind of future — had begun. I had long thought about what this day might bring. I thought of the potential ramifications for thousands, maybe millions, of people whose faces I would never see and whose names I would never know. I approached the large revolving glass door, fully composed. Or so I thought. Then came a sudden tightening in my stomach, a wailing inside of me unlike anything I had felt before. I stopped and said a prayer. God gave me strength. I pushed the revolving door and walked on, never to look back.

Going through that door would change my life forever. General Motors would never be the same. Nor would other large corporations in America who would open their doors to African Americans in leadership positions. Their progressive policies would eventually affect other parts of the world, especially South Africa, the land of apartheid. *New Yorker* magazine would later proclaim March 1, 1971, "a watershed for change in South Africa."[1]

The objective adopted by Adam Clayton Powell Jr., the most powerful champion for equal rights for blacks in America at the time, had been realized; his hopes had been fulfilled. For it was he who "discovered" me while I was a seventeen-year-old pastor of a small black church in a virtually anonymous West Virginia coal-mining town. It was he who urged me to come to New York after finishing my college education so I could work with him in Harlem. Later I did, becoming his assistant at the largest black Baptist church in the world. He would often say to the congregation and others, "Do you see this young man, Leon Sullivan? Well, I want to prove that I can take a gangling boy from the hills of West Virginia, who looks like he has never worn a pair of shoes in his life, and make him a successful minister and leader of our people."

Now here I was, thirty years later, in a way fulfilling Rev. Powell's prediction by walking into a meeting as the world's first black corporate board member. By God's grace, there were also other ways in which I had lived up to what Rev. Powell saw in me. By then I had established OIC (Opportunities Industrialization Centers), the largest, fastest-growing, and most successful skills training program in the United States, a program that through the years has helped millions of African American people get training and jobs. And I had developed and pastored one of the largest churches in America. From all appearances, even before that historic board meeting, Adam Clayton Powell Jr. was right about how God would use this gangling boy from the hills of West Virginia. But in some ways, the story was just about to begin.

It was 8:00 A.M. when I stepped inside the GM Building. Uniformed guards were waiting. They introduced themselves, then escorted me to the elevator and up to the twenty-fifth floor. As the elevator doors parted, I was greeted by a barrage of flashing lights, television cameras, and reporters. The arrival of GM's first black board member would be the main story the next day in the business sections of newspapers throughout America and around the globe. More importantly, this day would launch the struggle to help end an unparalleled condition of hate, prejudice, and injustice that, in its brazen disposition, had appalled and defied the entire world.

This book provides a record of how a struggle begun in a boardroom of the world's largest corporation played a major role in changing conditions of inhumanity in the Republic of South Africa in a time when some believed reforms could result only from a cataclysmic and bloody racial war. By God's grace and guidance, I had a different plan. What became known as the "Sullivan Principles" gave companies in the United States and around the world an effective, systematic way to break down the wall of apartheid through peaceful economic means. Largely using economic forces and moral persuasion, the Sullivan Principles ended racial discrimination and segregation in companies doing business in South Africa and helped end the apartheid system. These changes came about without the loss of a single life in any company during the entire time the Principles were active in South Africa.

This book tells, for the first time, the full story of how these Principles came into being, of how they evolved and were put into practice. It discusses how these same kinds of principles might be applied today in order to promote human rights, social justice, and peace in troubled spots around the world. The Principles are rooted in the assertion that when it comes to issues of justice and human rights, the actions of companies can be more powerful than the actions of governments. After all, governments need companies to develop their economies, but companies do not necessarily need governments to do business.

This book also tells the story of a movement, rooted in the success of the Sullivan Principles, to bring together Africans, African Americans, the African diaspora, and friends of Africa from around the world to meet on African soil in order to work together for the advancement of Africa and, in particular, for the development of sub-Saharan Africa. This book presents, for the first time, a far-reaching plan for economic, educational, and cultural development in South Africa, a plan that places democracy and peace at the center of a twenty-first-century "African renaissance."

In my book *Build Brother Build*, I wrote:

> When I plan for the future, my thoughts turn eventually to Africa. Somehow, I believe, slavery will be turned to the advantage of our future. The day will come when the continent from which my forefathers came will blossom into a paradise. I have a feeling that my ultimate freedom and my ultimate security are tied to the development of Africa. Of course I have no intention of forsaking America, for America is my home and I have helped to build her and shape her. But like the Jews and others who came to make this country what it is, I need an anchor in the past, a place my children can proudly call their ancestral home. My citizenship is here, but a part of my spirit is in Africa, also.
>
> I envision a bridge from America to Africa over which one day my children and my black brothers and black sisters will move freely from one side to the other and back again. The Bible has said, "The day will come when Ethiopia shall stretch forth her hands again," and I know that day is coming, though I shall not live to see it. The time is not far off when black technicians, artisans and craftsmen by the thousands and tens of thousands will visit a flourishing Africa, helping to mold that continent into a new greatness glorious to see.[2]

I believe that by God's grace and the hard work of God's people, the world will witness the emergence of a new Africa to the extent many today consider impossible. I believe this because I know it was once considered impossible for a black man to walk into a corporate board meeting in America. That mountain was moved, others have been moved, and still others remain to be moved.

The Bible tells us that "faith is the substance of things hoped for, the evidence of things not seen" (Hebrews 11:1 KJV) and that "if ye have faith as a grain of mustard seed" (Matthew 17:20 KJV), mountains can be moved. Moving mountains requires faith and determination, as well as the capacity to accept God's love and to recognize God's presence and power in ourselves and among the poor and needy of the world. I firmly believe that with faith and determination, there is no such thing as an impossible dream. Gandhi envisioned freedom for India from the British Empire at a time when the world believed it impossible. He used the strength of his mind, and he combined faith with action till his dream became real. Martin Luther King Jr. envisioned the end of legalized segregation in America. By the strength of his mind and faith and by the power of his actions, his dream was materialized.

Anything that can be conceived is within our reach. This includes moving the mountains that stand in the way of freedom, justice, and truth. A wise man once said, "Climb the tallest tree in the forest, and if you fall, at least you will land on the top of the shorter trees." My philosophy of life and ministry revolves around climbing the tallest trees we can find, of fighting the toughest battles. David went forth to meet Goliath. And as a result, mountains would be moved.

Notes

1. *The New Yorker,* May 14, 1979.
2. Leon H. Sullivan, *Build Brother Build* (Philadelphia: Macrae Smith, 1969), 178–79.

Chapter 2

Formative Influences

A S A CHILD, I knew — both instinctively and through what I was taught — that people were neither inferior because they were black nor superior because they were white. An incident occurred when I was eight years old that I have never forgotten. I bought a Coke at a drugstore, and when I went to sit down, a white man told me that black boys had to stand. But I knew better. I knew that a person was simply a person. People, of course, are different. Some are tall; some are short. Some have more talents and gifts in certain areas than others. But none of these differences makes any of us more or less of a person in the eyes of God. This simple, fundamental assertion lies at the heart of my philosophy of what it means to be human. Each of us has been placed into a different set of circumstances and conditions. Each of us is confronted with a unique set of challenges and opportunities. What we do with those circumstances and opportunities determines who we become as persons.

For as long as I can remember, issues of race and poverty have been at the forefront of my mind. And from my earliest days in Charleston, the capital of West Virginia, I was convinced that the solutions that would eventually lift the burdens of black people — and of the poor everywhere — would come from the guidance of God and from the people themselves. If people wanted something changed, they would have to go out and work for change.

I arrived at my convictions largely through the influence of my grandmother Carrie, a constant and powerful presence in my life who taught me early on the importance of faith, determination, faith in God, and especially self-help. She regularly reinforced the view that no one — not even God — would help me if I was not willing to help myself. I also encountered this message in the preaching I heard and in the lessons from the Bible I read over and over again. In admonishing me to "help our people," my grandmother said to me, "God can

6

lift a person if a person will help God lift them." My grandmother's influence is evident in a poem titled "Colored Man" that I wrote at age twelve:

> Stop your thinking God's against you, Colored Man,
> Stop your wild and cursed sinning, Colored Man,
> I know what you have to stand,
> I know how your race is banned,
> But give yourselves, your sons a hand, Colored Man.
>
> And stop your loud and boisterous talking, Colored Man,
> Learn to give and help each other, Colored Man,
> Conduct your life in such a way
> The whole world will have to say,
> "You're OK ..., Colored Man."

Because people can accomplish more working together than they can working alone, I believed from my youth that the church had an important role to play, even though most of the churches I attended did not directly address social issues. The services were filled with emotion; the preaching was lively and moving. Still, I was convinced that something was missing, that the church should be doing more. I held this view through high school and college. I carried it with me through my pastoral ministry. In fact, my call to the ministry was more practical than most. That is to say, given what I wanted to accomplish for people and for the church, I was convinced that pastoral ministry was the best way to do it.

My grandmother played a major role in steering me toward the ministry. Though poor in terms of material standards, she was rich in faith and inspirational power. She stressed the importance not only of serving God but of moving ahead on my own with every strength that God had given me. Another important influence was Rev. Moses Newsome, a young minister who came to pastor the First Baptist Church of Charleston when I was in my teens. His spiritual leadership was characterized by a remarkable commitment to help the downtrodden, especially black youth. Rev. Newsome reached out and down to the poorest and the lowest he could find. During this time when I was highly impressionable, I was watching him more closely than he probably realized. I admired him and determined this was the kind of man I wanted to be. I became a preacher at the age of seventeen and was the pastor of two churches at eighteen.

As young people inevitably do, I wondered about my future. Unlike teenagers in the majority culture, as a black youth I came to believe that my future would depend largely on the extent to which we in the black community could unite to help ourselves. This was the message I believed should be proclaimed not just in sermons but through our actions. The church had to be more than a voice. It had to demonstrate the will of God for humankind. And the will of God to me included reaching the needy, the unjustly treated, the poor. These convictions are as important to me today as they were over six decades ago. I believe that Christian ministry must be geared to action and that the problems of our society will be solved when people of faith take action.

Everything I saw and experienced in my youth, beginning with the chronic deprivation in the back hills of West Virginia, reinforced my view of what I was called to do. I would later see this same kind of poverty over and over again in the Black Belt, the Delta, Appalachia, and urban centers, such as New York City, Philadelphia, and Soweto. Early on, I came increasingly to the sobering realization that solutions could not be found in government alone. Nor were solutions forthcoming from the private sector. Politicians and social workers could in some cases alleviate the sting of living in poverty, but significant and lasting change would have to come through the church, especially in the black community, where the church was and is the most powerful and most free institution. My hope for a better future came from seeing ministers and congregations working together with others as agents for change, striving for real solutions in large part by encouraging people to take responsibility for improving their lives.

My personal mission as a Christian minister was to proclaim a pragmatic gospel, one that reassured people of God's love and God's desire to relieve the burdens of the underprivileged. In all my years of ministry, I have not found it necessary to change this essential message or my view of the church's mission. This was the message I advanced in my ministry in Harlem and later in New Jersey, Philadelphia, in the boardrooms of America, and ultimately in South Africa and across the continent of Africa. I preached — and continue to preach — that we need more Christians who strive day by day to work out the soul salvation of people and the salvation of the community. We need more people of faith grappling with the problems that affect people where they are. We need more people to take seriously the message found in the parable of the good Samaritan. Ministry must extend beyond the

Sunday-morning sermon. It must be active in the streets. It must tend to the material needs of people as well as to the needs of the soul, for a person's physical and spiritual beings cannot be separated.

These ideas formed the heart of my ministry philosophy when I moved from West Virginia in 1943 upon graduation from college to New York City. There I labored in Harlem with Adam Clayton Powell Jr., addressing the problems of youth, crime, and drugs. Little did I know that I was in training for other causes that lay before me. It was as though I were in school, engaged in a carefully planned training program of which I was not aware but through which God was preparing me for what was to come.

God has a way of preparing us, sometimes in spite of ourselves, for the work we are going to do. And so it was in all my work in the cities with community groups and movements. This work includes the March on Washington movement, led by A. Philip Randolph, one of the greatest black American leaders of the century. It was the early March on Washington in 1941 that moved the then president of the United States, Franklin Delano Roosevelt, to enact legislation that opened the way for blacks to have equal access to jobs in America during the days of World War II. Under the tutelage of Randolph were formed my ideas on nonviolent, direct action and on the development of the community through community-based organizations. It was he who taught me how to organize, how to mobilize, how to develop and guide nonviolent, direct-action efforts. And it was he who gave me the extraordinary opportunity to become president of the March on Washington movement at twenty-one years of age.

My experiences as assistant minister at the Abyssinian Baptist Church in Harlem, pastored by the dynamic Rev. Powell, reinforced my view that the church should be active in the community. An effective leader in the movement for black rights, Rev. Powell, more than anyone this century, articulated a plan for meaningful political action on the part of blacks. All of what I learned and experienced under him would one day find application in the land of apartheid. God was preparing me, teaching me, how to handle myself, what to do, when and how to do it.

Grace and I were two young souls trying to find our way in the world and striving to do what we thought was best to help others. After we served two years in Harlem, my young wife began to be concerned that the attention and acclaim I was getting was beginning to affect me negatively. Grace saw my feet rising from the ground, as if being lifted by a balloon. She let me know that my effectiveness in ministry was directly tied to my ability to keep my feet on the ground and that if I did not get back down to earth and do what I could to help the people, there would be nothing left of me. One evening, on a park bench across from the apartment where we lived, she gave it to me straight: "It's time for you to leave Harlem."

I had been in New York only for a short time when I met Grace. It was by far the most important meeting of my life. I met her on a blind date when a doctor friend had brought her to the apartment where I was staying. When I heard the footsteps in the hall, even before I had seen her, I somehow knew that something special was about to happen in my life. And when I opened the door and saw her, I knew I had seen Grace a thousand times in my mind and in my dreams.

Now Grace stood before me, telling me it was time to leave Harlem. Believing as I did that God had brought her into my life for a purpose, and with full faith in her integrity, I knew that if Grace thought it was time to leave Harlem, it was time to leave Harlem. I had arrived in New York from West Virginia wearing a hillbilly hat and carrying a bag, wrapped with a rope, which held all my possessions. In 1945, Grace and I left for New Jersey in much the same way, our few furnishings strapped on the back of a model-T Ford truck driven by the head deacon of the little church to which I had been called.

While in South Orange, New Jersey, at the First Baptist Church, I continued my formal education at Union Theological Seminary and Columbia University in New York City. I also began to experiment with new models of church ministry in such an area as community projects — building homes for the poor, organizing athletic teams, and pushing the village fathers to do more for black people with jobs and other opportunities. This kind of emphasis was needed in small towns where black people lived all across America. I put a high premium on education, and as far as I can recall, every young person in the church who finished high school went to college.

I will never forget my formative years of ministry in Harlem and in South Orange, New Jersey. They were a prelude, a training ground. I was still learning, exploring, developing ideas and skills. Then, after five years in South Orange, I was called to pastor Zion Baptist Church in Philadelphia. The time had come to test my wings.

Chapter 3

The Selective Patronage Movement

WHILE IN NEW YORK and New Jersey, I had worked with young people and community organizations and had also worked on behalf of civil rights. The move to Zion Baptist provided the opportunity to put my self-help ideas and ministry philosophies to work in the context of a major urban arena that had more than its share of problems and needs. I was anxious but also excited to discover if and how my most cherished ideals could make a difference.

Creating economic opportunities for blacks and other minority groups who had experienced discrimination stood at the top of my list of priorities. In the larger society, many mistakenly assumed that once the laws were changed to end segregation, all the problems of minority cultures would be solved. But black people learned from experience that social and economic discrimination would continue long after human rights laws were enacted as a result of the efforts of the civil rights movement.

As late as 1960, less than 1 percent of the managerial jobs in the United States were held by blacks, and of those most were with government agencies such as the postal service. A large proportion of blacks worked in service occupations, and many were still employed as domestics. Since jobs in private business were severely restricted, blacks entered the labor market in other areas, finding government jobs as postal-service employees, clerical workers, and lower-paid public servants. A limited number of opportunities were available in traditional professions, such as education, medicine, law, and the ministry. But when it came to jobs at banks, insurance companies, corporations, and retail stores, black people had virtually no chance. The doors were closed.

It was my mission to either get the doors opened or knock them down. This endeavor began with a group of four hundred black ministers in Philadelphia, of which I was the leader. Beginning in 1958, as

11

civil rights protests and demonstrations began to spring up, the four hundred of us launched what was to become a highly successful boycott campaign. The boycott was designed to eliminate employment barriers against black workers in the city. Using our pulpits as a common base, we persuaded the Philadelphia black community to use its purchasing power against companies who refused to comply with the request for fair job opportunities for black youths. In essence, we were saying that we could not in good moral conscience remain silent while members of our congregations patronized companies that discriminated in the employment of our people. We called our campaign "selective patronage."

Our campaign's success was rooted largely in an understanding of how corporate America thinks and works. Shortly after arriving in Philadelphia, I began to learn more about companies and what makes them tick. I joined a Philadelphia organization called ACES (Americans for the Competitive Enterprise System). To my knowledge, I was the organization's first black member. For years, I was very active with ACES and learned all I could about the ups and downs of the corporate world. In addition, I became an active member of the Junior Chamber of Commerce. I attended every meeting I could. I listened to the young executives talking about their businesses and their plans for the future. These young members of the Junior Chamber of Commerce were later to become chairpersons and leaders of their companies. The information and insights I gleaned would serve me well for many years to come.

Through my contacts with ACES, my active involvement with the Junior Chamber of Commerce, and my association with members of both groups, I found out that with most companies there was a thin line between making money and losing money and that the profit margins of some of the largest corporations were less than 3 percent. I also learned how vital the black purchaser was to the success of virtually every consumer company in the United States. I found that blacks, with 12 percent of the population at the time, were an indispensable consumer necessity for most profitable company operations. I found this to be true in every major city in America — every department store, food chain, soft drink company, bread company, ice cream company, and major retail establishment. All of them depended on the black customer to stay in business. I found that the black community as consumers in Philadelphia, Detroit, Kansas City, Atlanta, and in other cities throughout America was as important to the economic vitality and bond rating of a city as its tax base. Even today, selective purchase decisions of blacks in America can determine the future of much of the country's enterprise since automobiles, televisions, VCRs, washing machines, and computers are big items with black buyers.

The first step in our selective patronage movement was to form small visitation committees, which paid calls on targeted companies to tell them about the black community's needs. Members of these ad hoc committees were chosen on a rotating basis to provide as broad a leadership participation as possible. The committees acted on behalf of the group of four hundred ministers. Their initial task was to ask top company executives to open to blacks a certain number of jobs in specific categories of employment from which blacks had been previously excluded. The categories included clerical, secretarial, drafting, sales, and management.

If within a designated period, usually a month, the company had not met the ministers' demands, we would hold a meeting, usually scheduled for midnight at one of the churches. Members of the press were barred in order to allow the ministers the freest possible expression. We listened to the recommendation of the ad hoc committee reporting to the four hundred, then took a vote on whether to advocate selective patronage. If our decision was to so advocate, word of the recalcitrant company went out from four hundred pulpits across Philadelphia on the following Sunday. By Monday morning, three hundred thousand black people around the city had heard the message, even if they had not watched television, listened to the radio, or read a newspaper. Abiding by the recommendation, they either stopped buying certain items, commodities, or brands, or they stopped patronizing certain establishments.

These boycotts began in 1958 and achieved formidable results. The impact of the ministers' message was heeded throughout the United States, as similar projects took root in other cities. In just four years, the black community of Philadelphia successfully boycotted twenty-nine companies. Many other firms met our demands to prevent us from calling a boycott. In 1962, as a result of our efforts, some three hundred businesses in the Philadelphia-Delaware Valley area agreed to a policy of fair employment practices. For the first time, blacks began to appear in "good" jobs in private industry in ever increasing numbers throughout Philadelphia and its environs. In time, tens of thousands of jobs opened to young black workers as the message spread throughout the Philadelphia business community: "Get your house in order and employ blacks because the ministers are coming." In fact, it became good business practice to hire black workers to fill jobs in Philadelphia. The ministers had broken employment barriers; a new day had come for blacks in the City of Brotherly Love.

The success of the selective patronage movement prompted Martin Luther King Jr. to call on me to help him develop a similar program for America. It would be called "Operation Breadbasket" and was later led by Rev. Jesse Jackson. The success also led to the need to address another problem. Now that jobs had been opened to black people, we realized that in many cases blacks lacked the necessary skills to move into these jobs, for blacks in America had never been trained or prepared for the kinds of industrial employment opportunities created by the boycotts. We were discovering that integration without preparation led to frustration. The next step was to begin training people for available jobs. That thinking led to the establishment of the first Opportunities Industrialization Center (OIC), an organization that would eventually affect the lives of millions of people in the United States and abroad.

Chapter 4

The Opportunities Industrialization Centers Movement

THE NEED FOR JOB TRAINING and retraining in minority communities in the '60s was immense. Thousands upon thousands of people were out of work; many of them were out of hope. The training needed to be of high quality and would have to be done on a massive scale. Conditions called for a brand-new model, one in which programs would be developed within the communities where unemployed people lived. They could not be called *schools* because in the minds of the people, schools had already failed them. So we decided to call the new programs *centers*. And because we realized the importance of stressing opportunity, we decided to name them "Opportunities Industrialization Centers." Today these centers are known by millions throughout America and around the world as OICs. (See list of cities in Appendix E.) A new vision had been born.

Among our first priorities was to address the attitudes of the people. Many had given up hope, having been crushed by life's circumstances, including discrimination. Some had lost all feelings of self-worth. All their lives, black people had heard the message, "White is right; brown, stick around; black, get back." They had been brainwashed into thinking themselves inferior. Many blacks and Hispanics genuinely believed they lacked the intelligence to succeed in a meaningful career. Many were on welfare. The median age of those who came for training was about twenty-five, though most had dropped out of school by the eighth grade. Many lacked basic communication skills. Their poor hygiene not only testified to a low self-image but limited their ability to succeed in the business world.

The OIC conducted its training in two phases in order to serve its purposes most effectively. The first phase, called the *feeder program*, focused on attitude. We discovered that for the unemployed and poor

15

people who had lost hope in the system, the keys to learning were motivation, the development of self-esteem, and the formation of positive
attitudes. They had to develop self-respect. They had to try to put behind them a desire for revenge, as well as feelings of distrust, anger,
and hopelessness. To serve these needs, the feeder program consisted
of courses ranging from black history to etiquette, hygiene, and basic
grammar. Each course was designed to inspire trainees to lift their
sights above their present condition and to aspire to a better quality of
life. Our goal was to enable grown men and women to develop wholly
new images of themselves and their capabilities — in other words, to
be born anew virtually overnight.

The second phase of the program addressed specific skills training
for jobs that existed — or could be created — in the community. The
decisions regarding what was offered were not made haphazardly, for
we knew that if we trained people for jobs that did not exist, they
would be no better off than before. We concentrated on reaching, motivating, training, and placing people. Then we followed up to ensure
that the trainees maintained a high level of performance and remained
on the job.

Because no federal money for this sort of job training was available
in 1964, we looked to local government, businesses, and citizens to
help transform this idea into reality. One could say that ours was a
self-help strategy by necessity. With some lobbying, we convinced the
Philadelphia City Council to allow us to rent an old, abandoned jailhouse in a poor section of the city for one dollar a year. This jailhouse
became our headquarters. A former synagogue nearby became the
location for our first feeder program. We sought and received equipment for skills training from local companies and businesses, including
taprooms and pool halls. Schoolchildren collected bags of pennies.
I secured financial contributions from my own congregation, as did
other black ministers throughout Philadelphia. We got a $50,000 gift
from an anonymous donor, and a second mortgage on my house provided additional seed funds. (Later, on one occasion when money was
tight, Grace and I took out a loan against our house in order to meet
the payroll.) Recognizing that active community involvement was crucial to the success of OIC, we gathered a board of community leaders,
which chose the staff to initiate the program. In the early years we
also depended heavily on local volunteer counselors and teachers.

On a cold Sunday morning, January 26, 1964, the four hundred ministers who had led Philadelphia's boycott movement announced the opening of our first center. Politicians, businessmen and business-women, community leaders, bands, choirs, and Boy and Girl Scouts were in attendance. One of the largest crowds ever to assemble in Philadelphia gathered at the old jailhouse-turned-job-training-center to wish us well. Traffic was tied up for miles around. The next day our first students, 135 men and 165 women, filled the classrooms. Our waiting list quickly swelled to more than three thousand.

This first center trained students in typing, drafting, electronics, and machine tooling, as well as in the more traditional service jobs, such as waiting tables and cooking. Students strove to learn and to develop these skills quickly so they could enter the workforce as soon as possible. Absenteeism was almost nonexistent. The students knew they had to be diligent since ten people were waiting in line to take any unoccupied seat.

We had decided that every student who came to OIC must start at the feeder. Some believed they should be admitted immediately into the second phase of the program, but I did not want to stigmatize OIC trainees at the offset with the "high" and the "low." All would start together at the same place. I went through the feeder program myself to prove the point. Through an intensive counseling program, we were able to determine future assignments and to judge on the basis of progress how quickly a trainee should be moved out of the feeder program into an OIC skill training class and into a job, or directly into a job. We did this without exams because we did not want to scare people away at the beginning. Each person moved at his or her own speed.

Despite their impoverished backgrounds, these young adults attacked their studies with great enthusiasm and with a strong sense of solidarity. Groups of students created brotherhood funds, gathering dimes, quarters, and dollars to help one another in times of need, whether that meant securing food, clothing, or bus fare. Some trainees walked as far as five miles to and from the center each day. Our students knew what they wanted and worked to achieve those goals.

Remarkably, 83 percent of those first trainees quickly secured jobs. And through them, the OIC began to develop a reputation for training the best, the most dependable and effective, workers in town. Many possessed criminal records, which previously had given prospective employers pause. But once these men and women passed through

OIC, their pasts no longer mattered. In the eyes of employers, they had become new people.

From the beginning, we expected our program to expand throughout the city. A little more than a year after the first center opened, a second was established in West Philadelphia. Fund-raising for three additional centers began that same month. Before long, OICs were in every section of the city. The OIC had become a powerful movement among Philadelphia's unemployed poor. The program's slogan was "We Help Ourselves," and our symbol was a key with the message "To Open Any Door."

The success soon spread to other cities, as word got out about what was happening in Philadelphia. In June of 1967 I received a call from the White House. President Lyndon Johnson had heard of the OIC program and wanted to see it for himself. By then, OIC's success had enabled us to secure some small federal grants. Prior to President Johnson's arrival, the Office of Economic Opportunity in 1967 had allocated $6.5 million to further our expansion. On June 29, President Johnson arrived and toured two of the several centers that were operating in Philadelphia. At the old jailhouse, the president put his hand on one of the cells that still remained and said to America, "Having been here today, I think we are going to make it." That was the day the nation learned about OIC and its achievements; the president began to put the full force of his Great Society program behind OIC's efforts.

Thus, the time had arrived for OIC to assume a national role. The same urgent need that sparked OIC's development in Philadelphia existed in cities across the United States. As a result of selective patronage, boycotts, and other civil rights efforts such as the new "equal opportunity" laws, countless jobs were now open to blacks and other minorities. OIC filled the essential role of preparing people for the work they wanted to do. Within a few years, OIC programs were established in nearly one hundred American cities.

The underlying convictions and philosophy that gave rise to OIC programs are as relevant now as they were in the 1960s. The needs today in the United States and around the world for self-respect and the opportunity to learn a job and do it have not changed. The solutions offered by the OIC movement are as relevant now as they ever were, which is why OICs continue to thrive. Nearly thirty-five years after OIC's inception, it is the nation's largest skills training program for unemployed and underemployed people. Indeed, OIC has expanded from its black origins to serve disadvantaged persons of all races, colors, and creeds. In the West, many of the trainees are Hispanic and Asian. In Appalachia, most are rural whites. In the Deep South and in northern and eastern urban areas, the majority of trainees are black. In the Midwest, many trainees are American Indians.

OIC's successes, born of the spirit of the early civil rights movement, have not faltered with the changing social or political contexts or with its expansion into other ethnic communities. Amid the external changes, the emphasis on instilling pride and imparting skills remained constant. As the program has grown, it has adapted to the changing needs of the workforce and to the heightened aspirations of those it serves. The nearly one hundred OIC affiliates throughout the nation now offer courses in such areas as data and word processing, bookkeeping, and para-professional health care. OIC also provides training for both management and supervisory positions and has trained thousands of entrepreneurs through the years. In the Philadelphia OIC, more than seventy-five thousand people have been trained in skills for jobs, and thousands of them have become entrepreneurs.

Because OIC believes that the poor are entitled to assistance, we have tried to obtain public funding for our program, but we do not depend on it. While many local affiliates prospered under the funding, others were unable to adapt their comprehensive training program to government's decentralized and often fragmented models. Some OICs with unassailable records of effectiveness found themselves in a prolonged struggle with government officials in their jurisdictions. Through the years, OIC has had to be flexible in terms of its relationship with the government. When the government zigged, OIC zigged, and when the government zagged, OIC zagged. In 1982, for example, the passage of the Job Training Partnership Act marked a shift in priorities with the change from the Carter to the Reagan administration. This act repealed government-supported training programs. But through it all, OIC continued to expand and grow. While most government-supported programs closed, OIC programs kept going. The current emphasis in the United States on providing training and jobs has been the heart of OIC's mission for over three decades.

Among the keys to OIC's success has been its ties with the business community. An estimated twenty thousand businesses in the United

States work with OICs. Most of them have employed OIC trainees. The OIC National Industrial Advisory Council, consisting of CEOs and senior officers of some of the nation's largest companies, serves both as a conduit between OIC and the technical and financial resources available in the private sector and as an advocate for OIC in the public and private spheres. OIC has sustained its close ties with the business world in large part by entering into joint job ventures with private firms. For example, a number of local OICs have established high-tech training centers through partnerships with private firms such as IBM and General Electric.

OIC's connection with the business community through the years has provided local affiliates with comprehensive and current appraisals of the job needs of local businesses. As in the early days, OIC only trains people for jobs that exist or that can be created in the community. Toward this end, all OICs receive information on business job needs from Industrial Advisory Committees associated with local OIC affiliates. These committees, composed of local businesspeople, give OIC an inside view of the community's business sector, thus allowing the local affiliates to train specifically for available jobs. In addition, OIC pools information with other private job training programs, as well as with federal, state, and local job placement agencies.

While OIC operates on a national level to maintain these connections with the public and private sectors, the leadership structure of OIC reflects a commitment to serve local communities. All the chairpersons of OIC local boards sit on the national OIC board of directors. Under the direction of the board, the National Auxiliary and the National Clergy Support Committee serve to broaden the base of community participation at the local as well as the national level. In every city in the United States where there are OICs, hundreds of OIC trainees are employed in local companies, and thousands work in local, state, and federal jobs. In an OIC city, nearly everybody knows about the program because the OIC has helped someone they know — whether a family member, church member, or neighbor.

Local OICs are, for the most part, autonomous entities. The local OICs adopt the basic feeder program/skills training structure, receive technical assistance provided by the national OIC, and partake of federal, state, and local funds available for OIC. Because affiliates remain free to use these building blocks in whatever way they feel will best address the needs of their local community, the community-based aspect of OIC, so vital to its success, has been maintained.

To date, OIC has trained 3 million Americans for useful employment, and 2.5 million have been put to work. This is many more than have been trained in inner cities by the U.S. government. These people are earning more than $80 billion a year, and as a result, OIC-trained workers have added billions of dollars in tax revenues to the U.S. Treasury. Even with recent cutbacks of federal funds, OIC continues to provide a cost-effective and beneficial way to address this nation's employment problems, costing less than $2,000 per trainee a year. Through the tax dollars of OIC-trained workers, the United States has been repaid fifty times for every federal dollar invested in OIC programs.

Despite help and support from government and the business community, nothing has been more crucial to OIC's success than its ties to the church. I am convinced that without the help of God and the prayers of the people, OIC would never have gotten off the ground in the first place. From the beginning, I considered OIC to be part of God's calling of his people to love and serve humanity.

OIC works because OIC believes in the inherent dignity of human beings. Affirming that dignity means there must be an economic floor, some level of degradation and humiliation beneath which no American citizen should be permitted to fall. We fought for the opportunity for black and poor people to earn a decent living because we know that a job is the best welfare program of all. A person will either work or beg, steal, or kill. To empty the jails, help a man or woman get a job. The need to work is fundamental, which is why welfare reform must be tied to jobs if it is to succeed.

But while we prevail upon government, industry, and the community to help the poor by providing jobs, self-help remains as the key to OIC's effectiveness. Without inner resources such as motivation, discipline, and the will to succeed, no amount of external support will make a trainee independent and self-reliant. For this reason, OIC discourages training stipends, except for essential living and training needs. By extension, we are convinced that community-based organizations must eventually become self-supporting in order to institutionalize the principle of self-determination and self-help among black and Third World peoples. Self-help, however, does not mean selfishness or exclusiveness. The story of Jesus' miraculous multiplication of the loaves and the fishes is the guiding light of our mission. Time and time again, members of the OIC family are renewed by the returns from their shares in the business of developing human resources. The entire history of OIC has reaffirmed our faith in the miracle of sharing.

The formation of OIC led to the establishment of other programs designed not just to train African Americans for jobs but to help them develop enterprises to employ young people themselves. Thus I started another program of ownership in Philadelphia that led to the acquisition of properties valued at tens of millions of dollars. The vehicle for this community investment cooperative movement was what I called the "10–36 Plan."

One day I was reading the Bible's account of how Jesus took the five loaves and two fishes and changed these into enough food to feed a multitude with twelve basket loads left over. I decided the same idea of cooperation and involvement could bring about ownership benefits in a community of such supply that economic basket loads would be left over. I had long admired the work of Rev. Major M. J. Divine, who in New York, Philadelphia, and other places had inspired people to cooperate and to combine their resources to benefit themselves and others. One time when talking to Father Divine about how he could buy hotels with suitcases full of money, he replied, "Just get enough one-dollar bills together, and you will have enough to fill a suitcase and buy a hotel." I decided to get enough ten-dollar bills together to build businesses and enterprises and ownership for the black community.

One Sunday morning after preaching a sermon based on the loaves and fishes, I asked my members to invest ten dollars a month for thirty-six months to build housing and shopping centers and to create businesses. Six hundred members of my church volunteered to be a part of the 10–36 Program. The number eventually grew to more than four thousand, not only from my church but from other churches in the city. At the end of the first year, we had accumulated enough ten-dollar bills to build the first million-dollar apartment complex by blacks in the city of Philadelphia. We used carpenters, electricians, and plumbers trained at OIC to help build the apartments. By the end of the second year, we had accumulated enough ten-dollar bills to build Progress Plaza, at the time the largest shopping center in the United States to be built, owned, and operated by black people. We later built a second shopping center that was larger than the first in another part of Philadelphia. By the end of the third year, we were able to open factories, rehabilitate neighborhoods, and develop the Entrepreneurial Development Training Program, which taught management skills to more than four thousand blacks in Philadelphia who were running businesses or who planned to open them. Today, one-half of all the businesses in Philadelphia are run by blacks who received their management training from that Entrepreneurial Development Training Program in Progress Plaza.

To learn what has been built by blacks in Philadelphia who began with virtually nothing but a commitment to work together is cause for amazement. The accomplishments include shopping centers, housing developments, the Opportunities Towers for the housing of the aged and handicapped, neighborhood rehabilitation, many training centers, and, most of all, a community of people proud of their ownership. Again, these accomplishments are, not the result of government programs, but the result of several thousand ordinary people who were inspired to use what they had in their hands to work together without argument or dissension. Their children and their children's children will be the owners of these properties, which in the next fifty years will increase more than tenfold in value and will amount to a billion dollars, providing benefits and dividends to generations and generations coming thereafter.

Years later we would organize yet another initiative, the Self-Help Investment Program (SHIP). With their collective investment programs in cities, SHIPs could be a boon to minority business development and inner-city revitalization as well as help small-town development in the United States. Larger in potential scope than the 10–36 Program, it is my belief that SHIPs will spread throughout America in the twenty-first century helping with urban development and minority businesses on a scale never before envisioned by blacks. The program calls for one hundred people to invest $1,000 in small groups, in communities both large and small, to be used for neighborhood development and the creation of jobs. With SHIPs, pension funds, foundations, companies, and individuals provide supporting equity financing to help assure resources with returns so that projects can be successful. These SHIPs are being launched throughout America and, in time, will be formed in communities large and small throughout the United States.

The story of OIC and of similar initiatives is crucial to an understanding of who I am and what I believe. Many other OIC staffers
and I came from poor and working-class backgrounds. We rose above
poverty by God's grace and through family members, teachers, and
ministers who taught us and helped us to help ourselves. The values
and principles that led to OIC's creation and success are the same
principles that would one day find their way into South Africa by way
of my experiences on the board of General Motors. It is to that story
that I now return.

Chapter 5

A Turn for the Better at GM

A S A RESULT of the success of the selective patronage program in Philadelphia, I came to know Dr. Martin Luther King Jr. as an associate and as a friend. Many times we talked together about plans and strategies for the advancement of black people in America and black people everywhere, especially in Africa. It was from the successful program of selective patronage in Philadelphia that Operation Breadbasket, later led by the charismatic and effective Rev. Jesse Jackson, came into existence. To this day, the selective patronage program remains a viable and successful way in opening job opportunities for blacks throughout the United States.

Dr. King had been successful in Montgomery, Alabama, with bus boycotts. He asked me to meet with him and his associates in Atlanta to discuss how the selective patronage program had worked. As a result, the concept of selective patronage became the "economic arm" of the Southern Christian Leadership Conference. More importantly, I became friends with Dr. King.

Even in his death, Dr. King had something to do with my becoming a member of the board at General Motors (GM) and thus with my efforts to end apartheid in South Africa. On the Monday following the assassination of Dr. King, Jim Roche, the chairman of General Motors, was flying from a meeting in New York back to Detroit. As he peered through his airplane window, he later told me, "It looked like the whole city of Detroit was on fire." He said it was at that moment he decided something had to be done to improve race relations in this country and that he should start with General Motors and the board of directors.

At the time, activist Ralph Nader was focusing on corporate social responsibility. Specifically, his "Campaign GM" was pushing General Motors to do more for minorities. Through my involvement with various boycotts and, of course, with OIC, I had made several connections within the business community. In addition to all its other activities, one of OIC's missions was to urge companies to appoint black directors. General Motors did just that. And the person that the company chose was me.

I have never doubted that working to end apartheid was God's plan for my life, not my own plan. When I accepted the invitation to become a member of the board of General Motors, I had no idea where it would lead. In the years leading up to that appointment, I had no interest in South Africa beyond the hope — shared by many — that its system of injustice and the problems that went with it would come to a peaceful end. Though I was willing to support any initiatives in this regard, I had no intention of launching any initiatives of my own.

South Africa was secondary to me in part because of the many other demands on my time and presence. My church, which had become the largest in Philadelphia, was destroyed by a fire in 1970. I committed myself to rebuilding it. My OIC movement was growing rapidly, not only in Philadelphia but throughout the United States. In fact, it had even begun extending into Africa, Latin America, Great Britain, and the Philippines. I felt an obligation to provide leadership to the movement I had started, leadership that entailed such aforementioned activities as organizing community investment cooperatives in Philadelphia; building shopping centers, housing developments, and homes for the elderly and handicapped; and rehabilitating neighborhoods. I was also engaged in various civil rights activities in Philadelphia and other parts of the United States and was working on follow-up efforts with our highly successful selective patronage program. And given my close association with President Johnson and with key leaders of Congress, I felt it was important that my voice be heard in Washington. I wanted the nation's leaders to have my input on matters dealing with the problems of blacks, other minorities, and the poor in America. In addition, my responsibilities as a pastor meant I had to visit the sick, bury the dead, bless the babies, and visit the prisons. And amidst it all, Grace and I had a home to care for and a family to raise.

All this is to say that, during this time, I never envisioned that apartheid would become a focal point in my life and ministry. I did, of course, speak out against apartheid on a regular basis. I delivered speeches on college campuses against apartheid and urged others to do what they could to help. At GM board meetings, I voted in favor of the company using its influence to end the apartheid system. Then, on May 21, 1971, at the first stockholders' meeting I attended, I demonstrated why I had been chosen — by the intervention of God — for the board. Much to the chagrin of my fellow directors, I took the floor before three thousand stockholders and opposed the overwhelming majority of GM board members with regard to the company's presence in South Africa. As newspaper cameras clicked and television cameras rolled, I challenged General Motors to leave South Africa until apartheid had ended. My remarks included the following:

> My reason for speaking today . . . regards General Motors' involvement in the Union of South Africa. Blacks in the Union of South Africa are relegated to subhuman treatment without freedom of movement, without economic equality in wages for the same job performed, and without even basic, elemental rights. Apartheid must come to an end.
>
> To a great measure, the system of apartheid is being underwritten by American industry, interests, and investments, simply by virtue of our operations there. There are over three hundred American businesses and companies operating in the Union of South Africa today, including the General Motors Corporation. These companies, by their very presence, are helping to sustain the existence of this terrible practice I have alluded to today. Either the leaders of the Union of South Africa will end apartheid in the Union of South Africa, or one day apartheid will mean the end to the Union of South Africa — and everything General Motors has in it.
>
> But, even more than economic considerations or political considerations, American industry cannot morally continue to do business in a country that so blatantly and ruthlessly and clearly maintains such dehumanizing practices against such large numbers of its people. Admittedly, my concern goes even deeper. When I realize I am a black man and that the vast majority of those who are dehumanized are black like myself, I hear voices say to me: "Things will work out in time; things are getting better; let us slow down on this matter." But then I ask, "Why does the world always want to go slow when the rights of black men are at stake?"
>
> I want to go on record for all to know that I will continue to pursue my desire to see that American enterprises, including General Motors, withdraw from the Union of South Africa until changes have been made in the practices and the policies of that government as they pertain to the treatment of blacks and other nonwhites.

I tied my appeal for General Motors to leave South Africa to support for a stockholders' proposal by the Episcopal Church of the United

States calling for General Motors and other U.S. companies in South Africa to withdraw from that country.

Though outspoken on that day and before subsequent audiences throughout America and South Africa, I never intended to become fully engaged in the apartheid struggle. After I made the statement to the stockholders, the other directors did not know what to say or do. They were in a state of shock. Never before had a director of General Motors or any other large corporation made such a statement opposing a board position. Later, when I was receiving an honorary doctorate at Yale University with Henry Ford II, Henry said to me, "Leon, I would never let anyone on my board who would oppose me and my company as you have done. I like you and you are my friend, but my friendship for you would never, never go that far."

Thankfully, Chairman Roche defended my right to make my statement and fended off opposing views from my fellow directors. I would in time secure the cooperation of most members of the board, although some reluctantly. And later, the board placed its full support behind the Sullivan Principles. The action reinforced my conviction that if you believe what you are doing is right and if you have faith, the mountains of opposition can be moved.

But again, during my first few years with GM, it was not my intention to step out and provide leadership against the evils in South Africa. As far as I was concerned, my efforts on the GM board would focus on improving opportunities for blacks, women, and other minorities and on removing the glass ceiling that had prohibited the elevation of blacks within the company. I was also intent on developing black-owned GM dealerships, as well as black and other minority GM suppliers. It took a lot of hard work and constant pushing, but eventually these efforts bore fruit. Black dealerships and salespersons throughout the United States increased, and black suppliers doing business with General Motors grew from $3 million in investments when I joined the board to over $2 billion in 1990. In fact, at that time General Motors was doing more business with black-owned vendors and suppliers than the U.S. government was.

When I joined the board, there were only five black-owned GM dealerships in the entire country. As part of an effort to change this, I stationed some of my church members at four of the main intersections in Philadelphia at the busiest time of day in order to count the number of Cadillacs that went by and the number of those Cadillacs driven by blacks. The poll revealed that of 867 Cadillacs in an hour-long period, 510 were driven by blacks. I presented this information at the next board meeting, and as a result, a special push was made for the recruitment of black dealers for Cadillacs and other GM cars.

I came to this meeting knowing that once before blacks had been responsible for saving the Cadillac market. During his time as GM chairman, Alfred Sloane wrote a book that focused on how the Cadillac division was going out of business following World War II when a special effort was made to sell Cadillacs to black funeral directors, doctors, ministers, and other professionals. The Cadillac business became profitable again virtually overnight. Owning a Cadillac became a status symbol for black people. We could not buy homes, as whites did, because the housing markets were segregated. We did not have good jobs in business or in government. But we could own a Cadillac, and to do so became a statement of success.

On occasion, on a day's notice I would call and visit a GM plant somewhere in the United States to see for myself what was being done for the employment and advancement of blacks, women, and other minorities. The plant manager would have notice of only twenty-four hours, and he would scramble to see that favorable conditions were in place upon my arrival. On visiting the plants, I would ask to see the executive committee and key supervisors with expectations they would be integrated. I recall one occasion when the executive committee of the plant I was visiting included a black representative. I expressed pleasure at what I saw, for we were breaking new ground with black representation. But upon leaving the office, the black gentleman in the room caught up with me in the hall and whispered in my ear, "Reverend, this is the first time I have ever been in that room." He had just been put there to impress me. I laughed to myself. They thought they were putting something over on me. These visits became known as the "Sullivan Visits." Despite the window dressing, I know that my visits had a great impact on employment policies in GM plants. We worked with Jim Roche to set up a special program to recruit and train black dealers at the General Motors Institute located in Flint, Michigan. And in time there would be several hundred minority dealers and thousands and thousands of black salespersons in dealerships and black technicians in GM throughout America.

During my years at GM, at least once a year I would go to Detroit to meet with all the supervisors and executives dealing with equal employment opportunities, diversity, and the advancement of blacks, minorities, and female workers. During these daylong meetings — which became known as "Sullivan Days" within the company — with executives brought to Detroit from across the country, Europe, and even South Africa, we helped establish goals and landmarks for diversity of black, female, and minority employment throughout GM. At each meeting I would urge the executives present to stretch their plans and to do more and more in upgrading employment opportunities for minorities. I still meet once a year with all GM managers dealing with diversity and minority employment. I want to help keep General Motors on its toes.

At this writing, one vice president of General Motors who is in charge of building and selling several major GM lines is a black man. In every aspect of General Motors — from deposits in black banks and the greater inclusion of blacks in GM advertisements to changing the corporate culture in favor of fairer treatment of blacks and women — there has been progress. One day there will be a black GM president.

During the time of Sullivan Days and Sullivan Visits at GM, South Africa was still not a priority for me, but I could not ignore what was happening there. In fact, my interest in it began to grow. Because of all the things I was doing, I hoped my need for greater personal interest in South Africa would go away, that others interested in the problem would take the lead, and that I could get by with merely lending my encouragement and support.

My reticence perhaps was due in part to the daunting nature of the task. After all, South Africa had defied previous attempts at reform. Mahatma Gandhi worked to change the racist practices for twenty years before leaving South Africa in frustration, disillusionment, and discouragement. Nevertheless, I found myself reading more about South Africa and apartheid. In fact, I read every book and every news item I could find dealing with the problem, and apartheid increasingly troubled my conscience until I could not get away from it.

I realized I had to do something more to satisfy myself that progress was being made in South Africa. So in 1975 I decided to go there. It was not my first time visiting the African continent. I had heard about the injustices of apartheid in 1969 during my first visit to Africa when I met Emperor Haile Selassie in Addis Ababa, Ethiopia. The emperor gave me land and buildings to establish an OIC in the country. He also expressed his hope that before he died, something would be done about the conditions in South Africa. On that same visit, the first secretary general of the Organization of African Unity, Diallo Telli, one of the leading Pan-Africans on the continent, met with me and expressed his hopes that one day changes would come. He spoke of plans to mobilize an all-African army to fight against South Africa if the segregationist laws were not changed. But he told me that the Pan-Africanist efforts were not bearing fruit.

Now it was time for me to go to South Africa to see for myself what I could do. A whole new chapter in my life was about to begin.

Chapter 6

Encountering South Africa

S OUTH AFRICA encircles the small, independent kingdom of Lesotho. By the time I arrived there in 1975, Lesotho had been fighting off the encroachment of the Afrikaners for a century, refusing to be incorporated into the Republic of South Africa. I was there to establish an OIC training program and decided to tie this visit in to entering South Africa for the first time. Just as my walk across the street to attend my first General Motors meeting had done, this visit would begin a commitment that would affect the entire direction of my life. It would lead me, among other things, to play an important part in the dismantling of the apartheid system.

One cannot understand apartheid outside the context of African history. Humankind began in Africa. The book of Genesis refers to Ethiopia, establishing it as one of the world's first countries. For thousands of years before Christ, black nations, governments, and societies had existed and flourished. Long before the Europeans developed civilizations — while people in Europe were still living in caves and trees — parts of equatorial Africa had developed advanced systems of government. They had established vibrant cultures and created great and long-lasting dynasties. As early as 5000 B.C., African kings and potentates of immense wealth and power ruled on the African continent, from Cush to Nubia and the lands now known as Ethiopia. And the African prehistory territories now known as southern Africa and South Africa featured sophisticated art, systems of education, and industry that included the smelting of iron and copper and the mining and fashioning of gold. The early writings of Homer, Herodotus, Socrates, and Ptolemy featured stories of the great riches and strengths of ancient African peoples.

Fast-forwarding a couple of thousand years, we encounter one of the most interesting leaders of African history, Mansa Musa, who reigned in Mali from 1312 to 1337. His fame was such that the cartographers of Europe replaced the land's recognition as terra incognita upon the maps of Africa with the figure of Musa of Mali and substituted Musa on a throne, scepter in hand, for elephants, which appeared on maps for want of towns. During the fifteenth century, the sailors of Portugal searched for the land of Musa, regarded as one of the richest in the world.

Musa conquered new territories and integrated the older provinces into a great and mighty empire. A story is recorded of his journey to Egypt in which he was preceded by five hundred slaves, each carrying a six-pound staff of gold. A caravan of one hundred camels, each of them laden with three hundred pounds of gold, followed. Other camels carried enough provisions to clothe and feed entire villages. For one hundred years, the citizens of Cairo recalled how Musa had freely given gold to the poor and had paid inflated prices to the shopkeepers and traders in the city. It was all done without thought of political reward.

Musa erected a mosque and oversaw extensive developments of housing for the poor in Mali. And he built one of the most famous universities of the ancient world in Timbuktu. But he is only one example of the great kings and rulers who reigned for centuries on the African continent as it is known today, from the Mediterranean to the Cape of Good Hope. Prior to A.D. 1000, little is recorded about Africa south of the Sahara desert except loose bits and pieces. But what we do know challenges the popular view that historic Africa was a dark continent full of cannibals. In fact, much of the knowledge of industry, art, and culture known today in the modern world had its source in equatorial Africa.

The beginning of the slave trade marked an abrupt, shocking change to development in that part of the world. At the beginning of the fifteenth century (1441), the first dozen slaves were taken from West Africa to Portugal to be sold as shackled workers. With that, a new and terrible phase of equatorial Africa's history began. Slavery, though not new, took on a special historical role in the world with the advent of the African slave trade. The taking of slaves is as old as the known world. In ancient times, men and women defeated in battle were often taken as slaves and sold or given as gifts by conquerors for political and economic reasons. The slaves were black, they were white, they were red, and they were brown. By the end of the fifteenth century, however, the slave trade, which began in Portugal and spread to France, Italy, the United Kingdom, Persia, Asia, South America, and later the United States, became the most dominant and lucrative business in the world. The available statistics permit no more than a rough, impressionistic assessment of the volume and consequences of the slave trade. In the last half of the fifteenth century, white slave traders transported perhaps five thousand slaves a year from the African mainland to its offshore islands and Europe. But during the fifteenth, sixteenth, and seventeenth centuries, interest in slaves for American colonies grew and grew.

Explorations in the New World led to the need for workers, both for plantations and for industries and other labor associated with developing colonies and territories. The depth of the slave trade can only be estimated based on scattered evidence. But it appears that white entrepreneurs probably transferred, conservatively speaking, at least twenty-five million slaves from western Africa to the Americas before 1888, when Brazil officially abolished slavery and slavery was considered illegal in England and the United States. This figure does not include an estimated ten million Africans who lost their lives during the voyages. It also excludes about ten million slaves who may have been exported from eastern Africa to Arabia and Asia. Tropical Africa was therefore deprived of at least fifty million inhabitants because of the slave traffic. Most of the slaves were carried to America. There is no question that America became a strong and prosperous nation largely on the backs of slaves, people to whom the nation will always owe a debt.

The consequences of the slave trade were many. It deprived tropical Africa of its most creative and productive human resources — the young and healthy. The slavers skimmed the cream, leaving behind those inhabitants who were less able to keep pace with the changing times. Indigenous commercial activity declined. Knowledge of the old skills decayed. The traditional political processes, which had built African states on durable foundations, became less important than finding ways to deal with the problems of slavery. Ultimately, slavery taught the world to evaluate others based on skin color, producing the kind of racial antagonism that is so much a part of contemporary civilization in the United States and around the world.

Slavery is the greatest human tragedy in the history of the world. During World War II, because of Hitler and Nazism, Jews lost millions to Auschwitz and Dachau. But during the slave trade, which spanned four centuries, Africa lost tens of millions to inhabitable, foreign lands and millions more to the sharks of the seas. The stories and results of slavery are thoroughly recorded in the history books, but the pain of slavery lives on throughout the world, especially in America. That pain will never be adequately and fully described by any historian. Nor can the effects of slavery — which still haunt us today — be fully understood or easily, if ever, fully erased. Nevertheless we should applaud such efforts as the television miniseries *Roots* and the movie *Amistad* for moving the world closer to understanding.

In addition to the enslavement of millions of Africans in America, South America, and other parts of the world, a lesser form of slavery called *colonialism* existed throughout sub-Saharan Africa via the apportioning of equatorial Africa by European nations prior to World War I. This was in accordance with the Bismarck Agreement of 1884. The annexation of African territories continued to assure dominance of African people by foreign powers. Africans fought against this domination. In the anticolonial struggle, tens of thousands who resisted lost their lives. Eventually, the struggle for freedom and independence took hold, and with the support of others from around the world beginning in the mid-twentieth century, African countries began to gain their independence from foreign rule. Still, in some parts of Africa, this domination by whites over blacks continued to be strong, especially in the southern region once known as Rhodesia and now known as the Republic of South Africa, the land of apartheid.

For years in Africa, an oft-heard sentiment among whites regarding blacks has prevailed, especially in southern Africa: "We white people have not come to this country solely or even mainly to raise natives on the scale of civilization. Our main objective is to survive ourselves, to improve our conditions if we can, and to raise a family and to perpetuate our race." The view of the Africans regarding white rule has been that the white man "does not look upon the black man as a person; they just treat us like dogs. The only time they look after us is when they want money from us. I am a person, not a dog."

During the surge for African independence, frustrated settlers in central and southern Africa held tight to their racist views, believing themselves to be superior. Between the time slavery ended and the beginning of World War II, Africans lost hundreds of thousands of square miles to the colonialists of Europe. In Kenya, two thousand white settlers owned 40 percent of the colony's arable land. With the advent of Jomo Kenyatta and young leaders such as Tom Mboya and the rise of the "Mau-Mau," a radical movement among Africans to end colonial rule, the British lost their hold, though hundreds of white farmers and thousands of Africans lost their lives. But in southern Africa, the settlers gained absolute control, and in order to assure white domination over black labor, the noose was tightened more and more into what was ultimately to become known as *apartheid*, the complete separation of the races except for those workers in the mines, plantations, and the most menial of domestic occupations. This was done without opposition from the developed world, except Russia, and it was done with the acquiescence of the United States.

Whites have been settlers in southern Africa for three hundred years. Though they settled in the region for various reasons, most of them eventually became farmers. The rule of segregation of blacks from whites reaches all the way back to 1652, when settlers from Holland and Germany began to set up homes and to develop farms in that part of South Africa known as the Cape of Good Hope. In 1904, when white plantation owners and farmers began to populate that section of the world, measures were developed and "reserves" created to separate blacks from whites, except for the use of black labor on the plantations and with other private employers. In Rhodesia, whites created ways to minimize conflict between Africans and Europeans and to maintain the status of white rule over black workers. To have the quickest and most effective control was the goal of the white farmers. It was assumed that Africans who lived or worked on European-owned farms and who resided in the towns that began to develop in the regions would sell their labor at minimum pay. During this early period, blacks were compelled to carry "passes," or identification certificates, that forbade most forms of racial mixing. In Salisbury, the capital of Southern Rhodesia, laws were passed that even prohibited Africans from standing on the sidewalks alongside whites.

The division of the countries into European and African lands was systematically designed to destroy African resources, as well as to destroy the ability of Africans to maintain self-sufficiency. They were restricted to barren, urban locations. During the time before independence, discrimination, ghettoization, and impoverishment throughout sub-Saharan Africa led to underdevelopment and dependency. Africans were forced to work for the white man just to survive. This was especially true in southern Africa.

Following World War II, the Western powers developed methods that forced Africans to divide so that whites could rule and migrant labor could keep the wheels of South African production going. While all other African nations, having gained their independence, attempted to move in new directions, South Africa was still characterized by the politics of inequality, racism, exploitation, and oppression. In South Africa, the coalition of white workers and the rural middle class, consisting mainly of Afrikaners (descendants of the first white inhabitants of the southern region), formed the Nationalist Party as a way to hold blacks down. Blacks fought back by forming political parties and self-help and self-reliant welfare organizations. They also attempted to organize trade unions and appealed to human rights, calling for equal rights for all civilized people, irrespective of race and color.

From the vantage point of the oppressed, colonialism was nothing less than a tragedy rooted in settlers' economic self-interest and the perpetration of white domination over blacks and other nonwhites, whose numbers had grown as a result of Asian and Indian migrations. In South Africa, the whites in control had no thought of giving up their power. Thus in 1948 came a formal declaration of Grand Apartheid, the most separatist movement of the races ever devised and enacted in the known history of the world.

In 1949, in the face of mounting apartheid actions, the African National Congress (ANC) — an alliance of blacks, coloreds, Indians, and white liberals — formed an antiapartheid and nation-building program. Whites countered with their own campaign of white unity and militancy. The Nationalist Party–controlled government applied repressive and reactionary measures, such as the prohibition of meetings, police surveillance and harassment, and a ban on political parties. Those in power began to torture, banish, and imprison those who went ahead with such meetings, even killing their opponents. I was scheduled to meet with Steve Biko to discuss how programs such as OIC could work in South Africa, but he was killed before the meeting could take place.

Nelson Mandela, Walter Sisulu, Oliver Tambo, Chief Albert Luthuli, and others in the ANC formed an underground movement in their struggle for freedom. Other movements, such as the Pan-African Congress (PAC) led by Robert Sobukwe, took strong views against the white domination of blacks. In response, repressive laws were enacted against nonwhites. The Group Areas Act required the concentration of all South Africans by race. Measures were taken to oppose Communism, and of course anyone who criticized apartheid was considered a Communist. The Native Labor Act abolished the rights to freedom of association. Collective-bargaining measures made it illegal for African workers to form or belong to unions. The Criminal Law Amendment Act made it an offense to support any campaign against any law of the government. And the Mines and Works Act prohibited Africans from doing skilled work in the mines, although they were doing skilled work without the title or the pay.

Later, the government went even further to stop African determination and antiapartheid efforts. It enacted the notorious Bantustand Policy, which led to the Bantu Self-Government Act and the Bantu Investment Corporation. Under the act, Africans were divided into black homelands corresponding to the traditional ethnic groups of the Zulu, Sotho, Xhosa, Tswana, Tsonga, and Venda. They were to develop separately under some measure of self-government, though all matters of internal security, African affairs, and the budget were controlled by white South Africans. The Bantustand Policy was basically a "divide and rule" technique designed to weaken African nationalism and to buy time while consolidating white supremacy. The idea was to revise and revitalize ethnic rivalries of former years, thereby reversing the unifying factors of Pan-Africanism, education, urbanization, and nationalism being advanced by South African black leaders.

Nowhere have the racial lines been more clearly and forcefully drawn than in South Africa under apartheid. A person's political, civil, economic, and social rights hinged on membership in a distinct racial group. With apartheid, the government had fit everyone into a racial slot and had used the power of the police and the military to guard against racial crossings. Under apartheid, statutes in general usage at the time of my visit divided the population into four groups: Whites, Coloreds, Asians, and Africans. The central racial-classification law, called the Population Registration Act of 1950 and sometimes described as the cornerstone of apartheid, ordered the placement of every person in one of the official four groups. To keep racial lines from blurring further, the South African government enacted legal prohibitions against marriage and sexual intercourse between blacks and whites, which were, of course, often broken. The Prohibition of Mixed Marriages Act of 1949, which was later strengthened in 1957, outlawed sexual relations between blacks and whites and any "immoral or indecent act" involving a black and a white, whatever that meant. The Immorality Act of 1960 led to the prosecution of hundreds of people until 1980. The Parliament of South Africa made no attempt to make changes in this legislation.

Another pillar created to control and restrict the movements of the nonwhite population was embodied in the Homelands Policy, which separated blacks into tribal states while whites retained exclusive control over the remainder of the country, embracing 87 percent of the territory. Thus although blacks constituted 75 percent of the population, they were relegated to 13 percent of the land. The whites' goal was to avoid sharing political and, ultimately, economic power with Africans while at the same time retaining the use of African labor.

The Homelands Policy was one of the most ridiculous pieces of land regulation in the history of the modern world. It did not work because it could not work. The government was attempting to pursue a course of divide and rule with homelands for the most part scattered on bits and pieces of land rather than on unified territory. The Homelands Policy rested on the fiction that Africans residing in "white areas" were temporary workers rather than permanent citizens of integral parts of South African society. It attempted to ensure a continuing supply of African labor while avoiding the granting of full civil, economic, and political rights to African workers and their families. As one writer has put it, "According to the grand design of separate development, every African living in a Homeland area was required to become a citizen of the Homeland and would therefore become eligible for participation in the political process of the Homeland, but not in the affairs of the South African Government."[1] Millions of Africans were moved en masse from where they lived to remote areas designated for their particular ethnic tribe. They could be citizens of a designated homeland but could not be citizens of all-white South Africa. While millions of blacks resided in townships outside of the cities and on the outskirts of white areas for the purpose of supplying labor for the mines and factories and farms, there was no expectation nor any hope of ever becoming a citizen of South Africa with any power over their own destinies.

Another main pillar and a principal legal underpinning of residential and business segregation in the urban areas of South Africa was the Group Areas Act. It provided for the creation of separate group areas in towns and cities for Whites, Africans, Coloreds, and Asians, with the Colored group further subdivided into Indian, Chinese, Malay, and "other Colored groups." But despite widespread de facto segregation, residential intermingling had advanced far enough in most cities to prevent attainment of the goals of the Group Areas Act. In any place in the world, get a boy and a girl together, and they are going to mix somehow. You can put walls around them, on top of them, and underneath them, and a boy and a girl will get through those walls.

Yet the Group Areas Act was a continuing obstacle to the freedom of movement of the people, entrenching segregation in the amenities of everyday life. For example, people were restricted as to where they could dine or see a movie, what staircases, elevators, and public toilets they could use. In restaurants, seating accommodations were restricted between whites and nonwhites, if blacks were admitted at all. Sporting events and theater performances were divided into separate sections based on race. The Reservation of Separate Amenities Act allowed any person in control of public premises such as restaurants, businesses, libraries, parks, and beaches to reserve separate and unequal facilities for different races. The act abolished the power of the police or the courts to nullify such actions.

And there was the despised passbook system, which controlled the movement of Africans throughout South Africa. Passes for blacks in South Africa can be traced to 1800, when passes were required of blacks moving from place to place in the seeking of jobs. But of all these inhumanities, the worst was the relegation of blacks in South Africa to political obscurity. Blacks had no recognition as citizens in their own country and could not vote. These political realities and more obliterated any hopes for a better tomorrow and for freedom. This was the South Africa to which I had come.

As Nelson Mandela stated in an address at the ANC Convention in 1953, "There is going to be no easy walk to freedom for the Africans of South Africa." But on March 21, 1960, something happened that struck the conscience of the world. The context was a peaceful campaign against past laws and against the requirement that all black South Africans carry a passbook with them wherever they went. This campaign was organized in several locations throughout South Africa. It ended in the tragedy of Sharpsville, where police fired on men, women, and children engaged in a peaceful demonstration, killing 76 and wounding 126. Tragedies such as this planted seeds of discontent in the world outside Africa.

I arrived in South Africa early in the morning from Lesotho at the General Jan Smuts Airport in Johannesburg. The sky was red at the horizon. I was reminded of the English saying, "Red sky at night, the shepherd's delight; red sky at morning, the shepherd's warning." It was early in the morning, and the sky was red: a shepherd's warning. I had been told the General Jan Smuts Airport was the "freest" place in South Africa because of the large number of international travelers who went through there. Still, I saw blatant evidence of the segregation of races. All of the seating sections were still de facto segregated, one for whites and another for nonwhites. The cafeterias were the same. It was like being back in Mississippi.

Every black person I saw in South Africa had a large bulge in his or her right pocket, but I did not know why. Later, I found the bulge was the passbook required to be carried by every man, woman, and child over fifteen years of age as reference books describing every known action in their lives, including fingerprints, an identity card, and employment information that traced the history of a person's place of work from the time they had been approved for any job. Not only were these passbooks heavy and bulky to carry, but they constituted a dehumanizing symbol of black oppression. Getting rid of them would be high on my agenda for change.

I saw black workers sweeping and mopping floors, emptying the trash, and carrying things. I stopped one of the male workers and asked how things were going within his country. He looked at me with blazing eyes and said, "I am a man, and I am tired of being treated like a boy." This one comment revealed to me more than anything I could read or imagine about the evils of racial discrimination in the Republic of South Africa.

On entering Johannesburg, the gross inequities were painfully obvious. Thousands of blacks were walking along the streets individually or in pairs, their pockets bulging with the passbooks. There were few smiles on their faces. I saw people filled with gloom and despair. In the distance could be seen the great mounds of soil, rising hundreds of feet into the air from the diggings of the gold mines miles beneath the ground, where thousands of men worked every day in shifts around the clock and where terrible accidents occurred regularly, killing trapped miners by the hundreds.

I could see buses and trains headed to and away from Soweto, the township located twenty miles outside the city where blacks who did not live as domestic workers in the city were forced to reside. Buses and trains were filled to capacity; long lines of people waited in an eerie silence for the next bus or train to pass by. Signs marked the buses and trains either white or nonwhite, the eating places for whites or nonwhites, the benches for whites or nonwhites. Every attempt was made to make the separation of the races as complete as it could be. All this was happening as the world, including the United States of America, stood by making statements, forming commissions, and making reports about how terrible it was in South Africa while taking no action. The world was more concerned about profits to be made from South Africa's supply of gold, silver, and diamonds and was also concerned that Communism would take over and control the sea-lanes for the oil and minerals passing from the Indian Ocean into the Atlantic. Humankind's inhumanity to humankind was secondary — important, but secondary.

Then I entered Soweto, where more than a million people were living in what can only be called a massive shantytown, in hundreds of thousands of corrugated-roofed shacks. They had no sewers, no inside toilets. More than 80 percent of the people there had no electricity or running water. With few doctors and no dentists, they had virtually no access to quality medical care. The mortality rate of children and women bearing children was the highest in the world.

Through the center of Soweto was a wide, paved street lined with hundreds of vendors trying to sell fruit and other food in the open air. Along this main road could be found miles of hostels for migrant workers from neighboring nations, including Mozambique, Botswana, Zimbabwe, Swaziland, and Lesotho, and especially from the homelands. Alcoholism thrived in these hostels, as did prostitution. Tribal rivalries spilled out into the alleys and streets in ethnic battles that left thousands dead and tens of thousands injured and mangled each year. At the time of my visits, more people were killed per capita in Soweto than in any other place in the world, including even Harlem in New York, which had the highest homicide rate in the United States. In South Africa, more people were jailed each year — most of them black — than were jailed in any other place in the world. Most had no legal defense or any other recourse.

Nearly every black man or black youngster in South Africa had some type of jail record, mostly as a result of "irregularities" with the use of the passbook. While most whites lived with impunity and afflu-ence in the land, blacks lived daily in insecurity and massive poverty. And there appeared to be little chance for improvement. The fate of blacks in South Africa seemed sealed. Blacks were the have-nots in a land of plenty, the lifelong victims of white superiority and continuing domination.

Apartheid and the conditions it produced went against the grain of everything I had ever believed and worked to accomplish. The pain and frustration of this trip touched every level of my being. There was a time when apartheid was not at the top of my agenda. That time would soon be past.

Note

1. Foreign Study Policy Foundation, *South Africa: Time Running Out* (Berkeley: University of California Press, 1981), 51.

Chapter 7

Responding to God

"**W**HY DOESN'T someone do something about apartheid?" I prayed to God. God spoke back to me and said, "You do something about it. You are a member of the board of General Motors, the largest corporation in the world and the largest United States employer of workers in South Africa. You do something about it!" "But, God," I said, "I am one man. What can I do in a situation like this?" But God responded, "You do something about it...and I will help you!"

It was late afternoon when I finally arrived at the Holiday Inn near the airport where I was staying in South Africa. Many people were waiting there for me, for the news had gone out by radio and television and in the evening newspapers that I was in South Africa and had publicly invited any who wanted to talk with me to come to the Holiday Inn. Throughout the night I met with black and other nonwhite South Africans about the problems in the country. Everyone to a person asked me to do whatever I could to bring reform.

One of the most important of these spontaneous meetings took place the next morning when a group of civic and union leaders spent several hours with me talking about what steps might work. At the conclusion of our discussions, they prevailed on me to try a new tactic in addressing South Africa's problems. While they appreciated my call for companies to leave South Africa and supported the public statements I had made, they spoke of a more effective way to bring positive results more quickly. They urged me to attempt to galvanize companies doing business in South Africa, beginning with U.S. firms, for the purpose of initiating a campaign of corporate responsibility designed to end discrimination against all black and other nonwhite workers in the country employed in their plants and mines, to end segregation of workers, and to accept the rights of black workers to belong to black

44

and other unions that, up to then, had been denied them. This, they believed, would be an important first step in confronting the systems propped up by apartheid.

I listened but made no promises. Though I had been moved by what I had seen and heard, I knew I had much to do back home in the United States. Our cities were in trouble. Opposition to progress we had made on the civil rights front was mounting. Many black people still needed to be trained for jobs. The need to create black-owned businesses remained, as did the need for protests and demonstrations to end de facto segregation practices and remaining discriminatory laws in America. It was clear to me that the courageous efforts of black South Africans could benefit greatly from support outside the country, but I was not yet ready. Even though I sensed that God would provide support, the daunting nature of South Africa's problems and my corresponding feelings of inadequacy prevented me from making a firm commitment.

That afternoon, following my talks with various leaders, I checked out of the Holiday Inn, where I was staying near the airport. A porter took my bags to a waiting car and said to me, "I guess you know, with these damned white people, you are the most hated man in South Africa." Shortly afterwards, at the airport, an incident took place that would determine the direction my life would take for years to come. I checked my bags and along with several colleagues who had accompanied me walked to the waiting area for the plane. A policeman approached me, took me by the arm, and guided me to a small room not far away, leaving my friends to wait.

Once I was inside the room, the policeman ordered me to remove my clothes. I stripped down to my underwear as a guard checked my clothes. His attempts to intimidate me were clear, not only from his looks but also from the biggest .45–caliber pistol I had ever seen. I was not intimidated, but I was greatly humiliated. There I was — the pastor of one of the largest churches in the United States, the founder of the largest self-help movement for education and training in America, and a member of the board of directors of the largest corporation in the world — standing nearly naked in an airport room before a guard who was in no hurry to let me go. I asked him, "Why do you do this to me?" He responded, "I do to you what I have to do." At that moment I said to myself, "And when I get out of here, I will do what I have to do."

It was nearly an hour before I was permitted to return to my colleagues, who had waited for me at the steps of the plane. One of them was my closest friend — Rev. Cecil Gallup, pastor of the Holy Trinity Baptist Church in Philadelphia. I had known him for thirty years, as we had pastored together in New Jersey before coming to Philadelphia. Cecil rushed to embrace me, saying that they were about to call the United States Embassy to have someone track me down. I assured Cecil and the others that all was well, but I knew that not all was truly well. My soul was deeply troubled.

The incident in that little room in the airport brought back that childhood memory from Charleston, West Virginia, when I was attempting to sit at a lunch counter to drink a Coca-Cola. I was told, "Stand on your feet, black boy; you can't sit down here." The airport incident dissolved my hesitancy. I made up my mind to work against the evils of apartheid. This decision would alter my life, affect my family, set me on a course I had not intended to go. I had been standing on my feet against injustice in the United States from West Virginia to Harlem, to New Jersey, and then to Philadelphia. Now it was time for me to stand up again, this time against injustice in South Africa.

I made this decision with the full realization that whatever I might do would only be a part of a far broader effort, perhaps a mere appendage to the brave and courageous efforts of black and other South Africans who put their lives on the line for freedom and equality of opportunity in that country. I knew that already thousands of blacks and others had been imprisoned, beaten, tortured, and even killed because of stands they had taken. And I knew that for three hundred years blacks in South Africa had fought for their rights — from the days of Shaka, the legendary king of the Zulus, who fought the Boers when they attempted to take away their land, down to the leaders of the present day, such as Sisulu, Biko, Buthelezi, Motlana, Qoboza, Tutu, the great Mandela, and many more who daily put their lives on the line in the struggle for freedom. I chose to become a part of this heritage, hoping to act as a surrogate, to do something for people who were doing what they could for themselves and, as a result, were banned, exiled, imprisoned, or killed.

I arrived back in Philadelphia and immediately began preparing for a new kind of struggle. It revolved around a plan — proposed by South Africans themselves — to use the collective power of coercion by both morally and economically prodding corporations (beginning with U.S. companies) to change the laws of the South African government. It was something that had never been tried before. The seed had been planted to transform U.S. companies into a battering ram against the walls of apartheid until the walls came tumbling down.

Chapter 8

Launching the Sullivan Principles

THE SUNDAY after returning from South Africa, I preached at Zion Baptist to an overflowing congregation. My sermon title was "The Walls Must Come Down." I asked the children to take out a piece of paper and a pencil or pen and write down the date of the sermon: June 29, 1975. Then I said to them, "Write this: 'In fifteen years, apartheid in South Africa will be no more.'"

I spoke that day about what I had seen in South Africa and how the United States and the rest of the world had done very little to change the conditions of injustice and segregation that worked against blacks and other nonwhite peoples in the country. I spoke of my fears that South Africa would be thrown into a terrible, bloody, racial war unless something was done to end the atrocious racist conditions that prevailed. I told the children at Zion Baptist Church that history was about to be rewritten. I urged them to watch closely to see what God would do to change a situation that in the eyes of many around the world was unsolvable.

I began with a few lines I had written on a piece of paper, which I held up before the congregation. I titled this impromptu document "Principles of Equal Rights for United States Firms in the Republic of South Africa." Two years later, in stories published in the *London Times*, these Principles for Equal Rights would become known as the "Sullivan Principles." But in the intervening two years much work had to be done, and that work began a week after my sermon when I attended a board meeting at the General Motors Building in New York City on July 9. I reported on my visit to South Africa and asked the board to join me in the effort to end apartheid by taking the lead in organizing other U.S. companies to work together for change. I knew that if I could not persuade my own board of the urgency of this effort, it would be difficult to influence other companies. In fact, I announced that if the board withheld its support, I would resign

48

my position. Other board members and I knew full well that such a move would likely have great ramifications for the company, especially among African Americans, who viewed me as a symbol of hope and continued progress. The threat of boycotts against General Motors loomed.

My actions became part of the discussion among board members as they considered how to respond to my request. Others, no doubt, felt pressured into granting their support. But Thomas Murphy, who had succeeded Jim Roche as chairman of the board, was on my side. I had considered it a blessing to have Jim Roche serving as chairman of the company at the beginning of my tenure at GM. It was a further blessing for Thomas Murphy to be at the helm during this pivotal time. Influenced largely by Tom's leadership, the board ultimately agreed to support my initiatives in South Africa.

Following the board meeting, I had many discussions with various members of the board, some of whom had reservations about my actions. They believed that corporations should stay out of the business of governments. Several members characterized my actions as meddling and told me it would be impossible to achieve my goals. Some believed South Africa could not change without a bloodbath. Others were of the mind that things there were not so terrible, pointing out that blacks were living better in South Africa than they were in other African nations or even in some parts of the South in the United States. They voted to support me, they told me, not because they believed in what I was doing, but simply to go along with the rest.

No matter, the first step had been accomplished. I thought through my strategy and prayed about how I should proceed. I approached Tom Murphy and another friend, Frank Cary, who at that time was chairman of IBM and who had helped me with OIC, asking them to recommend a place where I could hold a meeting of chief executive officers from America's major corporations doing business in South Africa. I wanted to tell them of my experiences in South Africa and to request their support for the Principles I had developed. I wanted a place out of the way and free of public attention. This was not the time for publicity. Rather, I was intent on working behind the scenes to communicate my ideas as clearly as possible outside the gaze of public scrutiny.

Frank Cary suggested a place in Sands Point, New York, that served as a training center for IBM company executives. It was a remote

place, beautifully nestled in the New York hills. The date was set for
December 2, 1975. Tom Murphy and Frank Cary extended the invitation
to their corporate friends; chief officers and leading officials of
twenty-three major American companies in South Africa came to the
meeting.

After a brief introduction, Tom called on me to speak. I told these
executives what I had seen in South Africa, explaining how their
companies participated in oppressive, unjust systems. I spoke of the
dehumanization that existed in South Africa on a scale unequaled
anywhere else. And I urged them to combine their efforts, along with
the efforts of other companies in America, to work for change.

I appealed not only to their concern for racial justice but also to
their economic self-interest. I described my visit to Tanzania on my
way home from South Africa. There I had seen a rail line being built
by the Chinese from Tanzania to Zambia. I warned the executives that
if apartheid did not end soon, the stage would be set for a civil war in
the country. The rail lines would be a perfect passageway for Communist
soldiers from China, who would unquestionably use it in support
of South African blacks. Such a conflict would likely draw in the entire
Western world, I told them. All of Africa along with Russia would
join in the struggle. I warned that if this happened, Western companies
would in all probability lose everything they had. Many at the meeting
regarded the possible advance of Communism in the area as a major
concern. They feared that Communists would take control of the sea
route from the Atlantic to the Indian Ocean that was used for the
transport of oil and other minerals into the Western world. I believe
the fear of Communism and what could happen concerned companies
more than the welfare and freedom of the black population. I used
that fear to get the companies ready to fight apartheid.

I went on to suggest the development of a set of Principles of Equal
Rights for companies in South Africa. These Principles would be created
from the statement I had held up at my church months before.
In addition, they would incorporate ideas that had been sent to me by
several of the African leaders with whom we had met while we were
in South Africa.

That night at Sands Point a committee was chosen to refine our
ideas and to come up with a final draft, which would be presented
to company chairpersons of American businesses operating in South
Africa. Among the committee members were Tom Murphy; Frank

Cary; John Reid, chairman of Citibank; Brooks McCormick, chairman of International Harvester; and John Travalerious, president of Mobil. Over the next few months, committee members and their staffs met with me each week to complete the "Guidelines for the Principles of Equal Rights for U.S. Firms in South Africa."

As we worked toward finalizing the Principles, we often disagreed about what should be said and how. Many feared that their companies would be jeopardized by breaking the laws of the government. I responded by saying that while the Principles called for breaking the laws, the ultimate goal was to end them. At one point, frustrated at not getting the language I wanted, I decided to leave the meeting of the drafting committee and to give up on this whole approach. Brooks McCormick, who later became one of my closest and dearest friends and a supporter of my work in Africa, said to me as I was about to walk out the door, "Leon, don't leave. You have this thing where you want it at this time. Take what you have now and get all you want later."

One of the most difficult things about being an activist is knowing when to stand firm on principle and when to compromise for a time and be content with smaller steps of progress to reach the goal. I trusted Brooks's advice. And I'm glad I did. At first the language I wanted regarding recognizing unions and confronting the government head-on to end unjust laws was not strong enough. But the Principles would evolve, becoming tougher with each revision. When I was frustrated with the pace of their progress, I reminded myself that no company in America or anywhere else in the world had ever tried anything like this before. We were breaking new ground in our efforts to break the stranglehold of apartheid.

Developing the Principles was a rigorous process, but the most difficult part of the journey still lay ahead. I, and those who were behind me, had to convince leaders of companies throughout America not just to accept the Principles but to abide by them. Toward that end, for an entire year I traveled from coast to coast, meeting corporate executives in every major city of the United States, trying to convince them to become a part of this movement. Over and over again I was rebuffed and rejected. Companies did not want to buck the laws of a foreign government. Many believed that achieving political or moral goals fell outside the realm of business. Some executives said they wanted to wait to see what others might do; some, no doubt, did not like the idea of a black man trying to tell them what to do. More than a hundred meetings with representatives of corporations yielded twelve companies that were willing to support me. Even some of those did so reluctantly. I was determined to work with what I had.

On April 1, 1977, the Principles of Equal Rights, later to become known in America and around the world as the Sullivan Principles, were announced publicly with the names of the twelve signatory companies. Thomas Murphy of General Motors, Frank Cary of IBM, and Bill Travalerious of Mobil were at my side before the large press conference in Washington, D.C. Getting those twelve to sign capped two years of extensive work and travel. Not surprisingly, the first company to adopt the Sullivan Principles was General Motors. The other charter signatory companies were Ford, CalTex, Union Carbide, Otis Elevator, Burroughs, 3M, IBM, American Cyanamid, Mobil, Citibank, and International Harvester. Despite my satisfaction at having these twelve behind the Principles, I knew this was merely a beginning, for my goal was three hundred.

Before the announcement that morning, we had gone to the South African Embassy to inform officials of the Principles opposing segregation in their country. In their original form, the Principles called on U.S. firms with affiliates in South Africa to support the following operating guidelines:

1. Nonsegregation of the races in all eating, comfort, and work facilities.

2. Equal and fair employment practices for all employees.

3. Equal pay for all employees doing equal or comparable work for the same period of time.

4. Initiation of and development of training programs that will prepare, in substantial numbers, blacks and other nonwhites for supervisory, administrative, clerical, and technical jobs.

5. Increasing the number of blacks and other nonwhites in management and supervisory positions.

6. Improving the quality of employees' lives outside the work environment in such areas as housing, transportation, schooling, recreation, and health facilities.

The next day in South Africa, the story of the Sullivan Principles was blazing in the headlines of every newspaper in the country. The seeds for moving the mountain of apartheid had been planted.

Still people had their doubts. On one occasion, several GM board members expressed their skepticism as to how a few lines on a piece of paper could do anything to change a recalcitrant system that had defied change from every corner. "You will get something," they said to me, "but not what you are looking for." I had in my pocket a ball of yarn that Grace had been using to make something for one of the children. I took it out and grasped the loose end between my fingers and pushed the yarn across the table, and it fell unraveled on the floor. And I said to my fellow board members, "Apartheid is somewhat like that ball of yarn. If you take it by the end and hold it, then push it the right way, it will unravel to the floor." I continued, "I see the companies as the end of the yarn that I intend to hold in my hand, and I will push hard enough until apartheid unravels."

The Principles were not merely words written on a piece of paper. They represented goals and commitments to action.

Chapter 9

Applying Economic Pressure in South Africa

WITH THE PRINCIPLES in place, I followed up with a strategy I had used during the period when I was leading boycotts against U.S. companies and working for civil rights. I had persuaded companies to change their practices of employment by taking away their customers. I decided I must do the same thing to convince companies to become a part of the Sullivan Principles in South Africa. The goals were to improve conditions in the workplace, to increase opportunities for blacks in the communities where the companies operated, and to take a stand for economic and political justice in the country. The ultimate goal, of course, was to bring down apartheid.

Within a year, hundreds of church groups, institutional investors, and individuals were supporting the Principles through the ways they purchased and sold stock. They sent the message to companies in which they had investments that they would sell their stock if that company did not agree to sign and support the Sullivan Principles. In 1982, at the height of the Principle initiative, $500 billion in stocks and investments — representing pension funds, unions, universities, church groups, individuals, and city and state retirement funds — were behind me and the Sullivan Principles. In addition, on traveling to Great Britain to expand worldwide the Sullivan Principles effort, we secured the support of the Church of England and its foundation, which boasted the largest investment holdings among companies in the United Kingdom.

With the help of the Arthur D. Little Company, whom we engaged to establish methods of evaluation and the grading of the performances of companies in South Africa, an innovative system of grading, designed by D. Reid Weedon, was put in place. Three categories were created for the grading of company performance in the implementation process: *One*, making good progress; *Two*, making progress; and *Three*, needs to become more active. As interest from investors began to build, the companies felt a certain pressure to become signatories to the Sullivan Principles and to make good grades. Through the power of investors, scores of companies that previously said no began to say yes. Money talked. Company after company became a part of the Sullivan Principles. Pressured from several directions, companies began to work harder and harder to attain the best possible rating.

The rating of a company became a major item on corporate agendas in boardrooms throughout the United States. And the more the companies worked to implement the Principles in South Africa, the more changes, especially in the workplace, began to take place. Much of the credit for the success of this approach belongs to the Arthur D. Little Company for the grading system and to Reid Weedon and Daniel Purnell. Weedon, assigned by Arthur D. Little to work with us on the Principles, knew how to get our message across to the companies and helped me shape the grading system. Purnell helped execute the plan to monitor companies' progress. Without such grading and monitoring efforts, companies could have gotten by with merely giving lip service to the Principles. Many still did, in spite of the greatest efforts to avoid it.

After the first two years of the Principles, even though on paper they went against the laws of the South African government, every Sullivan signatory company in America had ended discrimination against black workers in company facilities in South Africa. Every company had begun to educate black workers for better positions. (Hundreds of black supervisors, administrators, and executives in corporations in South Africa today trace their career beginnings to the Sullivan Principles, which required the training and elevation of blacks to supervisory and management and executive positions.) Every company had begun to support black suppliers and small black businesses through contracts. Every company had initiated corporate responsibility efforts that reached into the communities where the businesses existed.

Companies were also helping with education, working to improve teaching skills and the conditions of schools. In some cases, they built new schools. Tens of millions of dollars were being designated for scholarships. At the high point of the Principles, thousands of black

South Africans were going to college in America on scholarships provided by companies working on their own or with other companies. The Principles also led scores of colleges and universities in the United States to grant hundreds of scholarships to black South Africans. Many of those who are now leaders of business and government in South Africa received scholarships in America because of the influence the Sullivan Principles had on school administrators, trustees, and companies.

The influence of U.S. companies had an impact on every segment of South African life, particularly in the cities, where most U.S. firms were located. Without the support of investors and stockholders, the Sullivan Principles would never have succeeded. Many of the companies had a humane interest in doing good in South Africa, but it was nothing compared to what they were doing based on economic self-interest. Yet it would be unfair to say that self-interest was the primary motivating factor in all cases. In fact, some company executives became so committed to change in South Africa that they took the risk of going to jail in order to do their part to help bring apartheid down. Extraordinary stories emerged from South Africa featuring U.S. company executives who actually became "radicals for change" and helped end conditions of segregation in entire regions. A general manager of one company in Port Elizabeth, for example, accompanied employees on "wade-ins" at the beaches as part of an effort to end segregation in the social realm. The effort spurred similar actions on beaches throughout South Africa and eventually put an end to separate white and nonwhite beaches altogether.

For the ten years the Sullivan Principles were active in South Africa, U.S. companies spent more than a half-billion dollars on programs to improve the quality of life for blacks, with support for blacks in South Africa and scholarships and other assistance in the United States. In places where U.S. companies were operative, education improved, thousands of schools were adopted and assisted by companies to improve education for black children, hundreds of clinics and many hospitals were equipped, and for the first time in history, South African blacks supervised whites. This model, provided by American companies, was once inconceivable in South Africa, where there was no evidence for hundreds of years of a black man's ever supervising a white man in a plant or in a mine or on a farm. Until the Sullivan Principles, a black man in South Africa never told a white worker what to do. But the winds of reform had blown, and as a result, the color of their skin will never determine the status of blacks in South Africa again. The Sullivan Principles created a revolution not only in job opportunities but also in the way black workers were viewed by white people in South Africa.

Each year from 1977 to 1987, the Principles became more ambitious and thus more difficult to implement. At meetings with company executives, held in New York twice a year, many complained of how we kept raising the bar, making "good progress" grades for companies harder and harder to achieve. But these Principles were by no means a static set of regulations. Our objective was not just to "shine the chains," as some critics at the beginning alleged, but to break the chains en route to achieving full freedom and justice for all. Provisions that were not originally part of the Principles were added as progress was made. We called for an end to job reservations, according to which black workers could not hold positions designated for whites. The Principles helped do away with laws forbidding the association of black workers and the creation of black unions. They helped eliminate restrictions on where blacks could live and buy houses. Largely as a result of the Principles and their demands, requirements for the carrying of passbooks ended, a goal that became especially important to me after my first visit to South Africa. Perhaps most importantly, the Sullivan Principles created a platform on which blacks and others could speak out for freedom and equal rights within a country where those who opposed the system had previously been routinely exiled, banned, jailed, tortured, or killed.

In 1980, I was invited to South Africa to deliver the Hoernle Memorial Lecture at the University of Witwatersrand. It was the most important annual address delivered in the country on the subject of race. Almost ten years before I had felt like David going to meet Goliath; this time I felt like Daniel about to enter the lions' den.

Chapter 10

Into and Out of the Lions' Den

REV. GUS ROMAN, my very close friend and coworker, strongly urged me to decline the invitation to deliver the Hoernle Lecture, warning me of the risk of going to South Africa. During this period, I had received many threats on my life from South Africa as well as from America. I had already found it necessary to move my family to different locations a number of times due to the intimidating and threatening actions against me, my wife, and my children. For several years, because of my great concern for their safety, my children were driven to school by a private driver. Threats against me came not only from whites but also from blacks, who for various reasons opposed my positions. I received numerous anonymous telephone threats and unsigned hate letters. During one period, trustees from my church accompanied me, following church services, to an apartment we had leased for security reasons. Because of the threats I was receiving, they wanted to be armed in order to protect me, and I had no problem with that. It was a time of assassinations in America.

I talked with Grace about my going to South Africa. We both felt great ambivalence but decided together that I should make the trip. We were willing to take the risk because we realized that to some extent the credibility of all I had stood for was at stake. I could not pass up this opportunity, despite the danger, to go to South Africa, completely reveal where I stood, and challenge the country to make changes. We agreed I had to be seen and heard, whatever the risk. We had come a long way from that remote meeting site in Sands Point, New York. Now it was time to deliver my message to the leaders of the South African government and to the entire country.

Since I was determined to make the trip, Gus Roman decided to accompany me and to stand (in most cases, literally) by my side. He was joined by Gary Robinson, a wonderful man who was head of the OIC International, and Daniel Purnell, executive director of the Equal

Opportunity Signatory Committee, which helped measure the compliance of companies with the Principles. When I got off the plane in South Africa, a fellow traveler on the trip, an executive of a major company, handed me a folder and said, "This is a speech I have prepared for you that has already been cleared. I think it says what you will want to say. Use it, and you need not let anyone know that I gave it to you." I was shocked and amazed. I shoved the folder back into his hands and said to him, "I have already written what I have to say, and it is not going to be cleared by anyone, except God Almighty. If the government does not like what I have to say, it can do what they want to with me, but they are going to hear what I have to say."

I was told — and I also sensed — that great expectancy had been generated surrounding my return to South Africa. The city of Johannesburg was astir. Hundreds of newspeople had come to hear my speech. Despite the expectancy, and as expected, my going into South Africa was neither easy nor pretty. On the front page of the *Rand Daily Mail*, a leading newspaper, the headline was "Sullivan lands — in a storm" (September 3, 1980). On the one hand, members of black trade unions sharply criticized the Sullivan Code for not persuading employers to recognize black unions. The union leaders also challenged me to state unequivocally the right of workers in South Africa to join unions of their choice and to insist that the black unions be approved by the state, and many black leaders asserted that the Sullivan Code was a toothless tiger. On the other hand, whites in South Africa, with few exceptions, opposed my coming to their country.

Before I left Philadelphia, I had received anonymous threats by long-distance telephone from whites and blacks in South Africa that I should not make the trip. These threats in particular prompted the precautions and guards that accompanied me throughout my visit. The precautionary measures did not go unnoticed by the *Rand Daily Mail*. Regarding the close security around me, the paper reported on September 6,

> He was surrounded at all times by a horde of security guards (including a senior executive of a security company) who would have done credit in both wariness and number to a visiting Head of State....
>
> A "Mail" reporter visited Fortress Sullivan this week and was told the great man was not talking to the Press. He stood up and took his leave.

He was then followed to the lift by a wary guard — presumably to make doubly sure that he did not burst into the Inner Sullivaranium and take a pot shot at His Excellency.

What would the good doctor do if he went to Belfast, we wonder? Send the Marines?

These were shaky times. But we made it.

While in South Africa, I met with black union leaders. Following these meetings and my speech at Witwatersrand University, my position in support of black unions would be emphatically clear, especially when I stressed that every company in the United States must recognize black unions. Indeed, the unfettered recognition of black trade unions was essential for the empowerment for black workers. I soon had the unions' support. But my visit did little to change the views of the white opposition because they believed I was trying to destroy their country. I was not trying to destroy South Africa, but I was trying to dismantle and destroy apartheid.

The time for the speech had almost arrived. Before I left the hotel for the university, I got on my knees to pray. Gus Roman, Daniel Purnell, and Gary Robinson knelt down with me, too. Gus later said that when he looked over and saw Gary Robinson on his knees praying, he knew this was serious business, for while Gary was a hard worker and a great leader and friend, he was not necessarily known as a praying man.

The auditorium at the university, called the Great Hall, was filled to overflowing. My speech at Witwatersrand University on September 4, 1980, outlined the Sullivan Principles and my thrust at that particular time. I spoke on "The Role of Multinational Corporations in the Republic of South Africa." With the speech I wanted to persuade companies from the United States and from elsewhere to use their clout and power in South Africa to bring an end to apartheid. I wanted to sound a message that would make it loud and clear that apartheid had to go and that America and the world should do everything possible to end the system. Excerpts from the Hoernle Memorial Lecture follow (see Appendix B for a transcript of the entire speech):

This evening, I come to your country as a black man with an appeal. It is an appeal for equality and for justice and for freedom for the black and other nonwhite population of South Africa. I come though not just for them but for all the people of your nation, white and nonwhite alike, because your destinies are tied together. For, "the laws of sacred justice bind oppressor to oppressed; and close as sin and suffering joined we march to fate abreast."

I ask you, therefore, as I speak to you here and to your nation, to find the national will to save your beloved country before it is too late and to provide full human rights and individual freedom to all your people and to let South Africa become South Africa, equally, for everyone. Above all things else, the need in South Africa today is for individual freedom and the recognition of the universal and inalienable rights of man. The notion must be confronted and dispelled that a white person is superior to a black person or a black person inferior to a white person or a person of any color inferior to another just because of the color of their skin.

I emphasize individual freedom because nothing will be more important to the future of your country than this. Without individual freedom for your black and other dark-skinned people, there will be no future peace in your land: the individual freedom to work where a person wants to work on the basis of one's ability and willingness to learn; the individual freedom to live where a person wants to live according to one's desire and circumstances to do so; the individual freedom to attend a school with equal access, without restriction because of color or race or tribe; the individual freedom to take equal part in choosing one's government and decide who shall make laws and govern lives, as well as to be part of those who govern; the individual freedom to move about without hindrance because of racial characteristics or identity; the individual freedom to speak as you please without fear; the individual freedom to be what you want to be and to work and to strive and to save and to own, as all others, for the benefit of your person, your family, your community, and your nation.

It must be sounded from your pulpits, taught in your classrooms, interpreted in your laws, and practiced in your nation. It must be realized here, as elsewhere, that if a nation is to be truly democratic, the fundamental premise of the equality of all people before God and man must prevail.... Racial discrimination has been with you a long time. Since 1660, less than a decade after the Dutch settled here, when a wild almond hedge was planted on a hill above Capetown and a pole fence was extended from it beyond which no black was to venture, South Africa has had its color bar. Since then black people have been constantly subjugated, and their labor exploited. David Livingstone wrote of inland South Africa in the 1840s and the widespread use of unpaid labor for the white farmers on the premise that "the people should work for us, in consideration of allowing them to live in our country."

These kinds of attitudes and practices have continued through the years, but racism took its worst and most dehumanizing form when, in 1948, South Africa structurally and officially adopted apartheid and made segregation the law of the land: enacting statute upon statute and piling indignity upon indignity upon its black and other nonwhite people. Apartheid and its policies of separate development, and all the laws and regulations that have followed, have made South Africa, in the eyes of the world, the most oppressive government dealing with human beings on the globe today....

...I cannot emphasize enough that I am a minister and a Baptist preacher, not a politician, not an educator, not a philosopher, not an economist, and not a businessman. I am a minister and a Baptist preacher, and I have gotten into this effort trying to meet challenges as they have arisen, as you will find later, step-by-step.

Also, I am a black man. There are eight hundred million of us in the world along with three billion other people of color, and we cannot permit a system that legally divides and segregates and degrades people simply because of the color of their skin, such as apartheid, to continue in the world today. Apartheid must come to an end, one way or another, and I intend to help bring it to an end if I can, hopefully, by peaceful means. My main personal objective is to help end apartheid. I want to see apartheid eliminated from the face of the earth. And the world must help make it happen.

Hurricanes are not deterred by national boundaries. Epidemics do not select persons because they are black, brown, yellow, white, or red. The seas indiscriminately wash many shores, and pollution from one nation can easily reach the shores of another. In a world such as ours where the few can dominate the many, no one knows what direction history will take. We must never forget Fascism and what happened because no one dared to stop it before it was too late. We must recognize there is a racial pollution here in South Africa that must be stopped; and it must be stopped now....

The Principles represent one of the most detailed and comprehensive industrial fair-employment charters ever voluntarily developed and activated in a united way by companies anywhere against racial discrimination in the world. If the Principles were followed and implemented by multinational companies in the Third World countries they would become a major force in the elimination of workers' inequities, widespread poverty, and pervasive ignorance and illiteracy in those countries....

Whatever might be said, it is clear that there has been some movement and some progress in South Africa as a result of the Principles. Therefore, I am encouraged but still very much dissatisfied because in relation to the need, it has all fallen far, far short of my desires and progress is far, far too slow. Conditions in South Africa are of such that the greatest urgency is required if the Principles and codes are to be effective enough to meet the needs at hand. Although there has been movement, the companies are not moving fast enough; in spite of the positive things that have been happening, the companies, overall, simply are moving too slow. The companies must be pushed more, for greater results. They are moving at the pace of a possum, when they should be moving at the speed of a hare. The companies are like a possum crossing a road, "taking their own good time." This includes American companies and other companies of the world as well.

To be sure, I am pleased by the leadership role the American companies have taken thus far in this progress, and I am pleased the Principles have been an important catalyst for change, and I am pleased for the recognition they have received, but I am far, far from being satisfied. They must do more to end discrimination, upgrade their workers, and promote equal opportunities outside the workplace. I acknowledge that some American companies are trying hard and doing encouraging things, but overall American companies must do more, and they must do them faster.

So, I will be returning to America and turning screws, more and more. I will be pushing all the companies, harder and harder to implement the Principles faster and faster, because the needs of black people in South Africa today are beyond description, and massive efforts are needed to eliminate their problems and to help them get rid of their oppression....

So, I will be supporting selective divestments against American companies that do not cooperate with the Principles and who fail to favorably comply with their implementation. I will, also, be "calling for" and urging strong United States government action against them, including tax penalties, sanctions, and the loss of government contracts. And, if change still does not come fast enough, I will consider stronger measures, including total divestment and, ultimately, a total embargo on all American exports and imports to and from South Africa.

In the past, companies have made excessive profits off of cheap labor,

lack of workers' rights, and segregated employment practices. We are just
not going to stand for it anymore. So...I will be doing all I can to get the
American companies to do more and to move faster to help in a definite
way to improve the conditions of black and other nonwhites here. And,
let it be heard in the corporate boardrooms of America that either their
affiliates in South Africa must shape up, or they should ship out....

Now, I am aware the companies cannot solve all the problems in
South Africa by themselves. It is a mistake to think they can. The problems here are far too deep and complex for that. In order to end racial
discrimination in South Africa, help is needed from many fronts: from
churches, unions, schools, governments, the United Nations, and world
public opinion, along with the companies. But companies have a major
role to play because they have been among the chief beneficiaries of an
unjust system, and they should be required to the utmost of their capabilities to help improve the conditions of the people and to help change
that system....

The Principles and the codes were never intended, as far as I am
concerned, to *appease* conditions, but they were meant to *change* conditions; some might have thought they were meant "to appease" and to
provide a cover for the companies to hide behind, but No! No! They were
not meant to appease or to cover up. They were meant to help change
the discriminatory conditions here; otherwise, as far as I am concerned,
they lose their purpose. If the companies of the world, with their Principles and their codes, fail to make a greater thrust inside and outside
the workplace soon, and if they fail to use their power and influence
to help persuade the South African government to end its racial and
discriminatory laws soon, then we will have missed the mark, and we
can all forget about our peaceful solutions. Time for peaceful change is
running out.

In Europe, and elsewhere, the voices of protest against racial injustice have been muted. Let them be heard again. Where are the liberal
churches? Where are they? Let them be heard again. Let them be heard
from London; let them be heard from Paris; let them be heard from Milan; let them be heard from Berlin, Stockholm, Tokyo...let them be heard
again. Where are you, Geneva, with your high-sounding platitudes on
freedom? Where is the world? There is a tragedy here. Where are you?

I am making an appeal today to companies of the world to use their
power and influence to help end racial discrimination in South Africa and
to help end apartheid. I ask the companies of the world to stop using the

Principles and codes as a camouflage and to realize they can no longer "do business as usual" in South Africa. . . .

Let the companies of the world in South Africa agree to face up to one of their greatest challenges and to insure the rights of black workers to association, to organize or belong to the union of their choice, if they choose, and the right to be represented in collective bargaining. For one of the greatest hopes for a peaceful solution in South Africa is cooperation "with" and "equality" of opportunity and benefits "for" the black and nonwhite workers. I implore you, don't suppress the workers. Let them organize if they choose, and work with them. To do less will be counterproductive. . . .

Also, let companies of the world agree to begin to expand their efforts outside the workplace, as described in statement 6 of the Principles. Let the companies of the world agree, beginning now, to assist in the initiation and the support of massive educational programs that will lead to the ending of illiteracy throughout South Africa and to the equalization of standards of education for every school and every child in the nation.

Let the companies of the world agree, beginning now, to assist with the development of training centers that will teach thousands and thousands of nonwhite youth with technical skills, as quickly as possible, and reach millions. . . .

Until apartheid has ended and there is clear, tangible evidence and demonstration thereof, no bank in the United States shall make any further loans to the South African government or its agencies and will give consideration only to specific, privately sponsored projects or programs, developed in cooperation with blacks and other nonwhites, which contribute to their social and economic advancement and equality and that do not support apartheid.

And it should be known that when I speak of the ending of apartheid in the bank statement and "clear, tangible evidence and demonstration thereof," I mean such things as the ending of the passbook system, the end to racially motivated banning and detentions, the rights of blacks to buy and own property anywhere in the nation, the ending of so-called independent homelands, equal protection under the law, and full citizenship rights and full political participation for blacks and other nonwhites equal to that of all other citizens in the Republic of South Africa. I will be pursuing support for this position or its equivalent throughout America, with the help of thousands of churches and bank depositors.

And regarding "new investments," I am opposed to new investments, except for retooling to remain competitive or for programs and projects that promote equality and improved social conditions for the nonwhite population until there are concrete evidences that apartheid is ending, including official meetings of white government leaders with black and other nonwhite leaders, such as a national convention, and a timetable with "common agreement" for full inclusion of blacks and other nonwhites equally in the economic, social, and political life of the country. At such a meeting or national convention, there should be real spokesmen for the people within the nation, urban and rural, and leaders like those in exile, banned, and like Nelson Mandela. Nelson Mandela must be freed!...

Recent developments have demonstrated to all that rising tides of discontent among the disadvantaged can change the course and the character of economic, social, and political systems. Historically, we know the revolutions that have shaken the world have come from lack of economic and political equality for the masses and lack of justice for the disadvantaged. Even today, the free enterprise system and the multinational corporations are being regarded by the disadvantaged of the world as dispassionate and unconcerned with the needs of the poor so long as they make their profits. And, as I see it, multinational corporations have, historically, been unresponsive to the needs of the poor, and for the most part, they are still so today. They have disregarded the human and social needs in the communities and environments where their plants and businesses exist. The great majority of the companies have been more interested in the bottom line than in helping people out of breadlines....

The Republic of South Africa provides the setting where companies can make significant progress in answering their critics by demonstrating clear and humanistic concern for the poor and the unemployed. They can use their vast powers and massive resources to help millions of people who have been cut off from opportunities to gain equality and equitable benefits from their labors and a better way of life. It is apparent that such direction is overdue and needed.

America, as the rest of the Western world, has a great deal to learn in this direction. The following comment appeared in an editorial in one of our great American financial journals, not long ago:

> It seems to us that the policy of American businesses makes little difference in South Africa, one way or another....most United States businesses in South Africa are expounding the sensible view that we provide goods and services to our customers, and profits to our investors; we obey the

local laws and try not to do anything beastly, and politics is the politicians' business.

It is this kind of view that must be proven wrong and dispelled because providing goods and services to customers and profits to investors might, unfortunately, have been considered sensible at one time, but not now. And observing local laws and trying not to do anything beastly is a day long gone. Today, humanistic interest had better be the concern of companies if, under the banner of free enterprise, they expect to survive. The greatest enemy of capitalism is not communism but the selfishness and lack of humanity of capitalism....

Just before the turn of the nineteenth century, W. E. B. Du Bois, a great black scholar and philosopher, warned, "The problem of the Twentieth Century is the problem of the color line — the relation of the darker to the lighter races of men in Asia and Africa." Here in South Africa, today that problem is seen at its apex. If it can be solved here, it can be solved anywhere.

For the sake of South Africa...

For the sake of all your people...

For the sake of the world...Let's all work to solve it.

That, by the grace of God, there might be found, in spite of the odds, a peaceful alternative to warfare in South Africa.

It can...it must be done.

South Africa, my black and white and other nonwhite brothers and sisters, may God Almighty bless you on the way and help you all in this struggle for freedom. Take each other's hands, and help build the new South Africa together, for everyone.

When I finished the speech, all the blacks stood up and cheered and applauded. Many could never have imagined ever hearing what I had just said in South Africa. Much of what I said directly opposed the laws of South Africa, most notably my call for the freeing of Nelson Mandela. The crowd surged towards the stage — I did not know whether they wanted to express their gratitude or to take other actions. But not wanting to take any unnecessary risks, Gus Roman and a couple of guards who had been provided for my protection rushed me off the stage, through a back door, and into a car that moved speedily to my hotel. The lobby was cleared when I entered, as was the elevator. Special precautions were taken throughout my stay.

Guards stayed in rooms on both sides of the one where I slept, and additional guards stayed in a room across from me. All of them were heavily armed.

The next morning, extensive parts of my speech were printed in all the South African newspapers, and much of it was aired throughout the day on television and radio. *The Soweton*, the leading black newspaper in South Africa, lauded my speech, expressing pleasant surprise that I had been so direct in calling for the release of Mandela. Such a call constituted an illegal act. An editorial in *The Soweton* stated, "The speech sounded good, but dynamite sounds better." Being a peaceful man, I would not call for violence. But after seeing what blacks were going through in South Africa, I could understand what the editorial was saying. At the next session of the South African Parliament a few days later, a speaker rose to ask, "How did that man, foaming at the mouth on television and criticizing our government, get into this country? His kind must never be permitted in South Africa again."

Over the next few days after the speech, I had many meetings with black and white leaders, including Gatsha Buthelezi, the leader of the Zulus, who later became a close friend. I also met with such leaders in the struggle as Nthato Motlana, chairman of the Soweto Ten; Bishop Desmond Tutu, one of the most brave, forceful, and inspirational leaders of our time; Rev. Beyers Naude, a white spiritual activist and a great defender of the black cause; and Cyril Ramaphosa, the brave and courageous leader of the black miners whom I strongly encouraged and supported, assuring I would do all I could to see that human rights for black workers, including the right to form unions, became a central tenet of the Sullivan Principles.

Minister Pieter Koornhaf, who was in charge of major matters pertaining to race in the country, called me on the phone and assured me that the decision had been made to end passbook requirements for blacks across the land. This was of major importance to me as I could never get out of my mind from my first trip to South Africa images of bulges in the pockets of every black man, woman, and child over fifteen years of age walking down the streets and roads of South Africa. I was also assured by the minister that rights for blacks to join and organize unions would follow.

While I was in South Africa, I tried to stay in touch with what was happening at home. A few weeks before I left for South Africa to deliver the Hoernle Lecture, I had been called by the White House and told that President Jimmy Carter was coming to Philadelphia and wanted to speak at my church. Though Grace and I decided that I should go to South Africa, I asked her to remain in Philadelphia and, taking my place in the pulpit, read a message to the congregation that I would send on that day from South Africa. It may have been the only time that a president of the United States ever came to speak at a church and the pastor wasn't there! But President Carter understood that my work in South Africa had become more important to me than almost anything else.

I sent the message in a lengthy telegram. I learned later that Grace, who had reluctantly agreed to stay behind, stood up and read it with a few insertions of her own. When she finished, the crowd stood up and applauded her for her presentation. President Carter brought the house down when he began his speech with a reference to "Amazing Grace." My wife has been known in Philadelphia by that moniker ever since, and I cannot think of a better phrase to describe what she has meant to me.

Before leaving South Africa, I met with representatives from the U.S. companies that were signatories of the Sullivan Principles. I thanked them for what they had done, for never before had firms from the United States or anywhere else in the world engaged a government to change its practices and its laws affecting workers and its people. But I also told them that when I returned to the United States, I would nevertheless be upping the ante and pushing for even greater reform.

The Principles had clearly transformed some company executives into activists for change. Whether motivated by moral principle or self-interest or both, U.S. companies in South Africa had become part of a corporate activist movement that would change the lives of tens of millions of people, both inside and outside the workplaces of South Africa. These companies had already accomplished what many believed was impossible: They had eliminated segregation within their companies. They had opened up places in South Africa where blacks and other nonwhites were previously forbidden by law to live. They had changed the way companies operated in relation to the government. Much of what they accomplished was in direct violation of South African law. But this was no time to stop or even slow down. These companies had to be pushed to go further.

My ultimate objective was, not to break the laws, but to end the laws that prohibited justice and equal opportunity for all. Thus, for the first time I informed company representatives that I would be calling on companies to engage in "corporate civil disobedience" in South Africa. I don't think any of them knew quite what I meant. They had heard the term *civil disobedience* but could not conceive of how it might be applied by companies. In time, however, extraordinary things would be accomplished under the corporate civil disobedience mandate.

My final meetings before leaving South Africa were with black community and union leaders. Before returning to the United States, I wanted to be sure that we were together on the objectives. They affirmed the direction in which I'd been heading and said they would do all they could from within South Africa to support my efforts. Over time, they fulfilled that commitment. In comparison, I received only lukewarm support for the Sullivan Principles in the United States, including from African Americans. Many could not conceive of a black man doing what I was doing. They figured I must be a tool of some person or entity. Truth be told, my faith notwithstanding, I even had trouble believing the changes that I witnessed could take place so rapidly. But I knew I was no tool to be used by anyone, but a servant of God willing to pay the price for freedom. What the world saw was what it got: a man who was attempting to move a mountain by applying the very principles he had believed in since his earliest days.

Ready at last to return home, I made my way with my colleagues to the airport in Johannesburg. For several hours we waited for the plane to leave, but it was mysteriously canceled. The U.S. government later had an attaché take us to his home, somewhere in the suburbs, where I slept until morning with someone sitting outside my door. The next morning, I was taken back to the airport and put on a plane. But I never saw my suitcases or clothes again; they could not be found anywhere. I did not care; I was glad to be returning home safely. Gus Roman said, in his own cryptic way, "Your clothes are being used as target practice." I'll never know for sure, but perhaps someone somewhere was trying to send me a parting message, and this was the best he could do.

Before arriving in New York, the airline hostess told me to remain in my seat until everyone had left the plane. I did not know what was going on. After all, the plane had landed safely in New York. After everyone else had left the plane, a man came back, took me by the arm, and led me up the ramp to the waiting room, around which FBI agents were hovering. They told me that while we were in flight, Gus Roman had sent a message to the captain of the airplane reporting that he had seen people on the plane he believed were members of the Afrikaner Broederbond, an Afrikaner militant group. Fearing trouble, Gus asked the captain to have the FBI at the airport for my protection. Whether or not they were Broederbond members, we may never know. What I do know is how thankful I was to have Gus Roman looking out for me. When I finally got in my car and was driving to Philadelphia, I breathed a great sigh of relief and looked up and said, "Thank you, Jesus." I was glad to be back home.

Not long after returning, I was interviewed by the *New Yorker* magazine for an article that appeared as a major story in the issue dated December 22, 1980. The interview took place during a break at a GM board meeting. The published article pointed out that some critics of apartheid had "denounced the Sullivan Principles — which call for integration of all plant facilities, equal pay for equal work, recognition of black unions, and the like — as cosmetic, and have denounced Dr. Sullivan himself, in part because of his association with General Motors, as a spokesman for the status quo in that tindery country."

The article quoted me as saying, "There's no question but that I ran into a storm in South Africa. I couldn't stay there long. I have to be in my church every Sunday. I'm not a businessman or an educator or a philosopher. I'm a *preacher*. So I didn't have time to inspect any G.M. plants there. I just went to talk, but I don't think anyone anticipated I would say what I did." Details of my formal speech in South Africa had been well publicized; the *New Yorker* article provided a forum to reveal some of the things I'd said prior to the speech.

Before the Hoernle Lecture, I had met with a couple of hundred resident business executives, all white and mostly the American managers of local subsidiaries of American companies. I'm sure most of them were expecting me to give them a pat on the back. But shortly before joining them, I had gone out to the black township of Soweto to get some feel of what apartheid really was like. I saw one million people living in a concentrated space in dilapidated conditions. The experience hit me hard and certainly did not put me in the mood to be offering anyone a pat on the back. Instead, I told them I was not satisfied with what they were doing: "If I were going to grade your performance on a scale of zero to one hundred, you'd average about an eight. You're not going to be able to use my Principles any longer as a coverup for your inadequacy. Shape up or ship out. I'm going to turn the screws on you." I also told them that the root problem in South Africa wasn't fair employment practices. It was apartheid. I called for a complete change in government, facilitated by a nationwide political convention of all races that would include the long-imprisoned Nelson Mandela. I talked about a possible total U.S. embargo against South Africa.

The executives couldn't believe what they were hearing. Had it come from a South African black person, he or she would have likely been imprisoned. Several who'd been planning to attend my speech changed their minds. Even some of the black leaders in South Africa were skeptical about what I could accomplish. Bishop Desmond Tutu told me shortly after I arrived, "Reverend, we appreciate what you're doing, but you're being used." But after he heard what I said, Bishop Tutu called me on the telephone and said, "I support you." And many others who had doubted before learned that I was not involved for the purpose of protecting business. What I cared about was changing an unjust system without a bloodbath.

I told the *New Yorker*, "I sometimes wonder why I'm doing all this. It's been such a long journey. I have no government behind me. I've got only faith, some economic persuasiveness, and a lot of guts. It's been slow going, but then you can't climb a mountain by jumping from the bottom to the top. I keep wondering: Is it possible for a society like ours to deal with things by humanitarian and economic means? Are there alternatives to war for solving social problems? Is it possible for a person who calls himself a preacher to bring about change in one of the most difficult areas of the earth? In terms of ministry, that's the greatest challenge. I'd like to go back to South Africa someday, but I don't know if they'd let me in now. I still have some clothes over there. My luggage somehow didn't get on my plane with me, and it hasn't turned up yet. Somebody suggested they're using my clothes for target practice. Well, there can't be many people who'd fit into them anyway."

When the interview ended, I walked right into the board meeting of General Motors and again urged them to do more to end apartheid. By faith, I believed the ultimate mission would be accomplished, but working toward that goal was often difficult and painstaking. Nearly everywhere I went in America and Europe I encountered opposition to my approach. Some of it came even from my closest ministerial friends, many with whom I had worked in the civil rights movement through the years.

But in the early 1980s, that began to change. Among those who would announce their support for my Principles were John Jacobs, president of the National Urban League; Benjamin Hooks, president of the National Association for the Advancement of Colored People (NAACP); Andrew Young, American ambassador to the United Nations; Rev. Ralph Abernathy, a close coworker and friend of Martin Luther King's; and Jesse Jackson. Many other lesser-known black church and community leaders in the United States also began to promote support for the Principles, and I also enjoyed the support of the Organization of African Unity (OAU). I had kept the OAU informed of my efforts against apartheid from the very beginning.

Through it all my support in Philadelphia remained strong. On one occasion the leading newspaper in the city carried articles criticizing work with my training centers and challenging our contention that we had trained a million people for jobs in the United States. And there were those at the newspaper who did not support my efforts in South Africa. When the articles appeared, the black community in Philadelphia went into an uproar. The paper did not realize that nearly every black household in Philadelphia had members who had been trained and put in a job through our training centers. Within the first week hundreds of blacks canceled their subscriptions to the newspaper, and during the next month virtually every black in Philadelphia, along with many others, had stopped reading the paper. It was said during the time that a black person in Philadelphia would not be seen in the streets carrying a fish wrapped in the newspaper. By the end of the year the newspaper, one of the most powerful in America, had to close its doors, and it never reopened.

In 1983, a commission supported by the Ford Foundation issued the report *South Africa: Time Is Running Out*, which was one of the most thorough documents dealing with apartheid of that time. The commission, chaired by Ford Foundation president Franklin Thomas, urged that the Sullivan Principles be followed by all U.S. companies in South Africa and supported by the U.S. government. Frank Thomas remained a friend and inspiration in the years to come.

There were times when I felt frustrated, alone, and misunderstood. Though I always knew God was on my side, it felt good to have a growing number of God's people behind me, too. The road ahead was still long, and I welcomed all the support I could get.

Chapter 11

Setting the Deadline to End Apartheid

M AKING THE SULLIVAN PRINCIPLES work as effectively as possible was a constant, delicate balancing act. For example, I wanted and needed publicity, but I also recognized that too much publicity could hurt the cause. At various times, some strong opponents of apartheid wanted me to push harder, while others thought if I pushed too hard, companies would quit trying to make reforms. My assessment of when to push ahead was based in part on my reading of the support I enjoyed both in the United States and overseas.

My plan from the beginning was to move forward in measured increments. First came the ending of segregation in the companies. Second came workers and union rights, along with initiatives to improve education and develop leaders for a postapartheid South Africa. In 1984, I determined that it was time to challenge companies to a direct confrontation with the South African government. I encouraged them to work towards eliminating not just the laws but all the customs that stood in the way of social and political justice. This resulted in the elimination of discrimination outside the workplace in such areas as housing, clinics, beaches, and schools. We had also ended passbook and job-classification requirements as well as regulations in the workplace favoring whites over blacks.

Still, unfinished business lay ahead, especially freedom for Mandela, equal voting rights for blacks, and the official dismantling of apartheid. The systems were in place to move on these fronts. Companies from all over the world began to support this goal. Targeted divestment and sanction campaigns, backed by massive stockholder support, had been making an impact.

In 1985, the time came for me to take the most significant step since unveiling the Principles in 1977. I brought the major issues to a head in an editorial published in the *Philadelphia Inquirer* on May 7, 1985, in which I announced to South Africa a two-year deadline for

74

the government to end statutory apartheid, release Nelson Mandela, and give black Africans the right to vote on an equal basis with whites. This deadline was reported extensively both in the United States and in South Africa. With that editorial, the last round of my fight had begun.

According to statement 7 of the Sullivan Principles, which was added in 1984, companies would be pushed to work to eliminate all laws, practices, and customs that impeded social, economic, and political justice. This meant those companies endorsing the Sullivan Principles would have to try harder to eliminate laws, practices, and present customs that impeded equal opportunity anywhere within their company operations or in South Africa, including the South African government and the environment in which the company did business. I called on companies to support human rights in ways that required dismantling the apartheid system itself and the freeing of Nelson Mandela. And this was to be done within the next twenty-four months. This seventh principle put the companies in direct confrontation with the South African government.

Several months after the announcement of the two-year deadline for ending apartheid, I appeared during halftime of a Monday-night football game on ABC. I took the opportunity to articulate and underscore my two-year ultimatum to an audience of fifty million people. That night, I lost a thousand white business friends who felt I had gone too far in turning the screws. Things began to heat up in America.

Antiapartheid efforts in the United States became stronger. Actions in the United States Congress took center stage. An omnibus antiapartheid act was being aggressively pursued, led by Congressman Bill Gray of Pennsylvania and Congressman Steve Solarz of New York, among others. Support from the Republican side of Congress was urgently needed to get the legislation through the House of Representatives, but the numbers were falling short. Republican congressman Jack Kemp, who aspired to run for president, called me during the heat of the discussion in Washington and asked me if he should support Bill Gray or not. I urged him to support Bill Gray and to go all out to get the full support of the Republicans in the House and the Senate. Within the next few months, the antiapartheid legislation passed with an overwhelming vote of Democrats and Republicans. President Ronald Reagan vetoed the legislation, but Congress overrode his veto;

the Anti-apartheid Act of 1986 became the law of the land. In the act, the Sullivan Principles were enshrined in legislation and were to remain so, even after apartheid had ended (as they do today), for assurances that U.S. companies would never again return to segregationist practices. A few days after the act had passed, Steve Solarz called me on the phone and said, "Leon, now two Americans have their names attached to American Foreign Policy Laws: the Monroe Doctrine and the Sullivan Principles."

As I continued to up the ante, I came to a greater realization of how crucial it was to gain the backing of British companies. The United States' economic stake in South Africa was relatively small, amounting to around $2 billion. The 350 American companies in South Africa employed approximately seventy thousand black South Africans, only 2 percent of the total black labor force. In contrast, half of the 2,000 companies actively operating in South Africa were British, representing an economic stake of $6 billion. I could use the companies from the United States as a powerful wedge, but they alone would not be enough to apply the economic pressure needed to dismantle apartheid. I needed the help of other nations.

I set out to make more of a concentrated effort to bring British companies and other companies of the world on board. Toward that end, I sought a castle in Europe, preferably one with a moat in order to set the proper tone, to create an aura of special importance and secrecy. I knew companies would be hesitant about a gathering that featured publicity and international scrutiny. I wanted a gathering that would be off the record to the world in order to enable everyone to feel free to state their positions. I lined up participants for the meeting while at the same time searching for the perfect place. At a public policy meeting of General Motors, I informed my colleagues that I needed a castle. John Horan, chairman at the time of Merck & Company and a very supportive friend, said he thought he could get me one. And he did: Leeds Castle outside of London, built by Henry VIII for his many wives. It even had a moat!

I then traveled throughout Europe and secured commitments from company executives in France, Germany, Sweden, Finland, and the United Kingdom to work with me, thanks largely to the support of England's former prime minister, Edward Heath, who at my request cochaired the meeting with me and who made every effort to get the top corporate officials of companies from the United Kingdom to attend. Roger Smith was helpful, as he always was, in handling staffing and transportation needs.

Prior to the first meeting at Leeds, I went to Rome to see Pope John Paul II. I wanted his support for what I was doing in South Africa prior to meeting with corporate leaders from Europe. At St. Peter's, he told me he knew of the Sullivan Principles and gave me encouragement to continue, with his blessing. I also asked the pope to do more to end apartheid. The pope's blessing and interest would prove helpful to me in my efforts to influence the executives.

In all, I coordinated three meetings at Leeds Castle: in 1985, 1986, and 1987. All made important contributions. Until now, no account of these meetings has ever been reported.

The date of the first meeting was March 8, 1985. Among those attending from America, Europe, and South Africa were chairmen and top executives of General Motors, Ford, Kellogg, Goodyear International, Control Data, Cadbury Schweppes, Citibank N.A., The Urban Foundation, Fluor Corporation, British Petroleum, Mobil Oil, CalTex, Shell Transport, Alfa-Laval, Barclays Bank PLC, The Premier Group Limited, Rio Tito Zinc, Anglovaal Limited, Barlow Rand Limited, SKF AB, Fagersta-Seco AB, and the Council of Swedish Industries. Never before had such an array of powerful company executives assembled to discuss South Africa at one place at one time.

We started with reports from various companies of what they were doing individually to change South Africa and to improve conditions for their workers. Then I delivered the following message to the chief executive officers:

I want to welcome you who have come today to Leeds Castle. No question is more important for discussion for leaders of the industrial world than future possible developments and the role for companies in the Republic of South Africa. The necessity for urgent changes in that country to ensure a just and free society for all its population is one of the most important and urgent needs facing the world today, and the contribution that can be made by chief executives of companies such as those represented here today can be decisive in helping determine the future course South Africa will take in dealing with its black population.

Already, equal-rights codes, such as the Sullivan Principles, the EEOC Code, the South African Seccola Code, and others, have been adopted and initiated by companies represented here and many other companies from various nations. The codes have unquestionably made a significant impact in South Africa as far as advancement for black and other non-white workers is concerned. In fact, a revolution in equal rights for black workers is underway within the workplace in South Africa, in plants and in mines, and in other businesses throughout the nation. It is a peaceful revolution, daily changing conditions and improving the quality of life for hundreds of thousands of workers. The effects of this revolution for equal rights within the companies are increasing every day, and if we strengthen these equal-rights codes and more closely monitor them and work to see that all companies in South Africa abide by them, there is no doubt they will have an increasing, major imprint on the problem.

However, it is clear the changes being brought about by our companies, and other efforts, are not happening fast enough to avert the kinds of cataclysmic developments building daily in South Africa that, if not averted soon, will lead to a bloodbath and the loss of millions of lives and the destruction of a nation, including your plants and businesses, and everything else with it. Such a development, beginning as a race war, would inevitably become an ideological war, quickly involving the whole continent of Africa as well as much of the rest of the world, particularly the Western nations and the Soviet Union, and could easily lead to a nuclear holocaust. The necessity for a nonviolent solution to the South African question is essential not only for industrial and strategic needs but for the peace of the world.

Being a realist I expect no miracles today. There are limitations to what even this group of companies can do. We have no mandate. Yet we have mutual interest, and of greater importance, we have a conscience. We generally agree that every step must be taken to avoid the massive violence and suffering and the untold destruction of property; in which case those who are not supporters of free enterprise will get a firm foothold in Africa, and all your investments will be in jeopardy.

Time, presently, is not on our side. Time for peaceful change in South Africa is running out, and if the large companies of the world do not move swiftly, very swiftly, to do all they can to help deal with the problems, it will be too late. Growing world opinion will continue to build against your companies, and the massive protests and calls for action against businesses in South Africa presently within the United States will not elude the shores of any nation.

I have come with no fixed agenda except that we be guided by our own conscience to find ways we, individually and collectively, might be most effective to help bring about equitable conditions of life for the South African black population, within and without the workplace, and that we rely upon the help of almighty God to guide us in the shaping of our views and conclusions.

It is imperative that we be honest and candid throughout our discussions, realizing that all we do with our good works within our companies is of little value if benefits stop at the doors to our plants and do not carry over into the families, the homes, and the communities where the people live. The companies must expand their efforts. The structure of apartheid must be dismantled. The window of freedom in South Africa must be raised.

We know that power is never relinquished without a struggle, but this time, the only alternative in South Africa for the sake of the world is a "peaceful" struggle that will remove all vestiges of discrimination — economic, social, and political — because of race or color. I hope we will discuss what can be done today to broaden the essential base of education and training, improve the social, economic, and political status of the black people, and what can be done to work with those within South Africa who are striving for a just and free society through nonviolence.

I made every effort to avoid the publicizing of this meeting, but we know it is not even remotely possible that so many contacts with so many important people can be made and assembled as we see here today in complete secrecy. Already the press has somehow learned of this gathering. Later, we will have to determine how to deal with reporting this meeting, particularly now that it is known.

To my knowledge, this kind of multinational gathering of chief executives of leading companies from around the world doing business in South Africa has never been held before. It is unprecedented and history making that this meeting is even happening, and all are to be commended for their attendance. It shows a strong awareness and desire on your parts, individually, to do something meaningful about the mounting problems in South Africa.

Now, let us get busy and see what we can do to help bring apartheid in South Africa to an end.

This introduction was followed by a full day of give-and-take. We discussed ideas and possibilities, as well as concerns and hesitations. We closed by deciding to meet again the following year. I did not get all I had hoped for, but this meeting was a beginning. It broke new ground in corporate international relations against the South African government's injustices. The wall was beginning to crack.

I decided to stay clear to the fullest extent possible of any publicity surrounding the Leeds meeting. As far as I was concerned, no one should know about who was there or what was said. If word got out, some companies might be hesitant to take action, and the plan could be endangered. But when that many high-powered people convene in one place, sometimes it is hard to prevent word from leaking out. The South African government learned of our meeting, and for this I was pleased. I wanted the South African government to know about the meeting to get them to move ahead to end the apartheid system. The gathering at Leeds Castle became a topic of discussion at the highest level of the South African government for some time to come. In top government circles, people began imagining for the first time what South Africa without apartheid might look like. They were beginning to grapple with the possibility of not being able to overcome a unified antiapartheid effort by the companies of the world. My plan to end apartheid was working.

Chapter 12

Running Out of Time

FOLLOWING THE FIRST Leeds Castle meeting, I immediately went on the road again, retracing my steps through Europe and then on to Canada and Australia, meeting with businesses, governments, and religious leaders to put more pressure on the South African government for fundamental change.

I also aggressively sought scholarships for young black South Africans to help them become leaders of a new South Africa. I knew educated black South Africans would be needed by the thousands. Also, I stepped up my efforts in the United States and gathered more support for my efforts from thousands of black churches, pension funds, and city and state governments. The criticisms against me remained strong in the United States in some circles really because many of these critics had little idea about what I was doing and how I was doing it. And I could understand their concern. If I were on the outside looking at me, I would not have believed what I was doing myself. In many ways my critics actually helped me because I learned from what they were thinking and saying to help me in my own efforts. I never condemn my critics; I learn from them. At times your critics can be more helpful than your friends.

In my campaign to end apartheid, I began to plan for a second Leeds Castle meeting. This 1986 meeting also brought together corporate leaders from throughout Europe, the United States, and South Africa. By and large, segregation in the private sector in the companies was coming to an end. But the structure of apartheid remained, and I continued to believe that the corporations of the world were in the best position to change that reality.

In a discussion with former Prime Minister Heath and several others the night before the meeting, I spoke of the need for greater efforts on the part of the companies to get the South African government to free Nelson Mandela and to end apartheid. I assured them that an all-out racial conflict loomed as a possibility. Though whites, of course, possessed the military might, blacks outnumbered whites four to one. At the time, blacks were marching in the streets of Johannesburg and firebombing government buildings and even jailhouses. They were becoming more defiant in their opposition to the continuing oppression. Demonstrations in the townships were met with an increasing incidence of "necklacing," the practice of putting a car tire soaked in gasoline around the neck of a black man, woman, or youth, believed to be in cahoots with the government, and setting the tire on fire. South Africa was officially in a state of emergency.

I told Heath and others in a private setting at the castle that time was running out for companies to address South Africa's problems in nonviolent ways, adding that if we were not successful with the companies, a race war was inevitable. Former Prime Minister Heath replied, "This means it is more urgent than ever that these meetings succeed because the world will not stand by and see four million white people go down." His statement reaffirmed the importance to me of our working even harder at Leeds the next day and in pulling out all the stops to get companies to help end the racist system. Everyone agreed that a race war in South Africa that would draw in countries from every part of the world had to be avoided at all costs. And I was determined to do what I could to avoid it.

On a lighter note, something unusual happened the night before the second Leeds meeting. I had decided to stay at the castle overnight, awaiting the arrival of corporate executives in the morning. I slept in a room used by King Henry VIII when he visited his wives, two of whom were disposed of on the execution block. I was awakened by strange sounds in the room and concluded that either it was the heat coming up through the ducts on this blustery night or it was the ghost of King Henry VIII moving around because he was disturbed with seeing a black man sleeping in his bed. After all, he was not known for his positive race relations. In any case, I turned over and went back to sleep.

Many serious discussions took place at the meeting the next day. I do not feel at liberty even now to provide details since much of what was said was of a personal and private nature. Suffice it to say that company executives left the meeting with a much stronger commitment to take more resolute actions, using their clout with the South African government to press for the dismantling of apartheid.

After the meeting at the castle, a reporter from the *London Times* met me in the lobby of a hotel in London, where I was staying the night after the Leeds meeting, and asked me to tell him what had transpired. He had heard about the meeting from some source, as had many others. It was hard to keep a secret given all the private helicopters and airplanes that had been landing nearby. I told the reporter I had nothing to say. He said that the Leeds meetings were world news, that the world should know what was going on, and that publicity would help my cause, but I refused any discussion with him. He looked at me, shook his head, and said, "I feel sorry for you." And he was right. I felt sorry for myself. I would have liked for the world to know what was going on. It was news. But I also knew that, given the commitment I'd made to those who came, if I talked to that reporter, I might never be able to get company executives together again, and the things I had in my mind might never be accomplished. Many a great cause to help people has failed because someone talked too much. I was not interested in publicity; I was interested in results. And so the Leeds Castle meetings got very little publicity, yet they were indispensable to the plan for changing South Africa. After all, the government could put black people in jail for doing something it didn't like. But it could not jail a company. Companies and money they brought to the table would increasingly do my talking for me in Pretoria.

When I was last in South Africa, I had indicated to company executives that I might call them to corporate civil disobedience. I determined in 1986 that the time had come. On May 2, 1986, I sent the following letter to the chairmen of the nearly two hundred American companies remaining in South Africa who were signatories to the Sullivan Principles:

Dear Chairman:

The purpose of this letter is to inform you of the broadened initiatives I am advocating that signatory companies to the Sullivan Principles should take in the light of the unprecedented turmoil in South Africa. My goal since the inception of the Principles has been to assist with the total elimination of South Africa's apartheid system. It is very clear that until the system is actually removed, the crises in South Africa will worsen. Therefore, this letter is a call for your company and all other United States signatory companies to increase, intensify, and broaden their efforts to maximize their impact in South Africa. I am, therefore, requesting today that each company should individually and collectively work toward the common objectives outlined.

First, I am stressing that U.S. signatory companies continue their present programs in keeping with full adherence to the Sullivan Principles. These programs have demonstrated their value, and the human and financial resources expended on each of these activities should be continued and expanded upon. Special emphasis must be given immediately to increasing the number of blacks in management positions "to assure that as quickly as possible there will be appropriate representation of blacks and other nonwhites in the management group of each company at all levels of operations" as detailed in Principle 5.

Second, I am advocating that U.S. signatory companies increase their activities in the areas of the Fourth Amplification, which calls for U.S. signatory companies to actively challenge all apartheid laws. I am therefore requesting that U.S. signatory companies individually and collectively issue public statements opposing the existence of apartheid and calling for its total abolition — including full and equal citizenship rights for all blacks, the freeing of Nelson Mandela, and full and equal participation of blacks in the political process, and that you take every possible action to help bring this about.

Third, I am calling upon the signatory companies to follow a stringent course of "corporate civil disobedience," which means U.S. signatory companies should not administer any unjust laws or discriminatory practices or requirements pertaining to the apartheid system at any of their company operations. Also, I am asking the companies to use their legal and financial resources to the fullest possible extent, wherever their companies are located, to assist blacks in the equal use of all private and public amenities, such as parks, beaches, hospitals, theaters, public transportation, schools, and housing.

I am urging you, as chief executive officer of your company, which is a signatory to the Sullivan Principles, to support these initiatives. The coming year will be a crucial one for United States' companies, and companies from around the world in South Africa, to do all they can to contribute to the unequivocal freedom of South Africa's black population.

Sincerely,
Leon H. Sullivan

The letter and the appeal for corporate civil disobedience created shock and astonishment throughout the American business establishment. I received many letters expressing a wide array of sentiments, though most of them conveyed dismay and anger. The general view of the corporate community could be summarized by the question, "What is Sullivan trying to do?" I received a call from the chairman of one of the more powerful companies who asked, "What are you trying to do to us, put our managers in jail?" I responded, "Absolutely, if it is necessary to achieve the objectives."

I pushed forward because the momentum of progress was on our side. Demonstrations and protests against apartheid in South Africa reached their height in our country's capital. They included a very important and successful campaign waged at the South African Embassy in Washington. Each call for greater action brought tension. But I knew we'd faced it before and had overcome. This was no time to turn back.

The months were moving on, and the two-year deadline was coming to an end. The third Leeds Castle meeting of worldwide corporate chief executives took place in March 1987. Grace accompanied me this time. I opened the session with a statement about the work the companies had done and now must do in the months ahead:

There are times when the people of the world must stand up together and be counted against social evils. Today, those from around the world who represent the mainstream of our society, our governments, our companies, our churches, our universities, our unions, our community groups, and our political organizations must stand together for justice in South Africa and say, as forcefully as we can, that the time has come for the human evils practiced in that country to come to an end.

The people of the world must say it to the parliaments of the nations, with calls for antiapartheid legislation and stronger sanctions against the Pretoria apartheid regime; we must say it to the companies of the world who still do business in South Africa, to use their powerful influence to bring an end to the despicable apartheid system and to work aggressively for full and equal political rights for the black population. We must say it to the United Nations, to speak out resoundingly against apartheid and to act more forcefully for justice in South Africa; and to representatives of the governments of the world in the United Nations, particularly America and Britain, to cease vetoing actions for sanctions and embargoes against

South Africa, until apartheid is finally ended. And our world leaders, especially President Ronald Reagan and Mrs. Margaret Thatcher, must let their voices be heard against the evil system because they are the most powerful leaders in the world, and their strong positions against apartheid would make a difference. They, and other heads of all governments, should speak out against South Africa's inhumanities and atrocities. If the world had stopped Hitler in time, there might not have been a World War II.

We have seen the grievous humiliations and deprivations against black people in South Africa long enough. The world has seen the whippings and the jailings and the killings of little black boys and girls long enough, and it is time for an end to it. The time is now. We have seen the hopelessness and the frustrations of blacks, young and old, striving to be free and the disheartening spectacle of people, black and white, struggling against seemingly insurmountable odds for basic human rights. The world must say to the South African government and to Prime Minister Botha, with every moral, political, and economic force at our command, that enough is enough and it is time for a change.

It is for this reason in May of 1985, I set a deadline that if, in twenty-four months, statutory apartheid was not ended and the main pillars of apartheid abolished, including the Group Areas Act, the Population Registration Act, and the Separate Amenities Act, and if there is not a clear commitment of the vote for blacks with full and equal participation, I would call for the withdrawal of all American companies from South Africa and a total United States embargo against that country. That deadline is May 31, 1987. Up to now, the apartheid regime has only accommodated gradual reforms.

I am aware my position represents a controversial one, and I know the suffering that will occur for many blacks in the loss of jobs will be considerable, but somewhere and somehow a stand must be taken that, hopefully, will bring some definitive resolution to the apartheid conditions that can lead to fundamental change, and human rights and benefits to millions, without a massive and bloody war. Something must be done to "wrench" the South African government to decisive movement. In this regard, action by the Americans is imperative.

I would prefer not to urge the withdrawal of the American companies. I would rather not do so because the American companies, following the Sullivan Principles during the ten years since they were initiated in 1977, have done more to bring about change and reform for black workers in

South Africa than any other force we know, including all the governments of the world and the United Nations put together. But the tide of human aspirations of blacks from bondage in South Africa is rising, and the urgent need in South Africa today is not just fair employment and equal job opportunities or equal rights in public places but freedom: freedom and justice and human dignity for the black population, especially the right of blacks to participate equally in determining those who govern them, and we must see the freeing of Nelson Mandela.

South Africa is at the crossroads. It is my view that, within this year, South Africa will either go the direction of a unitary free South Africa as, for the first time, we see whites and blacks standing together in the interest of a free South Africa or in the direction of a chaotic revolution that will lead not only to the destruction of South Africa but the devastation of the entire southern region of Africa. Also, what starts as a racial war will surely become an ideological war, possibly bringing the United States and Russia together in a massive atomic conflagration. Peace in South Africa and peace in the world could hinge on the rapid eradication of apartheid in the Republic of South Africa.

I am working day by day with company executives from around the world to help bring as much economic, moral, and political influence to bear on the South African government as possible for the dismantling of the apartheid system before May 31st. I would prefer the American companies and other companies represented here today remain in South Africa to continue your effective programs of equal rights, education, and economic and social advancement. I am hoping for a miracle. But if the South African government does not move to dismantle the apartheid system by the end of May 31st, as things are now, I will take my stand and call for the American companies to leave the country, along with all other companies present here and from other parts of the world.

I know the opposition to such a position will be great, in South Africa and in America, and in the world where there are companies represented at this meeting. But somewhere, and at some time, a line must be drawn and the South African government must be required to choose between either the continuation of American and other companies and their mutual economic interests or the elimination of apartheid.

Following the statement, I observed that the executives had very little to say. At last, one of the representatives from a major company in South Africa spoke up and said, "Reverend, we are here for one purpose. We want to know what you are going to do about your deadline." I told the executives that if the conditions of the two-year deadline were not met and Nelson Mandela were not freed, I would call on all U.S. companies remaining in South Africa to leave and would support a full U.S. embargo of South Africa except for economic activities addressing humanitarian and education needs. Grace told me later that after my response, I was facing twenty-eight blocks of ice.

Further along in the meeting, the executives agreed to let the leadership of South Africa know, individually and collectively, that it was essential for the sake of South Africa that every effort be made to end apartheid with all possible speed. I later learned that the executives present at Leeds had indeed contacted the South African government at the highest levels to urge the leaders to make fundamental change before the deadline. In fact, it was the urging of these company executives in private and in public discussions that later helped to lead to the freeing of Nelson Mandela. The companies' loss of money and their push on the South African government to free Mandela, perhaps more than anything else, led to his release.

Many messages were sent to me by company executives in the United States asking me to defer acting on the deadline. Black delegations from South Africa came to see me in Philadelphia, urging me to extend the deadline and remain with the Sullivan Principles in South Africa because, they said, the country was at last turning around and my objectives were being achieved. Several delegations came with petitions. One of them had twenty-five thousand signatures of people asking me not to call the companies out. They said hundreds of thousands of black workers would lose their jobs if I did. I was so concerned about these requests that I decided I would go to South Africa myself to see firsthand what was happening and to learn the sentiment of the people on the ground. However, my application to enter South Africa was refused, and I was told that I would not be permitted to go into South Africa at that time. I had been banned. The Associated Press carried stories throughout America. One paper in Boston reported, "The banning of Leon Sullivan from South Africa is like the banning of a book in Boston. It does him more good than harm."

Despite such incidents as bannings and attempts to hinder our efforts, I set June 3, 1987, as the time for my announcement on the

ultimatum. Many wondered what my decision would be. Most believed that I would not call on companies to leave but that I would
remain engaged in South Africa with the Principles. Only Grace knew
what my decision would be. Even when I had my statement written, I prepared two announcements: one saying that the companies
should stay and one saying that the companies should leave. I wanted
to be sure that even from my office there could be no leaks. No
one would know what my position would be until the day of the
announcement.

Chapter 13

Companies Leave South Africa

G RACE WENT WITH ME to Washington to hear the announcement of my decision on the deadline. I met first with the representatives of companies who had supported the Sullivan Principles, as I'd told them I would do. All of them were there at the DuPont Plaza Hotel. It was a standing-room-only crowd. Next door there was a gathering of television, radio, and news media.

First I told company representatives about the remarkable accomplishments of their efforts and the Principles. I told them that what they had done had made history and that South Africa would never be the same as the result of their efforts. I went on to say that the conditions of the deadline had not been met: statutory apartheid had not been ended, Nelson Mandela had not been freed, and blacks did not yet have the right to vote equal to whites. I told them of my decision to request that all U.S. companies in South Africa withdraw and that the United States declare a full embargo against South Africa except for humanitarian and educational purposes until the conditions of the deadline were met.

I left the room to a standing ovation. As I left, many of the executives were crying. We had, in the past ten years, developed a relationship unparalleled in the history of corporate responsibility and corporate relationships. The Principles had introduced social responsibility to corporations of America on a scale never previously envisioned. We had been through a lot, and the intensity of this moment was playing itself out.

I then went next door to address the large numbers of newspeople waiting there. I told them what I'd just told the company representatives. Following is the text of the statement I made to the press:

I have assessed, to the best of my ability, the situation as it now exists in the Republic of South Africa, and I have reached the decision the time has come for American companies and the United States of America to take a definitive stand against the evils of apartheid. Therefore, today, I am calling for the withdrawal of all United States companies from the Republic of South Africa and for a total United States embargo against that country until statutory apartheid is ended and blacks have a clear commitment for equal political rights, and I am calling on the president of the United States to end diplomatic relations with South Africa until the atrocities against black people end and apartheid is dismantled.

As of May 1985, I stated if in twenty-four months statutory apartheid was not ended and there was not a clear commitment of the vote for blacks equal to whites, I would call on the companies to leave South Africa and call for an American embargo. The conditions have not been remotely met. Therefore, after careful, painstaking, and prayerful consideration, I am making this statement.

This action comes after years of effort with the Sullivan Principles to help, along with other thrusts, to bring about fundamental change in that country, and I want it clearly known, I am proud of the work of the Sullivan Principles and proud of the efforts of those companies who have followed them. The Sullivan Principles, initiated March 1, 1977, ten years ago, have been a tremendous force for change in South Africa.

When the Sullivan Principles were introduced ten years ago, a black man did not even have the legal status as a worker in South Africa. The Principles broke new ground for blacks rights in South Africa that had not existed for three hundred years. They have caused a revolution in industrial race relations for black workers in that country.

These equal rights standards, followed by many American companies, have led the way in promoting equal pay for equal work, fair employment practices, recognition of independent and free black trade unions, extensive educational training programs, the promotion of blacks to management and supervisory jobs, the initiation of hundreds of black-owned businesses, the building of schools and health facilities, and the improvement of the quality of life in many other ways for hundreds of thousands of blacks, far, far beyond the small number employed by American companies.

The Sullivan Principles have been a catalyst for change throughout the Republic of South Africa. Also, in recent years, as the Principles have evolved, some United States companies have begun to challenge the apartheid system itself and have begun to practice "corporate civil disobedience" against apartheid practices, regulations, and laws.

Many United States companies engaging in this effort have left a notable record in corporate social responsibility in South Africa. Whatever
happens in the future, the efforts of many of the companies to change
conditions for blacks have been outstanding. Yet, in spite of these and
other efforts, the main pillars of apartheid still remain, and blacks are
still denied simple basic human rights in their own country and are still
deprived of the right to vote.

In spite of appeals and protests and cries for change and justice within
South Africa, repression grows; thousands are jailed without trial, including little children; people are brutalized, beaten, and killed; dissent is
ruthlessly suppressed; and the press is muzzled. Intransigence to fundamental change continues, and today the government pushes back even
minimal progress and reform. South Africa has become a nation of oppression and a police state, and the continuation of apartheid and its
inhumanities against blacks goes on. There is no greater moral issue in
the world today than apartheid!

Somewhere, somehow, it must be said, as loudly and as clearly and as
firmly as possible, that what is happening in South Africa to black people
is immoral, and it is wrong, and it must be brought to an end—not ten
years from now or five years from now or three years from now but now.

The winds of change have reached South Africa, and the winds will
not be subdued until the people have no less than their full economic,
social, and political freedom. And violently, or nonviolently, black people
in South Africa are going to have it. And nothing can, or will, end the
rising surge of the people's aspirations for their freedom and for justice
in South Africa but the elimination of the apartheid system itself, which is
the root cause of the nation's problems.

South Africa is at the crossroads. Either South Africa can go the direction of a unitary, free South Africa or the direction of a chaotic revolution,
with the killing of millions of people, the destruction of a country, and the
devastation of the entire southern region of Africa, leading to the possibility of the confrontation of the world's great nuclear powers at that
strategic point of the world, as a race war would certainly become an
ideological war. And should the United States become involved in such a
war, as most assuredly we would one way or the other, race riots would
break out in every major city in the country, far worse than anything ever
seen in the history of America.

It is in the interest of peace in South Africa and peace in the world and
peace in America that apartheid must be ended. The evils of apartheid

are broader than South Africa. Apartheid is against the will of God and the humanity of man; and like Nazism and Fascism, it must be stopped. America and the world must draw a line and speak out and act against it. If the world had stopped Hitler in time, we might not have had World War II.

It is clear the South African government does not intend to end apartheid on its own. Since the recent elections, the government has become more defiant to further change. Therefore, something must be done *now* to dramatize the issue before America and before the world. Every moral and economic and political force must be brought to bear to help influence the South African government to move towards dismantling the apartheid system, while there is still time. In this regard, America, as leader of the free world, should take the lead, including our companies and our government, hoping others in the world will follow.

Therefore, today, as the strongest possible American nonviolent protest against the continuing existence of apartheid and with the maximum nonviolent use of moral, corporate, and governmental force against that inhumane system, I call on all American companies to withdraw from the Republic of South Africa until statutory apartheid has been abolished, and Nelson Mandela has been freed, and there is a clear commitment of the vote for blacks, in accordance with agreements reached with authentic and representative black South African leaders.

Also, I call on the United States to enact, with urgency, a total United States economic embargo against South Africa, all exports and imports, including gold and diamonds, and to seek South African sources' vitally needed materials elsewhere or to seek alternatives or to stockpile or to recycle or to do without.

I further call on the Congress to consider stringent penalties against United States trading partners who assume markets left by departing United States companies and who continue to do business in South Africa, such as the Japanese.

I, also, call on the president of the United States to break all diplomatic relations with South Africa until atrocities against black people end and apartheid is dismantled.

Should, *at any time,* the South African government abolish statutory apartheid, free Nelson Mandela, and commit itself to equal voting rights for blacks, in accordance with agreements reached with authentic and representative black South African leaders, restrictions against American companies operating in South Africa should be lifted, and American companies should be free to return to the country, along with unlimited United States investments in a unitary, free South Africa.

This call for withdrawal excludes philanthropic and educational initiatives and the media.

This is my message to the companies of America, the Congress and the president of the United States, and to the government of South Africa. The guidelines for company withdrawal from South Africa are as follows:

- Companies should begin the process of withdrawal immediately.

- Withdrawal should be completed within a nine-month period. Companies should sell their businesses only to buyers who agree to promote equal rights for blacks, to black labor representation, and to company ownership plans making possible broad black participation.

- Companies should end all business relationships with buyers, including logos, trademarks, components, materials, consulting services, and other supporting contracts, excluding certain special consideration for support to undeniably black-owned and -initiated businesses.

- Emergency medical-supply needs should be dispensed through recognized world humanitarian organizations.

- Companies should favorably consider relocating in neighboring nations (such as Botswana, Lesotho, Mozambique, Swaziland, Zambia, or Zimbabwe), thereby helping strengthen regional and local economies with industrial development, growth, and jobs.

- Individual and institutional stockholders, including pension funds, unions, churches, universities, and other fiduciaries, are asked to support this call for withdrawal with the selling of holdings in noncooperating companies, or votes on disinvestment stockholder resolutions.

- Government bodies — municipal, state, and otherwise — are asked to support this call through the disapproval of purchase agreements or contracts for goods or services to companies choosing to remain in South Africa, as well as through the sale of investments or securities held in those companies.

The announcement was the lead story on all three major American television networks, along with CNN and many local television stations around the nation. The same was the case in South Africa itself, for the announcement hit that country like a bombshell. I went on the *Today Show* to further emphasize my statement and to call on all U.S. companies remaining in South Africa to leave.

Over the next few weeks, the walls of apartheid began to crumble. Six months after the announcement, forty U.S. companies had announced they were leaving South Africa. In ten months, this number had grown to seventy, including General Motors, IBM, and Mobil, all of which were among South Africa's leading U.S. companies. Within twelve months of the announcement, South Africa lost $1 billion in company investments. Within two years after the announcement, statutory apartheid had ended, and a year later, Nelson Mandela was freed from prison. Three years after the announcement, blacks had the full right to vote. And four years after the announcement, Nelson Mandela was president of a democratic, free South Africa. The ball of yarn had fully unwound. The walls of apartheid had come down. It took fifteen years — almost to the month — after the first announcement about my plans in the Zion Baptist Church of Philadelphia.

We organized the Post-Antiapartheid Council in the United States at the end of apartheid in 1993 just prior to the election of Nelson Mandela. I continue to maintain surveillance over the practices of U.S. companies to make sure they do not fall back into the same kinds of practices they followed previously. The Antiapartheid Council still remains in existence because the Sullivan Principles mandated by the United States government still remain law for U.S. companies operating in South Africa. The time could come when in some form the Sullivan Principles may have to be used again…and I want to be ready. But today we can be sure that South Africa will never return to the horrid and legalized days of apartheid. The mountain many thought immovable had indeed been moved.

Chapter 14

Reflections on the Sullivan Principles

THROUGH THE YEARS, both the Sullivan Principles and I had many detractors and vigilant opponents, especially between the years of 1978 and 1986. Sometimes it seemed to me that the world was divided; half of the population praised me, while the other half maligned me for what I was doing. Nearly all said my efforts were well meaning, but many felt what I was doing could result only in cosmetic changes.

I listened and believe I understood their concerns. If I had been someone else looking on, I would perhaps have been a critic, too. I recall one occasion at a New York City church where leaders of the antiapartheid movement had gathered to discuss the Sullivan Principles. One woman spoke up and said, "Reverend, you are polishing our chains and we want them off." I nodded my head in consent because, at that time, the Principles had been launched only a year before. What she said was true. All we were doing at that time was polishing chains, getting rid of petty apartheid by ending segregation in locker rooms, restaurants, rest rooms, and water fountains. But I also knew what no one else in that room knew: I knew my plan, my strategy. And I knew that with the help of God and others, I would see every pillar of apartheid fall to the ground.

In large part, the strategy that lay behind the Principles called for determining what was ultimately right and what was possible in the short run. The principles were incremental in nature. Apartheid could not be brought down in a day, a week, a month, or even a few years. Through the years, those who knew me became familiar with an expression I am found of using: "TTT." It stands for "Things take time."

When I became a member of the board of General Motors, I supported U.S. withdrawal from South Africa. I changed my mind because I concluded that, at that time in history, full-scale withdrawal was not the best way to accomplish the ultimate goal of bringing relief to the people. Things take time. On the other hand, I wanted to make sure that things did not take too much time. If progress slowed too much, some understandably questioned whether progress had stopped altogether. So it seems that through the years in which the Principles were active, I was forever meeting with people on one side and urging patience, while I myself was impatiently turning the screws on those who were content with the progress being made.

Peter Kinder, Steven Lydenberg, and Amy Domini, authors of *Investing for Good*, assessed the response to and the strategy of the Principles in this way:

> The Principles did not meet with universal approval. Some activists saw them as a license to continue business as usual with the South African government. And in the short run, they were right. But what the critics did not foresee was the Principles' long-term significance.
>
> The signatories — at one time, seventy companies — had agreed to do *something* about an evil. The nation's largest international companies acknowledged that they had moral obligations, duties not quantifiable on financial statements. For one hundred years, corporations had wrapped themselves in the doctrines of social Darwinism and substantive due process to argue that they were purely economic entities. Their only role, they argued, was to maximize their shareholders' wealth.[1]

The philosophy behind the Sullivan Principles was no different from the approach I had developed in my boycott days at the height of the civil rights movement. In that regard, the Sullivan Principles were nothing new, for the fundamental premise behind them was that people — individually and collectively — can and should use their economic influence to make a moral statement or to take moral action. Ultimately the Principles accomplished their mission because enough people cared about injustice to do something about it. All I had to do was to persuade them to take action together. Collective economic power and consumer strength enabled the Principles to succeed. We had the support of institutions such as Yale, Oberlin, Notre Dame, Columbia, Tufts, the University of Pennsylvania, Princeton, MIT, Tulane, and a hundred other major stock-holding institutions.

Investor groups such as CalPeRS, with stock holdings in corporations in America and in the world valued at over $100 billion, the New York Pension Fund, with investments almost as much, and supporters such as the Massachusetts State Pension Fund, the Oregon State Pension Fund, the Calvert Fund, and others came together to support the Sullivan Principles at the peak of their influence. They helped account for $500 billion in investment support behind our efforts in South Africa. This kind of potential influence remains today.

With a single letter or telephone call or the threat of a single stockholders' resolution on any public policy issue, CalPeRS can influence the actions of the largest corporations in the world in matters of public policy and human rights. What must be understood, however, is that such powerful blocs of influence ultimately consist of the collective actions of individuals. Thus it was not the "big people" — the executives and company presidents — who ultimately made the difference. Rather it was the ordinary person who transformed the Sullivan Principles from just a few lines on a piece of paper into a formidable and influential doctrine against apartheid. I recall one meeting in New York City attended by representatives of more than one hundred companies where a man rose and said, "Why do we sit here as representatives of the largest companies in the world and let this one man standing there tell us what to do?" My response was, "But you do not have to do what I tell you to do. Just go and tell your chairmen and boards of directors that you do not want to do what I am telling you to do and see what your stockholders and consumers have to say."

I have found through the years that the support of people at the grassroots level on matters affecting the advancement of race is far more dependable and formidable than assistance from the top. Jesus said, "The poor you shall have with you always" (John 12:8). And in a way, it's good at times that we do. In all my efforts ranging from Harlem to Philadelphia and to South Africa, I found that those on whom we could most depend were not those who have the most in our community but those who have the least. In matters pertaining to human rights, if you have the ordinary person on your side, the big shots will follow.

Consumers at the grassroots level were kept informed about what companies were doing or failing to do. Here, the black churches in particular played a major part. Companies' ratings — that is, how they fared in following the Sullivan Principles — were put on the bulletin boards of thousands of black churches throughout America, published widely in black newspapers, and made available to community-based radio stations. Many companies lost sales in the black communities because their companies were at the bottom of the rating list. Because of individuals acting together, companies and governments had no choice but to listen. To ignore the voice of the people was to risk financial suicide.

After it became clear that supporters of the Sullivan Principles were taking the 1987 deadline seriously, the pace of positive change in South Africa quickened. Had that not been the case, I had other strategies in mind, including a call for companies to refuse to pay taxes to the South African government and to put their tax funds into escrow until apartheid ended. I was also prepared to launch a diamond boycott in America, believing that it would spread throughout the world. A year prior to the deadline, I had met with Harry Oppenheimer, at his invitation, in his Park Avenue apartment in New York City to discuss my views and future plans for the Principles in South Africa. He was leader of the largest diamond cartel in the world. I told him that if the conditions of my ultimatum were not met, I intended to launch a massive nationwide boycott against the purchase of diamonds. I felt that such a boycott would be especially influential among African Americans and blacks of the African diaspora worldwide. When I told him of my plan, I could see him shudder.

Oppenheimer knew such a boycott would have an important impact on diamond sales in the United States. I suspect that black women probably wear diamonds more than any other group in America. For them and for their husbands and boyfriends, diamonds are a status symbol, the primary token of love and affection that can be given to any woman. I had plans to reach into every black household in the United States using thousands of black ministers across America to announce the boycott on a Sunday morning two months prior to Christmas Day. I intended to make the wearing of diamonds a badge of dishonor for every black woman — or any woman who wanted to see the end of apartheid. I knew the boycott would spread from the black community into the white community and that "Buy no diamonds until apartheid is ended" would become a rallying call throughout the nation. Oppenheimer took the message back to South Africa, and the DeBeers diamond organization got busy making the potential diamond boycott in America known to government authorities.

I sometimes wish I had been able to go through with the diamond boycott. It would have been exciting to see the response of black communities in America upon given a chance to make a direct statement against apartheid. However there was yet another tactic I had in mind that I am glad I did not have to carry out. Every major television show in the United States had asked me to appear to discuss the Sullivan Principles. The *Larry King Show* asked me several times. I shied away because I realized the negative impact too much publicity can cause. But if apartheid was able to withstand the diamond boycott, I was prepared to appear on a popular television show, break a water glass on the desk, and with a piece of that broken glass, and with thirty million people watching, severe the little finger from my right hand in protest against the apartheid system. I was also prepared to announce that I would come on again six months later to cut off a second finger and six months after that, a third, until my cause had succeeded and South Africa was free. I knew that whoever would let me appear would have the largest television audience of the week.

Some would deem such an approach not just radical but desperate. The truth is that this was a time for desperation. I was determined to do anything short of violence against another person to call attention to this cause and complete the task I had begun. Interestingly enough, several years later during a near-death illness, I lost the use of the very three fingers I was planning to sever from my right hand.

Let it be said that I am proud of the role the Sullivan Principles played in bringing an end to apartheid, but I have always emphasized that they played one part among many. One cannot talk about how apartheid ended without recognizing the 250 years of struggle and sacrifice against white rule over blacks from the time of the Zulu chief Shaka to Nelson Mandela. We must recognize the building pressure within the country from lay leaders such as Steve Biko, who gave his life in the struggle. We must acknowledge the determination of the ANC (the African National Congress), the PAC (the Pan-African Congress), labor groups, and religious leaders, as well as the fearlessness of black youth in the streets of the townships like Soweto, many of whom died in the struggle for freedom. Black South Africans in exile in Zimbabwe, Tanzania, Ghana, Mozambique, Lesotho, and Namibia fought nobly against the best-equipped and best-trained military on the African continent. The voices of black and other nonwhite South Africans who had been exiled from their homeland screamed to the world about the injustices rampant within their country, helping to raise the consciousness of the world.

In America, the actions of churches, colleges, universities, cities, states, and counties against the continuation of apartheid played an important role. Then there were the seldom-mentioned antiapartheid import-export regulations initiated by Congressman John Evans of Delaware early in 1978. It was the first legislation to include the Sullivan Principles for companies in South Africa doing business with the Import-Export Bank. Recognizing the need to use powers of the United States government to help deal with the problems of apartheid, Congressman Evans seized the opportunity to use the Export Control Act to require South African companies doing business in the United States to comply with the recently annunciated Sullivan Principles. This made it possible for the United States government to use federal regulations to require South African companies to follow and implement human rights requirements of the Principles. This action by Congressman Evans played an important role in the opening salvo of the United States government against the injustices of the apartheid system.

The efforts of the National Council of Churches, led by Timothy Smith, a most effective antiapartheid campaigner, helped push companies to oppose apartheid. And there was Randall Robinson, who provided vital leadership in sensitizing Washington, D.C., to the evils of apartheid. The work of hundreds of student protest groups on college campuses all across America compelled trustees of colleges and universities to take stands with stock divestment actions.

We must recognize also the efforts of people such as Dr. Beyers Naude, a respected figure within the Dutch Reformed Church. This church had played a major role in the institutionalization of apartheid. It had interpreted the tower of Babel story as an act of God to divide the races and preached that Ham, described as the forerunner of the black race, should be beneath and subjugated to the white race. It was the white Dutch Reformed Church that, from 1932 on, sent delegation after delegation to the government to support proposals for racial legislation. The church worked hard to devise practical policies of apartheid that could be implemented by the government while formulating theological constructs to justify the policies. It was these plans the church finally presented to the Nationalist Party in 1947. The Nationalist Party accepted them, and the program won at the polls in 1948. The church had argued through the years that "because Noah cursed Ham's descendants to become 'the lowest of the slaves,' this effectively relegated blacks to a permanent status as servants."[2]

Dr. Beyers Naude put his life on the line to challenge the positions of his own church. His challenge led to the end of the Calvinist

church's theological subjugation of blacks that assigned to them an inferior racial status. Naude was one of the many nonblack heroes of the
antiapartheid movement. Among others is Helen Suzman, who aggressively challenged the government and spoke out as a member within
the all-white parliament of South Africa through the years. Perhaps
most importantly, we must recognize the thousands upon thousands
of people of all colors who played a part but whose names will never
be known.

So again, while I emphasize that the Sullivan Principles played a
part, it is perhaps best for me to leave it to others to assess their significance. In an important report dealing with the Principles, author
S. Prakesh Sethi commented,

> The experience of the Sullivan Principles offers a unique opportunity
> to learn about the possibilities and challenges of creating universal
> standards of conduct for multi-national companies.... Nowhere in the
> annals of the history of international business, especially the history of
> multi-national companies, has there been such a unique and profound
> experiment as the operations of the U.S. companies in South Africa
> under the white-dominated regime which practiced legalized apartheid.
> The Sullivan Principles constituted the first voluntary code of ethi-
> cal conduct applied under realistic operating conditions. The Principles
> possessed a large measure of moral authority for validating corporate
> actions and, where necessary, for exhorting companies to undertake ac-
> tivities they might otherwise consider ill-advised on purely economic or
> political grounds.[3]

A special report dealing with conflict resolution published in 1997
and issued worldwide by the Carnegie Foundation included a section
on the Sullivan Principles and their importance. It stated that the
Principles "remain the primary example within the business community of voluntary implementation of a code of ethics for operating
within a country." The report went on to state that although the
Principles were not without their critics, most would agree that they
"served as a powerful symbol of the international community's opposition to apartheid and provided much-needed support for black South
Africans."

A scholarly analysis of the Sullivan Principles appeared in Karen
Paul's *The Nonprofit Sector in the Global Community:*

> The final amplification of the Sullivan Principles in 1984 put Sig-
> natories in the position of outright defiance of the South African

Government. Normally, multinationals operating abroad are expected to stay out of politics, to refrain from attempting to exert undue influence on the government, to respect local laws and customs. But United States companies in South Africa with the [Sullivan Principles] were being asked to lobby actively to create pressures for changing South African laws, to support those who challenged the government and to take a positive stand on social issues — in short to become an instrument for social change.[4]

Perhaps the greatest legacy of the Sullivan Principles is, not what they did to help end apartheid, but what they have done to help improve the lives of blacks through education and the building of schools, the opening of clinics, and the supporting of hospitals — advocating a better way of life for black youth and advancing equal political rights. This legacy is being seen more and more now and will continue in the future. The Principles have helped prepare a generation of black and nonwhite leadership to lead and mold a nation in the effort to become a prime example to the world of a nonracial democracy that works.

When the walls of apartheid came down, there were young black men and women prepared as a result of the Sullivan Principles to take leadership in businesses and in government. In addition, thousands of black-owned businesses had been established as suppliers and contractors to companies attempting to implement the Sullivan Principles. These black-owned businesses are multiplying every day, making it possible for black entrepreneurs to have a piece of the economic pie in South Africa. Legal defense groups and organizations were formed, supported by companies complying with the Sullivan Principles, providing legal redress for thousands of blacks who, even today, need lawyers to stand in court with them in cases where the legacy of apartheid remains; and for the first time unions are open to blacks.

Companies in South Africa that supported the Sullivan Principles were changed in ways that go well beyond issues of race-based discrimination. In 1997 the internationally recognized Investor Responsibility Research Center in Washington, D.C., reported on a survey of seven hundred American companies doing business in South Africa that showed philanthropic spending by United States signatory companies to the Sullivan Principles has been increasing since the ending of apartheid. It goes on to state that the American companies "clearly recognize that socially responsible investments can augment public awareness for the companies' name and products and earn goodwill from both the American company public and the South African government." According to the report, companies with a commitment to social responsibility have an edge over those who do not.

The report also reveals that Sullivan signatory companies had gotten into the habit of giving generously: "Several Sullivan corporations continued to support drought relief and educational projects in rural areas that have little ancillary benefit in their business image." All this continuing progress by U.S. companies and companies from other parts of the world, who in time adhered to the Sullivan Principles, have added to the record of the continuing influence of the Principles on the improvement of the quality of life for blacks and other nonwhites in the new democratic South Africa. The report continues, "Managing Directors of Leading United States Companies in South Africa said that companies did not support such extensive or formalized social investment programs elsewhere and that their South African programs reflected Sullivan's historical impact." The report also states that by far "the greatest area of United States corporate social investment in South Africa is educational because, in an increasingly competitive global environment, companies hope to insure the quality of labor needed at all levels of their operations." This is consistent with the Sullivan Principles' strong emphasis on education.

The efforts of the Sullivan Principles to dismantle racial segregation extended beyond South Africa into every neighboring country of southern Africa, including Zimbabwe, Swaziland, Zambia, Angola, and especially Namibia, which had equally been caught in the clutches of apartheid and whose money was tied to the South African rand. On October 1, 1997, I visited the Republic of Namibia and met with President Sam Nujoma, who said to me, "Namibia would not be free today had it not been for the Sullivan Principles."

During that visit to Namibia, I was approached by an Afrikaner who recognized me and told me that he had heard me speak in 1978 about the Sullivan Principles and the need for white South Africa to change the way it treated blacks. He let me know that the speech turned his life around and that he had committed the rest of his years to fighting racial prejudice in South Africa. "Reverend," he said to me, "you planted seeds that have grown into great trees. Your Principles helped to free a nation." Stories such as these confirm my faith and make all the frustration and stress I experienced in association with the Sullivan Principles worthwhile.

The Sullivan Principles became the forerunner for corporate responsibility in the United States and the world in endeavors to deal with social and political issues. History will record that with the Sullivan Principles 184 United States companies, though some half-heartedly, during 1977 to 1990 prevented the loss of perhaps a million lives and helped to bring human rights and freedom to South Africa. In future years the model of the Sullivan Principles will be used as the standard for corporate responsibility around the world in nations with problems of social justice and human rights.

Despite the progress, however, some companies have failed to live up to affirmative-action commitments. I am concerned that large-scale unemployment among blacks, if not addressed, will lead to riots and racial turmoil, threatening peace and security in South Africa. At the writing of this book, I continue to keep watch, prepared to do whatever is necessary.

Notes

1. Peter Kinder, Steven Lydenberg, and Amy Domini, *Investing for Good* (New York: HarperCollins, 1993), 93–94.

2. Douglas Johnston and Cynthia Sampson, *Religion, The Missing Dimension of Statecraft* (New York: Oxford University Press, 1994), 182–88.

3. S. Prakesh Sethi, "Working with International Codes of Ethics: Experience of U.S. Companies Operating in South Africa under the Sullivan Principles," *Business & the Contemporary World*, no. 1 (1996): 129–30.

4. Karen Paul, *The Nonprofit Sector in the Global Community: Voices from Many Nations* (San Francisco: Jossey-Bass Publishers, 1992), 108.

Chapter 15

Principles for the World:
The Global Sullivan Principles

I HAVE BEEN ASKED many times if Global Sullivan Principles could be effectively applied with companies in other parts of the world where human rights are in question, places such as China, Cuba, Mexico, or Nigeria. My answer is yes.

Some argue that problems in South Africa were different and unique and that the impact the Sullivan Principles had there would not be possible in other countries with human rights problems. I could not disagree more heartily. There is nothing about the Principles that made them uniquely effective in South Africa. The Principles revolve around basic realities of economics: the need for all to survive and the desire of companies to prosper. As I've stated previously, companies can often accomplish more than governments in the effort to advance human rights. Companies need governments, but not as much as governments need companies to provide jobs that produce taxes that enable governments to do their jobs. The bottom line is that no nation can survive without businesses.

The world addressed a major evil when it dealt with apartheid. But there are many other evils: child labor, worker abuse, discrimination against women and persons of color, neglect of the environment, and many, many more. There is nothing to prevent the application of Sullivan-type principles in an attempt to address these problems. Sometimes, however, an appeal to companies to do something is complicated by the fact that the companies themselves are the perpetrators. The goal of the Global Sullivan Principles is to appeal to individuals in ways designed to get companies' houses in order and then to appeal to companies to get governments' houses in order.

Obviously, the particular goals or calls to action will vary from place to place based on the situation, but the basic principles remain the

106

same. In all cases, wherever possible, the principles must be developed in cooperation with the companies themselves so that they can claim ownership in the human rights initiative. In addition, the principles must be simple and direct, and they must address the most vital needs for change. They must be adopted in keeping with both short-term goals and long-range plans.

As in South Africa, it is important to come up with ways that accurately and meaningfully measure compliance with the Principles. The cooperation and active participation of institutional investor organizations, individual stockholders, churches, and consumers, as well as the cooperation and support of the United States government and other governments, are important to the success of Global Sullivan Principles, though no one of these by itself is essential.

Multinational firms from the United States and other nations can play a formidable role in the promotion of human rights and justice. They can serve the poor and disadvantaged through, among other ways, job training and education programs. With the right incentive, multinational firms can have much the same impact in other countries as they did in South Africa. With that in mind, I offer the following:[1]

Basic Requirements for Global Sullivan Principles

In order to be effective, Global Sullivan Principles require that multinational companies adhere to basic economic and ethical requirements. Companies adopting the principles will publicly express their support for fundamental human rights in all operations; implement equal and fair employment practices for all employees and for others seeking jobs with the company; prohibit all manner of discrimination in operation because of color, race, gender, age, class, parental origin, tribe, province, or ideology; provide equal pay for equal work; end all forms of work exploitation and unacceptable worker treatment (such as child labor, physical punishment, female abuse, or involuntary servitude) and insure that the workers' right to association is not infringed upon; end all forms of intellectual piracy and support company "property rights" in all nations; improve the quality of life of the community outside the workplace in education, protection of the environment, sustainable development, housing, health, and the safeguarding of children; abstain from the purchase of goods or services from those who do not comply; help with training and jobs for workers formerly discriminated against culturally, racially, or ethnically, including training and openings for supervisory and management positions, and assure racial and gender diversity on policy-making committees and boards; support social, economic, and political justice wherever the company does business; promote race, ethnic, and religious understanding, locally and nationally; and help with the culture of peace among nations.

The Global Sullivan Principles must be a set of corporate responsibility standards voluntarily developed by companies themselves, intended to affect companies large and small and to influence communities and nations for human rights and greater justice for disadvantaged people in local communities and worldwide.

The final Global Sullivan Principles should be drafted with representatives of multinational companies, and support for them should be sought from recognized international bodies committed to justice, human rights, and peace and also from institutional investors, other shareholders, consumers, and religious and governmental bodies within the United States and throughout the world.

These Principles should in no way contravene existing corporate codes of conduct or principles but rather make these more effective.

Regarding the use of the Sullivan Principles on a broader international scale, it has been said,

> Experience with the Sullivan Principles must be seen within the context of a growing challenge that Multi-National Companies have to confront in their overseas operations. As they pursue their economic activities around the world, Multi-National Companies face an uncertain and highly turbulent socio-political environment. One can see ample evidence of such a turmoil in business-society relationships both in the United States and in the international arena. These turbulences characterize the new domains that define business-society relationships, the relative strengths of various stakeholders, and above all, the arenas where business-society conflicts need to be resolved.
>
> In the international arena, Multi-National Companies have been confronted with demands to curtail their activities and modify their operational procedures in order to protect the poor and the uninformed consumers in Third World countries; to preserve the environment; and to contribute to a more sustainable development. Multi-National Companies, therefore, need to develop a more pro-active approach to their strategic goals and operational policies that takes specific cognizance of the public good as well as private gain.
>
> The Sullivan Principles offer an excellent framework for developing commonly accepted operational principles that would provide Multi-National Companies with guidelines for instituting standards of

conduct that: (1) take cognizance of different economic and competitive conditions in different countries; (2) involve all significant stakeholders in the process; (3) are flexible enough to provide individual companies with room to maneuver; (4) are based not only on economic realities, but, equally important, are rooted in the concept of basic equity and fairness for those who are least able to bargain for themselves; and, (5) have the force of world public opinion to prevent individual companies and countries to escape compliance.[2]

Periodic reporting is crucial to the successful adoption of the Global Sullivan Principles, and adherence to the following guidelines will ensure the accuracy of such reporting. Multinational signatory companies to the Global Sullivan Principles will (1) report progress on compliance on an annual basis to stockholders and other concerned institutions and individuals, (2) have all reports on implementation audited by outside certified public accountants and made available for release to interested parties, (3) inform all employees of the company's annual implementation reports, and (4) invite input on ways to improve company performance. In addition, there should be a continuing review and assessment of the Principles in light of changing conditions and political circumstances within given countries as well as periodic on-site monitoring evaluations for company implementation results.

The Global Sullivan Principles are particularly applicable to prevailing conditions in China, especially given the concern in the United States about China's human rights policies. Indeed, such principles for China could be amazingly effective, especially if companies in China with United States trade relations were required to report to United States government trade agencies on their implementation of Social Responsibility Global Sullivan Principles, with penalties for noncompliance. Results from examples set by the companies and their human rights activities would spread across China. Actions of the companies would also link human rights and commercial and government practices in China to the government's "most favored nation" trade status, which is so much in question.

Adopting Global Sullivan Principles for China is an essential and urgent need for the United States. American companies are more and more unable to compete with Chinese firms because of cheap and exploited Chinese labor. As Chinese imports into the United States continue to grow, as they are now at a rapidly increasing rate, many American companies competing with Chinese firms for business in the

United States or in China will either have to relocate or go out of business, costing America thousands of jobs and billions of dollars in lost income. American firms vying with Chinese ones for business must have a level playing field in order to compete in the United States and in China and, thus, survive. Global Sullivan Principles can help level the field.

Perhaps most significantly, I believe that Global Sullivan Principles can play an important role in the world by promoting a culture of peace. Of course, the pursuit of peace cannot be separated from the issues of freedom and justice that have been raised. People cannot be held down forever. To be sure, situations of injustice will inevitably be addressed; the question is whether they will be addressed through violent or nonviolent means. With the end of the cold war and the collapse of apartheid, many wrongly believe that war is on its way out. The truth is that the world remains a very violent and dangerous place. It is a world replete with hatred; greed; divisions among states and nations over borders, boundaries, and land; and hostilities among people because of race, color, gender, tribe, and religious beliefs.

Time may be running out. Nuclear power resides today in the hands of nations large and small, even in poorer countries like India and Pakistan. Every student trained in physics knows how to make an atomic bomb. An unseen spark in Israel, Palestine, Bosnia-Herzegovina, Iraq, Iran, or elsewhere could set off a major nuclear conflict.

Carl Sagan in his book *Billions and Billions* poignantly describes how the ballistic projectiles launched from the cannons at Gettysburg had a range, at best, of a few miles. This battle was only a little over a hundred years ago, and the amount of explosives used in the most formidable of the cannons was some twenty pounds — roughly one-hundredth of a ton of TNT. It was enough to kill a few people. The most powerful chemical explosives were used eighty years later in World War II. The United States used the first atomic bombs to annihilate two Japanese cities. Each of those weapons, delivered after a voyage of sometimes a thousand miles, had the equivalent power of about ten thousand tons of TNT. That is, one bomb was enough to kill a few hundred thousand people — one bomb. The measure of destruction of people destroying people goes on. A few years later, the United States and the Soviet Union developed the first thermonuclear weapons: the first hydrogen bombs. Some of them had an explosive yield equivalent of ten million tons of TNT, enough to kill a few million people. Now, strategic nuclear weapons can be launched from any place on the planet.

Each of these technological triumphs advanced the art of mass murder by a factor of a thousand: from Gettysburg to the blockbusters, a thousand times more explosive energy; from the blockbusters to the atomic bomb, a thousand times more; and from the atomic bomb to the hydrogen bomb, a thousand times still more. A thousand times a thousand times a thousand is a billion; in less than one century, our most fearful weapon has become a billion times more deadly. But we have not become a billion times wiser in the generations that stretch from Gettysburg to the present. (All of this is not to even mention the biological and chemical weapons that are capable of mass destruction of human life.)

Questions and issues of economics, in addition to those of freedom and justice, are fundamental to human existence. We cannot avoid them. Economics pervades every aspect of our lives — what we eat, where we live, where we work, and how we die. How we deal with resources, manage land, and distribute wealth are all affected by moral judgments and considerations, or the lack thereof. Indeed, economics wields a major influence on individual human lives and on the survival and development of civilizations. Through the ages, wars have been started and promulgated in the name of business and economics. Today, corporations have an opportunity to be forces for peace. More than any other institutions, businesses have the power to influence economic realities.

I am not so foolish as to believe that the Sullivan Principles, so successfully applied in South Africa, could in and of themselves achieve the victory of peace over war. But as I look at my little grandchildren, I want life and peace and security for them. I have only a little time left on earth to go, but their lives are just beginning.

Of all I have done — including my work in the civil rights movement, promoting employment opportunities for minorities, working to develop sub-Saharan Africa, and helping to bring down apartheid — I hope that the Global Sullivan Principles for multinational firms in Africa, Cuba, China, Mexico, and throughout the world will one day become my most important and lasting contribution. How far, on a global scale, could a charter for corporate responsibility based on Global Sullivan Principles go in dealing with the deep, complex, and

fundamental problems of peace and social, economic, and political justice in a world that is divided in so many ways by hostilities, unsettled
misunderstandings, competition, fear, and hate? I do not know, but I
would like to find out. I believe such principles deserve a try.

Notes

1. The suggestions for Global Sullivan Principles are intended as a framework
from which to begin deliberation and discussion. If initiated, the final version should
be publicly and widely announced after meetings and due consideration with global
companies showing commitment and interest in social justice, human rights, and
peace.

2. S. Prakash Sethi, *Business and the Contemporary World* (Berlin: Walter de
Gruyter and Company, 1996), 146–47.

Chapter 16

Blazing New Trails

A T THE LIBERTY BELL in Philadelphia on July 4, 1993, I had the pleasure of meeting Nelson Mandela for the first time in the flesh. He and F. W. de Klerk had come to Philadelphia to receive the Liberty Bell Award for the work they were doing together to unite South Africa. At that time, it was crucial to have a Mandela and a de Klerk, who were prepared to give up power for the good of their country without a fight. I found de Klerk to be a good man who wanted peace and order for his nation. I believe it was in the plan of God for South Africa to have these men on the two sides of the fence to try to work together.

My conversations with Nelson Mandela led to friendship. He thanked me for what I had done and told me he wanted American companies to come back to South Africa. Soon after, I appealed for them to return, and they began to do so in large numbers. Mandela also asked me to help with the training of young men and women in South Africa who had dropped out of school and with other unemployed youth who needed to be trained for jobs. I promised I would help. In July 1995, I opened the first South African Opportunities Industrialization Center (OIC) at Qwa Zulu Natal in the city of Petermaritzburg, where Mandela was first put in prison and where Mahatma Gandhi had labored unsuccessfully for twenty years to bring an end to South Africa's system of race discrimination. The OIC in Qwa Zulu Natal has become one of the largest and most successful training programs for unemployed youth in South Africa; OICs are now being established in provinces throughout the country in order to train youth by the tens of thousands for jobs.

With Mandela moving to the helm in South Africa and with the return of American companies, it was clear that the Sullivan Principles had successfully run their course there. It was time for me to move on to other things. The OIC movement continued to spread rapidly

113

throughout the United States and would take on increased relevance as the country moved toward stricter standards for gaining access to government welfare. I was finally able to concentrate more of my time and effort working with the International Foundation for Education and Self-Help (IFESH).

IFESH had been created in 1988 at the peak of implementation of the Sullivan Principles to provide sub-Saharan Africa's poor developing countries with self-help methods relating to education, food, health, jobs, businesses, and other areas. Since it started, the work of IFESH has spread throughout sub-Saharan Africa and other poor parts of the world. It has provided teachers, developers, training centers, schools, farmers, medical assistance, business development, and employment. As of this writing, IFESH has affected millions of lives with self-help projects and programs in Africa, Latin America, and Asia. In recommending support for IFESH from the United States government, Congress in 1994 stated, "IFESH is blazing new trails in human development needs in Africa and other developing countries and we recommend its support."

Under the auspices of IFESH, by 1997 five hundred master teachers had assisted in training twenty-five thousand teachers in Africa, with the number planned to grow to one thousand teacher placements over the next four years. One hundred sixty IFESH Fellows (called the "Sullivan Marines") from sixty American colleges and universities have gone to twenty African and Asian countries to assist with development work. IFESH has dug thousands of wells in Nigeria and trained one million Africans to use them to irrigate farms. It has provided extensive health education for the containment of HIV/AIDS and has trained 250 of the best and brightest African bankers to become the banking leaders of Africa. IFESH has also started many skills training centers, assisted some two hundred thousand Africans with cures for river blindness, and has built hundreds of schools. In addition, IFESH has established training schools, orphanages, and work centers in Peru and sent medical teams to Africa to establish medical clinics and perform heart surgery, in some cases in parts of African where it has never been done before.

In 1998, at the recommendation of the Congress of the United States, additional funds were made available to IFESH to expand its programs for teachers, bankers, and human development in Africa. IFESH was now becoming a major player for education and human development needs in Africa and other countries. In the words of former Secretary of the Treasury William E. Simon, who serves on the board of IFESH, "IFESH was on the way to being a significant private foreign-aid organization helping the poor and disadvantaged."

IFESH was organized initially with the great help and assistance of Brooks McCormick of Chicago, a grandson of the founder of International Harvester. We are extremely fortunate to have the assistance of some very supportive and loyal members sitting on its board of directors. Among them are Dr. Andrew F. Brimmer, former governor of the Federal Reserve Bank; Dr. Edward D. Eddy, former president of Rhode Island University; Hon. William E. Simon, former U.S. secretary of the treasury; Rev. William H. Gray III, president of the United Negro College Fund; Donald M. Kendall, former chairman and CEO of Pepsico; Hon. Lawrence S. Eagleburger, former U.S. secretary of state; Hon. Louis W. Sullivan, former U.S. secretary of health, education, and welfare; Maceo K. Sloan, president of Sloan Financial Group; Esther B. Ferguson, well-known advocate for Africa; and Dr. Blenda J. Wilson, president of California State University at Northridge. I must also mention Lamond Godwin, a remarkable man who has helped with IFESH every step of the way. It was he who put together the first IFESH Debt for Human Development plan, which has helped thousands in Africa, Peru, and elsewhere.

As I considered all I wanted to do with my remaining years, it became more and more clear to Grace and me that we had completed all of what God had called us to do in Philadelphia. It was time to move on to climb another tree in the forest and to help move another mountain.

And I cannot overstate the love and respect I have for the church many in Philadelphia and throughout the United States know as "Great Zion." I could not have done what I did from the mid-'70s and through the '80s without their approval and wholehearted support. In fact, I cannot imagine a church anywhere being more supportive. I will always thank God for the Zion Baptist Church in Philadelphia, which provided the essential practical needs for my work. The people responded to all my requests. The church provided the resources necessary to send me where I wanted to go and to do what I wanted to do. Money for my projects and programs was never a problem. Because of the support of my church, I was fiercely independent and self-sufficient. I was beholden to no one but God, Zion, and Grace. My church made me free, so much so that in Philadelphia, I was called "the Lion of Zion." With my church behind me, I believed I could move any mountain.

But the time had come to move on. Upon leaving Zion Baptist, Grace and I moved to Scottsdale, Arizona, where we set up offices for IFESH. God had been developing in me a vision to aid in the economic development of sub-Saharan Africa and also to unite the black diaspora, especially African Americans, who had been separated for four hundred years from their African roots. I wanted to start a movement to improve education for the people of Africa and bring democracy to them, and I wanted to work for the advancement of the African continent so that tribal hostilities could be brought to an end and so that the world would begin to view Africa with the respect and dignity it deserves. There was yet another mountain to be moved.

Chapter 17

Building a Bridge

I HAD HEARD and heeded the call from God and from Africa and from African Americans and others of the black diaspora to try at last to unite people of African heritage with Africa, to make a link, to build a bridge from America and other parts of the world to Africa among peoples of African heritage that would never be broken again. The building of this bridge would lead to a series of landmark African–African American summits.

Because of what I consider to be God's miraculous intervention, I am convinced that my work in Africa is part of God's plan. The story of this miracle begins with a meeting I had in February 1990 with African envoys in Washington, D.C., to discuss a summit of African and African American leaders. The purpose was to facilitate the advancement of Africa. We decided to call the effort the "African–African American Summit." I would be the chairman and the convener of the plan.

During the formative stages of the first summit, which was to be held in 1991, I took a trip to the Central African Republic primarily to establish an Opportunities Industrialization Center (OIC) project in the country with the support of our International Foundation for Education and Self-Help (IFESH). And then it happened. On my return to the United States, I became very ill and had to be rushed to the hospital. While I was there, an undiagnosed infection began to spread from my right hand up my arm. To this day, the doctors do not know how the infection began or what exactly it was. But within twenty-four hours, the infection had spread and begun to eat away the flesh of my right arm. The best doctors the hospital could produce were befuddled. None had ever seen this kind of infection before.

In the afternoon of the second day, two doctors came to my room. I was wracked with fever and had no energy. Because of the way the infection was progressing, they feared for my life. One, a leading surgeon, drew a black line on my right shoulder to mark where the cut would be made to remove my arm the next day. He was convinced that the amputation was necessary to save my life. The other doctor seemed equally convinced that my constitution was not strong enough to survive such an operation. So one said, "Either this will be done or the Reverend will die," while the other said, "Cut off his arm and he cannot live." As they left, I heard the men talking with each other. The prognosis did not seem good.

People at Zion Baptist, who had been informed that I was gravely ill, consequently held prayer meetings in the homes of hundreds of church members. The message was also sent to the OIC programs throughout Africa and other parts of the world. In towns, villages, and cities across Africa, Europe, and South America where there were OICs, thousands prayed in my behalf. That evening at around the midnight hour, I too looked up in the darkness and prayed to God. I told him there was something else I wanted to do. I wanted to bring my people in Africa, America, and other parts of the world together. I wanted them to learn to believe in themselves, to become stronger, and to advance the race. I said to God, "I would like to have a little more time to do it, if I can." And in his own way, God said to me, "I know what you are going through, and I know what you want to do. Don't worry. I am going to give you a little more time to do your work." I went to sleep.

I woke up early that next morning, and the infection had been stopped in its tracks. Water mixed with blood was coming out of two little holes that had opened on either side of my arm, just below the elbow. The fever that had ravaged my body for two days was gone. That morning, while Grace was with me, a woman I had never seen before came into the room. We assumed she was a doctor. She was dressed in black. She looked at me, examined my arm, cleaned the wound, and wrapped it with new bandages. She then turned to me and said, "You are going to be all right." Then she left. Grace and I never saw her again. We did not know who she was or where she went. We asked the nurses about her, and no one had seen her or knew who she was. Grace and I called her the "angel doctor in black." By that afternoon, I was sitting up in a chair. By evening, I was walking through the halls. But the infection left its mark, something to link my past with the present. It left me without the use of three fingers on my right hand — the same three fingers that at one time I was planning to cut off in protest against apartheid.

During my recovery, during which time the open wound on my arm was covered with skin grafted from the side of my right leg, I began to organize the First African–African American Summit. It was to be held in Abidjan, Côte d'Ivoire, and hosted by President Houphouet-Boigny, a friend who offered to open his nation to this first gathering of African and African American leaders and people. From my sickbed in Arizona, I called more than six hundred people — teachers, doctors, ministers, businesspeople, civil rights leaders, politicians, youth leaders, and anyone who, I believed, had an interest in the advancement of Africa. The telephone bill was higher than the doctors' bills. Something within me told me that it had to be done and that the effort must not fail. I knew that if the first summit was not successful, it might be the last summit. I was determined to make the hopes of W. E. B. Du Bois, Marcus Garvey, George Padmore, Kwame Nkrumah, and others from the United States, the Caribbean, and Africa a reality. As I reflect on things now, I believe my being sick was a part of God's plan, for I had to be tied to a sickbed in order to get the job done.

Over the next year I along with our small committee of African diplomats completed the organization and the launching of the First African–African American Summit, one that would prove to be a seminal event for future relations between and among African Americans, Americans, and Africans. We took three hundred African Americans, of whom 90 percent had never before flown over an ocean, to that first summit in Abidjan in 1991. It was the largest contingent of African Americans ever to return to Africa. I called them the "Historic 300," for it was they who opened Africa as a new frontier for future youth of the African diaspora.

President Houphouet-Boigny, one of the most honored African leaders of his time, has since passed on, but I will never forget a statement he made in his address to the thousands present at that first summit: "They will return to the tree one day, and when they do, we will be here waiting to receive them." At the summit he presented his country's first dual-citizenship passports, making Grace and me citizens of Côte d'Ivoire. His action launched a dual-citizenship campaign for African Americans who wanted to have two citizenships — one in America and one in an African country. A number of African Americans are now dual citizens. In future years, I foresee thousands of blacks of African heritage formally associating with the African country of their choice, where they will help in practical ways with education and the economic and cultural advancement of the nation. People of African descent will do in future years what the Jews have done in holding dual citizenships with Israel, what the British living in other lands have done in holding dual citizenships with Great Britain, what the Italians living outside Italy have done since the days of the Roman Empire in holding dual citizenships with Italy. In the twenty-first century and beyond, African Americans and others of the black diaspora by the thousands will hold dual citizenships in Africa.

The 1991 African–African American Summit in Abidjan, Côte d'Ivoire, was a success, despite the doubters and skeptics who could not imagine anything meaningful or lasting being accomplished. From the opening day, it was clear that something extraordinary and unusual was happening as hundreds from America, who were brought across the ocean on a special chartered plane, came together with hundreds of Africans from nations across the continent. Representatives from a hundred companies attended, including many major firms that had never done business or invested in any African country but South Africa. They were looking for new markets and new opportunities. And they got them. Hundreds of educators came, along with doctors, lawyers, community activists, union leaders, barbers, beauticians, and just ordinary people who wanted to be a part of something new that was happening in Africa. What surprised me most was that five African heads of state came along with prime ministers from northern Africa and cabinet ministers and top government officials from twenty-six African countries.

Newspapers from America, Europe, Africa, and Asia reported, "Something is happening in Côte d'Ivoire that has never happened before." History was being made. At the summit, Principles and Recommendations of Action were developed and approved, which later were expanded. They called for advances, on scales never before attempted, in education, business and investments, food production, democracy, and peace.

By the time of the first summit, debt relief for African countries had become a main concern for African leaders, for a debt of more than $300 billion was saddling their poor countries. Most of the countries could not even service their debts, much less pay on the principal. As the unpaid interest accumulated, the debt continued to mount. In a special, closed session at the Abidjan Summit, the African heads of state appealed for relief from the heavy debt load. President Quett Masire of Botswana called the debt "an albatross around our necks."

Results from the 1991 summit began to take shape immediately after it adjourned. Upon leaving Africa, we immediately began to work towards the alleviation of the debt. We met with the director general of the United Nations, Javier Pérez de Cuellar, and asked him to call a special session of the United Nations to deal with African debt. He agreed. Six months after the 1991 summit, the first official UN meeting for African debt relief was held at the United Nations in New York City. Representatives from all the nations of the world, including those from the most powerful countries, attended the sessions. Four thousand U.S. participants converged on the United Nations for the deliberations, coming by bus, train, and car from cities all across the country. Leaders of corporations attended, including the heads of General Motors and Colgate-Palmolive and the president of J. P. Morgan. There were representatives from the United States Treasury, the United States Department of State, and the White House. At that meeting the call was made for the first time in UN history for massive debt relief for sub-Saharan African countries. At the meeting all the developed nations of the world and the Paris Club, which regulates debt for developing countries, were called to cooperate in lifting on a massive scale the ominous debt on African countries. It was the first big push for debt relief for Africa.

Immediately following the United Nations meeting, I made a move of my own. I proceeded with an intensive, all-out follow-up for African debt relief. I visited the heads of state of the largest and most powerful nations in the world holding debt on African countries. I started with the United States, arranging a meeting with President George Bush, with whom I had become friends as a result of my OIC programs at home and abroad. I asked for his help with debt relief for sub-Saharan African countries, having been told by African leaders that the United States had been dragging its feet on debt relief for many years and had done little to help with the problem. President Bush agreed to work with me, and on that day, he forgave $2 billion of sub-Saharan African debt.

The stage was set for me to do much more. Encouraged by the response from President Bush, I went to Europe and met with President François Mitterrand and asked for his help. As a result, France forgave $6 billion in debt, and more was promised. I then went to Bonn, Germany, and met with Chancellor Helmut Kohl. He committed Germany to supporting our efforts "as long as benefits from the debt relief are not used by African leaders for tanks and chalets." President Mitterrand and Chancellor Kohl took the leadership in taking our message to meetings of the leaders of the seven most developed nations in the world (the G-7) and received a commitment from the leaders of the United States, Germany, France, England, Italy, Japan, and Canada to intensify debt relief for sub-Saharan African countries. President Mitterrand, Chancellor Kohl, and President Bush kept their word and supported us; without such action there would not have been much progress in African debt relief.

I then went to Paris to the Paris Club, where I secured the leaders' commitment to make debt relief for sub-Saharan African nations a priority. My appeal was for 80 percent debt relief for the African nations with the interest on remaining debt to be converted into local currencies for education, health, and other human development purposes and with the condition that the benefits would be tied to accountability by the African leaders, as Chancellor Kohl had stipulated.

I then went to the World Bank and the International Monetary Fund (IMF) in Washington and spoke to the leaders of both multilateral organizations, appealing for their cooperation. At the time, more than half of the debt in Africa was held by the World Bank and the IMF. It was essential to have their cooperation, and I was assured of their support. Large-scale relief began to follow, all tied to structural readjustment and accountability.

By the time of the Second African–African American Summit, held in Libreville, Gabon, in 1993 and hosted by President Omar Bongo (who provided extraordinary support to that and later summits), we had secured $10 billion in debt relief, and plans were underway with the Paris Club and other treasuries of the developed nations for much more. By the time of the third summit — held in Dakar, Senegal, in 1995 — we had secured debt relief for sub-Saharan African nations totaling $30 billion. By the fourth summit — held in Harare, Zimbabwe, in 1997 — we had secured $60 billion, and we were working on $100 billion more.

The success of the summits went well beyond the efforts at debt relief. Some skeptics had thought the summits would produce little more than good speeches, some posturing, and some politicking, along with a lot of black leaders trying to get their names and pictures in the newspapers and their speeches on radio and television. Some of these skeptics likened the summits to sending up a rocket that goes nowhere fast only to flicker out and fade away.

But I had promised myself and God that something worthwhile would come out of these efforts to help the poor and the needy of Africa, especially the children. God had given me a little more time to do what I wanted to do, and I was determined that the time I had left in my life would be put to the best possible use. This mission was important to me because Africa had been marginalized by the rest of the world. Much of the world believed that, outside of Africa's minerals, exceptional climate, animals, and forest preserves, little more could come out of sub-Saharan Africa, with South Africa being the exception to the rule. But I had made up my mind to show the world that these opinions of Africa were not true. A continent where, over a period of four hundred years, a third of the people had been taken away in slavery, leaving behind the old, the very young, and the very weak, could become a cornerstone of economic, social, and political progress.

I became involved in Africa believing that God would help me move the mountains that stand in the way of the African people. I look forward to the day when black youth everywhere will stand alongside their peers in every other part of the world, proud and confident in their economic, educational, and social equality. We can learn science and math; we can become mechanics and engineers; we can develop banks and financial institutions and businesses. We can do what we prepare ourselves to do.

During this period, I was especially fond of using the expression "TTT." Things take time — I knew it would take time to see a new, stronger Africa fully recognized by the world. And I knew it would take work: much, much work and prayer and sacrifice and education and determination and faith. Reaching the goal of equality with other parts of the world will take decades, even generations, but I know it will happen with the help of African Americans and others of the black diaspora and with help from America and other world powers. It will happen if those of us who care do not give up. Perhaps it will not happen in my day, but surely it will in the days of my children or my children's children. Perhaps it will happen sooner than anyone thinks it can.

From the beginning of the summit movement, I believed that if Stanley could do what he did in Africa and if Livingstone could do what he did in Africa and if Rhodes could do what he did in Africa, although our goals were far from the same, then I could do what I wanted to do for Africa, with the help of God. This time it would be, not for diamonds or gold or money, but to uplift black children who, for four hundred years, have had the foot of the world on the back of their necks.

By the time of the third summit in Dakar, Senegal, in 1995, which was hosted by President Abdou Diouf, the African–African American summit movement had come of age. America and the world began to take notice. The impossible had become possible, and Africa, in the minds of many in America and the world, would not be the same again. It would no longer be known as a place of animals, Tarzan, cannibals, and backward peoples. For the first time since the emancipation of blacks in America, black people would begin to identify proudly with a new and hopeful Africa. This growing pride needs to be nurtured and claimed. For many African Americans and others around the world, Africa is still a dark, undesirable continent. This misperception must be destroyed. The world has done a job on the black man's head that needs fixing, but as a result of the summits, progress is being made. If it continues, people will begin to see Africa in a new light.

At the Dakar Summit, reports revealed formidable accomplishments that had followed the summits in Abidjan and Libreville. Reporting about the summits in May 1995, the leading newspaper in Botswana, one of the most respected in southern Africa, wrote the following in an editorial entitled "Hope for Africa":

> A vision hatched by Leon Sullivan to unite the Africans and African Americans in a common goal of improving the quality of life among Africans appears to be the most practical in this decade.
>
> The accomplishments since the summit's first meeting have been phenomenal. A number of declarations adopted by the summit at its two previous summits have been translated into reality with a verve unparalleled.
>
> Rather than rhetoric that has become so characteristic of continental meetings such as the OAU, the African–African American summits have concerned themselves with the day-to-day problems of the people. The focus of one summit after another has been on education, health,

food production, jobs, industrialization, economic growth and the promotion of a deeper and better understanding between the Africans and their counterparts in the diaspora.

These are the cornerstones of a better life. And indeed, in each, the summit movement has scored remarkably. A glaring example of the summit's pragmatism is acquisition of the Thirty Billion dollars ($30 billion) in debt relief for the continent.

Yet as Sullivan put it, the achievements so far made are a scratch in the surface in helping with the greater needs of the continent. More lies ahead. And the future success will be in keeping the summits as, in the words of President Masire, "a people to people movement."

It is disturbing to note that whereas the African Americans from across the spectrum attended the summit, the Africans were represented by bureaucrats. No doubt the people on the ground such as businessmen, doctors, architects, journalists, engineers, teachers, and other professionals would have been a better choice of representation at the summit. Otherwise, the absence of this arrangement denied those who would have been interested an opportunity to make crucial business contacts.

Sustaining the summit as people-based perhaps bears the potential of finally realizing the historical dream of uniting the continent. After all, unity from above has proved to be impractical, as demonstrated by the failures of the OAU.

The summit movement activities are also unique in that while they are underlined by pragmatism, they are all encompassing. They are as economic focused as they are social, cultural and scientific. The underlying philosophy here is that one aspect cannot be meaningfully developed in isolation. They are interwoven into a fabric that finally defines a human society.

Over decades, attempts to establish viable continental groupings in Africa have been undermined by failure to take cognizance of this philosophy. Politics and politicians played high while all other social aspects were consigned to the background. This is an approach that history has proved wrong.

Perhaps at long last in Sullivan's vision a thing can be learned.

At the summit in Dakar more than four thousand delegates and participants attended the meetings. There were eighteen African heads of state and government, one of the largest outpourings of prime ministers and presidents from African countries to assemble since the earlier days of African liberation. There were two hundred companies represented, including the largest companies in America as well as major companies from Europe. And large numbers of African

American businessmen and businesswomen came to Africa for the first time, looking to do business. There were hundreds of religious leaders and hundreds of educators, including presidents of some of the largest colleges and universities in America. There were doctors and nurses and students and politicians and community leaders from all across the United States. And there were hundreds of ordinary citizens, mostly African Americans. Almost all of the delegates had never before flown across an ocean; many prayed all night long.

In Dakar, announcements were made regarding the successful campaign to recruit a thousand teachers from the United States for the teaching of teachers in African countries. At the time, three hundred of these teachers had already been assigned to work in African countries, providing thousands of African teachers with new skills. One hundred fifty African bankers, called the Best-and-Brightest, had already been brought to the United States and returned home, trained with the most modern and advanced banking skills available to help upgrade the banking systems in Africa. And by the fourth summit in Harare in 1997, the number of teachers had grown to 500 and the number of bankers to 250. Announcements were made of the digging of fifty thousand wells in Africa and successful programs for the eradication of river blindness. OICs were being established in many new countries of sub-Saharan Africa where they did not already exist. At the forefront of OIC development in the United States, Africa, and elsewhere in the world have been the churches—Christian and Muslim. OIC would not exist in the world without the leadership of churches. Also, $500 million in new investments by American companies had been made in sub-Saharan Africa, along with programs to improve health, especially in rural areas, with the goal of establishing clinics in every country where they did not exist in sub-Saharan Africa along with the improvement and the building of hospitals.

Following the summit at Dakar, a small army of skilled surgeons, physicians, and nurses from American hospitals returned to Africa to help with the improvement of medical conditions. During that time, the first heart bypass surgery in the history of Dakar, Senegal, as well as all of West Africa, was performed under the direction of Dr. Albert Olivier, one of the most outstanding heart surgeons in America, who just happens to be black. A program to continue with the improvement of health conditions in sub-Saharan Africa, called the Rev. Leon Sullivan Medical Project for Africa, was also well underway.

President Bill Clinton, with whom I had talked about the Dakar Summit, at the time urging him to visit Africa, sent Ron Brown, secretary of the Department of Commerce and one of the most respected African American leaders in the United States, to represent him at the summit. Ron brought a tremendous, inspirational message geared toward greater American corporate participation, investment, and joint ventures with Africans and African Americans. The later loss of Ron Brown in an airplane crash while on U.S. government business was great not only to America but to Africa. It was also a loss to the summit movement because he had made a commitment to work with me in whatever way he could with future summits and their follow-up activities. Fortunately, a new cabinet member, U.S. Secretary of Transportation Rod Slater, has stepped forward to take Ron's place and has become a great help to me and Africa.

Following the Dakar Summit, new and bolder programs were launched to improve economies in Africa as well as the education and health services of Africans, especially the children. This included a major focus on containing HIV/AIDS, which has become one of the greatest scourges and deliverers of death on the African continent and in the world. Recognition and respect for the summit took hold and grew around the world.

By the time the Fourth African–African American Summit was held in Harare, Zimbabwe, in 1997, nearly every major nation in the world would send representatives. The black diaspora was there from the United Kingdom, the Caribbean, Brazil, and Canada and from every city and state in the United States. People came from every part of Africa; there were prime ministers and high government officials from Morocco, Tunisia, Algeria, and Egypt. Almost every news agency and major radio and television network was there, including ABC, CBS, CNN, and the BBC. The summit in Harare would be top news around the world.

Chapter 18

Preparing for Harare

THE 1997 Harare Summit was of special importance because it was the twentieth anniversary of the introduction of the Sullivan Principles. This was one reason the decision was made that southern Africa should be the location. The summit was organized as no event of its kind had ever been before. The planning was extensive and meticulous so that everything would happen when it was supposed to happen, especially during the last two days when more than twenty African heads of state and leaders of government would speak during plenary sessions and scores of committees would be working behind the scenes putting content into the speeches and formulating a plan of action that, following the summit, would lead to the education and human development of tens of millions of people and, especially, children. For something of this magnitude, work and planning are paramount for success.

All the African–African American summits with friends of Africa were different from any summit gathering held before in Africa or any other part of the world. Usually, summit gatherings are organized and carried on by nations. Those who attend are heads of nations and the top government officials from countries around the world. The African–African American summits with friends of Africa broke new ground in the way these kinds of continental gatherings were organized. For the first time these summits were convened and organized by a private citizen who, with the help of hundreds from Africa and the United States, had "the gall," as some observers called it, to call heads of state and government together with others to make plans for a continent. The amazing and unexpected thing was that when the call was made, the heads of the nations came.

The large number of helpers for the summit was like a volunteer army: young and old, educated and uneducated, Christians and Muslims and all religions, mostly black, but with some whites. One of the most important preparations for the Harare Summit took place six months before the event when I, along with Dr. C. T. Wright, traveled to Johannesburg, South Africa. We were there to make plans for the thousand Americans who would be stopping first in Johannesburg on their way to Harare for a special visit to Soweto, where many of the antiapartheid demonstrations had been held.

During a brief, three-day stay in Johannesburg, we talked with leaders of the South African government who were making plans for a large reception for the Americans. We wanted to be certain that everything would be in place. It was the Easter season, and I went to Soweto on Easter Sunday morning and spoke at three churches to announce the coming of the Americans on their way to the summit in Harare, Zimbabwe, which was to be held later in the year on July 21. The sermon I delivered was called "A Message to the Churches of Soweto." In it, I described my experiences in South Africa during the initiation of the Sullivan Principles along with my plans for the future with the Principles in their country and the coming of the Americans to Soweto on their way to the summit.

I was amazed on entering Soweto at the reception I received from the people, for I did not know the Sullivan Principles were so well known there. I had no doubt that the businesses and the South African government knew about the Principles, but I was not expecting to find that they were so well known and appreciated in the grass roots. As is my usual practice when traveling through places like Harlem, North Philadelphia, and Watts, I stopped the car to get out to meet the people and talk with them to find out how they were faring. Every time I got out of the car in Soweto, there were people who recognized me and came up to me to thank me for what I had done for the country. Even though in all things I try to remain composed, these actions from the people, so spontaneous and unexpected, moved me as anything seldom had. I did not realize how much the people in Soweto knew about my attempts to help them. Not only did they know, but they appreciated it greatly and tried to express it to me on that day. Most black people in America didn't know what I was doing in South Africa, and many of those who did know didn't really care. But the people in Soweto who were there in the struggle knew all about what I was doing. And they definitely cared.

One of the men who came to embrace and thank me had been with Nelson Mandela in prison and was a well-known freedom fighter in Soweto. He insisted on getting in the car so he could take me to his church and present me to his pastor. After meeting me, the pastor introduced me to his congregation, literally thousands of people attending the worship service in a huge tent. The congregation stood up and applauded. I spoke about my joy in being back in Soweto with them in a free, democratic South Africa and about the blessings of God in helping with their freedom. And as I left, the crowd stood again, singing and applauding. It was a scene I will never forget.

At the last stop, at one of the largest charismatic churches in Soweto where I was scheduled to speak, the Faithway Bible Church, I was presented by the pastor, Dr. Nguako David Thevehali, who had traveled in the United States and observed the OIC work in Philadelphia. He was an enthusiastic supporter of the self-help concept. I spoke to the people to affirm their courage in the struggle and to tell them of plans for future development. Following are excerpts from my sermon on that Easter Sunday.

You fought in a great movement for freedom, and the struggle you made reverberated around the world. What I did was only as a surrogate because you were the real warriors. It was you who fought the real battle. It was you who went to the jails. It was you who had your heads beaten. It was you who were the vanguard in the struggle, but I want you to know back in the United States Leon Sullivan was there. And I have come back today, this Easter Sunday morning, to thank God and to tell you what an example you are to the world. You do not realize in Soweto the example you have been for millions of people all over the world who will have struggles for human rights and for freedom. And when they said it couldn't be done today, we look at Soweto and look at South Africa, and if they can do it with God's help, it can be done around the world. So, I have come back to Soweto. The last time I was here, they had the police around me, and they had guns around me, and they had guards around me because they didn't want me here. But today, thank God, Jesus is around me. Yes, yes, yes. Today Jesus is around me.

Now we have something else we are going to do, and I wanted you to know about it, Brother Pastor, you and your great church, because I wanted you to be among the first to hear it. The Sullivan Principles are not over. Apartheid is ended, but your children still need a whole lot of help. They need help still for skills and jobs. They still need help and health benefits and human improvement. You still need help for the development of businesses so you can own something for yourselves. You need something not only to be politically free, but you need to be economically free.

Before I go to Harare, Zimbabwe,...I am going to bring one thousand Americans...here to Soweto so they can be with you at least one day....Will you meet us when we come? [The response was a great "Yes!"]....We are building thousands of schools in Africa, and, Brother Pastor, I am going to build some of those schools in Soweto. We are sending thousands of teachers to help upgrade your teachers, and I am going to send some of those teachers to Soweto. I am going to open OIC Skills Centers. I have just opened one in Qwa Zulu Natal, and I want another OIC here in Soweto to train your girls to be able to work those computers and to train your young men so that they will be able to be plumbers, electricians, and carpenters. So you will be able to build things for yourselves and...start businesses of your own. That is what we are going to do in the new Sullivan Principles. So I want your children to have hope. Jesus still lives. Have hope; help is on the way. Your children who are unemployed, help is on the way. God is already here, and we are coming. "The Americans are coming. Meet us when we come."

And so I say to you, "Walk together. You are not alone." This Easter Sunday morning God rolled the stone away, and he is going to role the stone away again for Soweto and South Africa....There is going to be a new day....And you know that Jesus is here this morning. You can feel him. He is everywhere, and things in South Africa won't be the same for a thousand years. The struggle is not over; human development and education are needed now. We must empower the people so they can stand shoulder to shoulder and eye to eye with the white people in this world. You can do anything anyone else can do if you believe it. Your children can be anything they want to be if they believe it. So, have faith. God is with us. Meet me when we come to Soweto, and let us send a message to the world that it will never do to us again what it has done before. Thank you very much. Praise the Lord. Glory hallelujah.

When I finished my sermon, the applause and singing lasted a half hour.

On Monday, the day after visiting Soweto, I spoke on a popular television show, *Good Morning, South Africa*, which was carried throughout the country. I told South Africa that we would be coming through Johannesburg and Soweto on our way to the summit. I wanted the nation to be poised to receive us.

Later that day, I traveled on to Harare, an hour and a half away by plane, to meet with President Robert Mugabe of Zimbabwe and other leaders of the nation. We wanted to be certain that ample preparations were being made. I was pleased to find that President Mugabe had pulled out all the stops to insure that the summit in Harare would be successful. The country was preparing for our coming. I also met with business, religious, and community leaders to champion their maximum participation in all of the summit activities. When I left for America, I knew that South Africa and Harare were ready to receive us. The planning had paid off. During the last days of preparation, scores of committees were working in Africa and in America with many schedules formulated and plans laid. We were coming to South Africa and Soweto, and we were coming to Harare. And we were organized like a finely tuned machine.

Chapter 19

Historic Harare

FROM TWENTY GATEWAY CITIES in the United States on the evening of July 18, 1997, a thousand Americans of diverse backgrounds and viewpoints boarded airplanes that carried them to airports in London, England, and in Frankfurt, Germany. They arrived at this first stop on their journey to Africa in the morning, and after sightseeing and resting in prearranged hotels at the two airports, the summit delegation from the United States, augmented by delegations from the United Kingdom, the Caribbean, and Brazil, attended a reception, then boarded planes for Johannesburg, South Africa, where the thousand delegates were to visit. That Sunday evening, a great reception was hosted by the South African government. The highlight of the evening was the presence of Nelson Mandela. A moving experience, just being near this great man was something most in the delegation would never forget. Speaking to the delegates who crowded the presidential reception room, the president said, "The time for great unity among us has come."

Nelson Mandela is an icon of freedom for the world during the second half of the twentieth century. He is one of two great men, the other being Martin Luther King Jr., who have helped shape the future for justice and human rights in the world. I found Mandela to be one of the kindest, most gentle and inspiring people I have ever known. At the time, he was the most respected leader in the world, and I am pleased to have him as a friend.

On Monday morning, the one thousand delegates boarded buses and were taken to a church in Soweto, the township outside of Johannesburg that was the center of major protests against the apartheid system. It was a great day for me personally. I remembered well my visit to this church in 1980, during the days of apartheid. Then I was guarded by police with dogs and guards with ready guns, but on this day in 1997, I was surrounded not by police and guards but by a spirit of love, happiness, and joy. The changes that others had fought for had been realized. South Africa was a free and democratic nation with Nelson Mandela, a black man who had been in prison for twenty-seven years, serving as president. The happiness I felt that day amid the singing, the clapping of hands, and the cries of "Welcome Americans" that rang out inside and outside the church brought tears to my eyes. The walls had come down, and I was thankful that we had played a large part in helping to bring it about. It was another reminder of how faith can move mountains.

The large church was Regini Mundi. In the middle of town, it was one of the churches I had visited the previous Easter Sunday and was where most of the demonstrations against the apartheid system had been held and where there were great funeral services for many black youth of Soweto killed during the apartheid days. There were still bullet holes in the walls and the ceilings of the church kept there as a reminder and memorial to the terrible days of the apartheid struggle.

At the special service, a large choir sang moving and inspiring songs. The leaders of Soweto, including its mayor, all assembled with our summit delegates in the church. In addition, hundreds of ministers and other religious leaders of churches from Soweto and surrounding areas attended the service. Also, a thousand residents from Soweto sat and stood behind us, crowding the church to its capacity, with thousands more listening to the service from loudspeakers outside.

On that great day, African Americans and residents of Soweto and other parts of South Africa had come together with hundreds more of the black diaspora from every part of the world to celebrate a new day for South Africa. New hopes for the future were brought to all of Africa and Africa's children. It was a great and inspiring celebration. A number of great black American leaders spoke, along with some youth from America. Leaders from Soweto and other parts of South Africa gave moving talks. The leaders of the women of Soweto and leaders of black women from the United States spoke, as did South African political, civic, and religious leaders.

After the highly emotional service, the delegates from the United States along with others from the United Kingdom, the Caribbean, and Brazil boarded waiting buses that drove us to the airport, where we boarded planes that would carry us to Harare for the formal opening of the Fourth African–African American Summit. On the buses and on the planes, there was singing and jubilation all along the way.

Whatever might happen afterwards in Harare, we thought, our experiences in South Africa with Nelson Mandela and in Soweto had already made the summit a success well worth the time and cost of coming.

It was 4:00 P.M. when our plane landed on the airfield of Harare. Thousands of Zimbabweans met us with singing and dancing as we left the planes. I saw some of the delegates, men and women, who bent down and kissed the ground, happy to be back at their ancestral home. Still singing, the delegates took waiting buses to their hotels, where they were directed to their rooms. The delegates' bags, which had been stamped with their names, addresses, their hotel in Zimbabwe, and their room numbers, were quickly delivered. The moving of four thousand bags from the planes to hotels at the different stops in London, Johannesburg, and Harare was an achievement in itself. Within a few hours after arriving, the delegates were settled and had begun to take walks around Harare. Never before had a thousand Americans been moved about anywhere with such order and precision. The summit got off to a great beginning and continued so through the entire proceedings. It was indeed the "Optimum Summit."

It was imperative that this summit be successful. I knew the eyes of not only Africa and the United States but of all the world were upon us. And I knew that whatever we could do that was positive, practical, and effective to help the poor and disadvantaged of Africa, especially the children, would pay great dividends with future support from the United States and other supporters from Europe, Asia, and every other part of the world.

My children, Howard, Julie, and Hope, were all very much involved with the summit and at different points with my work in general. My son, Howard, an engineer, was the lead person on the ground in Harare to work with the leaders of Zimbabwe in all the preparations. A few days before the opening of the summit, I was concerned about possible problems. I called Hope, a young lawyer, then thirty-three years of age. She had helped put the summit together along with Larry Branch, a former top executive with Merck & Company who had worked with me during the Sullivan Principle days in making various arrangements for the Leeds Castle meetings. When I asked Hope how things were going, she said, "Daddy, you have nothing to worry about. This thing is organized so well that only an act of God could mess it up." I was pleased because I knew the summit was in good hands and under control. Julie, trained in communications and education, was the one responsible for sending five hundred master teachers from the United States to Africa, the largest Teachers for Africa program ever attempted. I must say I am proud of my children and all the help they have given me through the years.

I knew it was hard to steer clear of all problems with anything the size of the summit. I knew you could not bring six thousand people together with different ideas, ideologies, personal motives, and feelings and have everything go well. But I strove for optimum results. Yes, there were glitches here and there. Yes, some feelings were rubbed the wrong way. But the Harare Summit was a tremendous success. Nothing like it of such magnitude had ever been seen and done so well in Africa before.

At 8:00 A.M. on Tuesday morning, there was an opening religious service of unity, reconciliation, and cooperation. Hundreds of ministers, pastors, priests, and other religious leaders talked and preached on the theme of greater unity among the leaders and the churches. Groups represented included Baptists, Methodists, Episcopalians, Pentecostals, the Church of God in Christ, Evangelicals, Catholics, Muslims, Sikhs, Hindus, and more. The goal among the clergy was to mold thousands together into a united body, recognizing differences of faith but uniting participants in the main purposes of advancing sub-Saharan Africa and educating and helping the children.

Following my opening address (which is found in chap. 22) and the addresses of more than twenty heads of state and government and other distinguished participants, such as the secretary general of the Organization of African Unity, leaders of the World Bank and the International Monetary Fund, envoys from nations of Europe, and leaders of the United Nations Educational, Scientific, and Cultural Organization (UNESCO), the summit conferees got down to serious business, and many spectacular decisions to help with the future of sub-Saharan Africa followed. Final reports of Principles and Recommendations of Action were presented to an overflow audience in the convention hall of the Sheraton Hotel, where the main sessions were held, while an array of follow-up groups made plans to put the recommendations into action.

Among the many highlights of the Harare Summit were memorable speeches, down-to-earth reports, and commitments for widespread follow-up throughout Africa and in the United States, the Caribbean, and Europe. Many heads of state inspired the great gatherings with messages of unity and hope; these leaders included our host, President Robert Mugabe; President Abdou Diouf of Senegal; Sir Quett K. J. Masire, president of Botswana; President João Bernardo Vieira of Guinea-Bissau; Yoweri Museveni of Uganda; King Mswati III of Swaziland; President Menes Zenawi of Ethiopia; and President Sam Nujoma of Namibia. Other inspiring speakers included Rev. Jesse Jackson; Coretta Scott King, wife of Martin Luther King Jr.; Dorothy Height, leader of the National Council of Negro Women; Dick Gregory, the famous entertainer and civil rights activist; Marion Barry, the mayor of Washington, D.C.; David Dinkins, the former mayor of New York City; and many others who joined in the appeal for unity in Africa, including well-known leaders from across Africa and the Caribbean. Other leaders who provided an inspiring presence included representatives from a White House delegation led by Secretary of Transportation Rodney Slater, who had a special message from President Bill Clinton lauding the work of the summit and promising U.S. support for summit recommendations.

In the opening summit meeting, President Mugabe said,

> The U.S., perhaps for too long, has tended to regard Africa as a marginal part of the world which "belonged" to Europe. Ours has been a continent in which the United States became interested only as a stage for the cold war. We are confident that image of the continent is behind us all. This old negative image of Africa will only be fully erased if we continue to see many Americans coming to seek opportunities in Africa, to engage fully in the many business ventures that are on offer. It is our reverent hope that our American brothers and sisters will take that message back to America.

Corporate executives with several chief executive officers from industrial conglomerates such as Shell Oil International, Chevron, Procter & Gamble, Owens-Corning, and Caltex, spearheaded American industrial presence in Harare. The message of democracy and economic liberalization was echoed again and again at the summit by leaders from both sides of the Atlantic Ocean. Said President Mugabe to the delegates, "The time has ended for African governments to be led by soldier come, soldier go. We must work together."

Delegates from more than fifteen state legislatures in America were present. Lois Deberry, president of the National Caucus of Black Locally Elected Officials, stressed, "I consider this to be the real Africa. In order for us to go back to the States to educate our people, we have got to know truth no matter how bad it hurts. That truth is beyond the reports of progress of some individuals, to the reality of poverty on the continent which still finds most people 'drinking water from a river, trying to survive.'" Representing those present from the Caribbean, Celeo Alvarez Casilo, president of the Central American Black Organization in Honduras, exclaimed with great passion, "It's a great opportunity for communication with black people in the world. We need more organization, more communication for development, especially because the problems of blacks in Latin America are easily overlooked."

As the many speakers gave their remarks, delegates throughout the great audience wept. The sessions on government, business, and health, among others, were unforgettable successes with follow-up plans coming forth with each gathering. I exclaimed at one of the sessions that "we are here and we will never be separated again," and I thundered, "This is a new day for Africa and African American unity, and we have returned with something to give back to Africa at last."

In spite of nearly three centuries of slavery in America, African Americans have emerged in 1997 with vision, skills, jobs, and wealth, with a purchasing power of some $600 billion and with more college graduates, doctors, dentists, lawyers, engineers, preachers, M.B.A.'s and Ph.D.'s than all the rest of the black population of the world put together. And in Africa there are more minerals, diamonds, gold, silver, copper, bauxite, oil, and coal than in any other place on the globe. I knew that if we could ever begin to put the two together, the African Americans with what they had and the Africans with what they had, the two could work together so that, one day, there would be a new era of opportunity and advancement for coming generations in Africa unequaled in any other place in the world. I had seen what the Jews in America and the Jews in Israel could together, what the Poles in America and the Poles in Poland could do together, and what the Irish in America and the Irish in Ireland could do together, all for their mutual good. I knew the same could be done by Africans and African Americans and others of the African diaspora, working together for their common good. I knew no people can be a free people without a base, and Africa is the base for black people, without which we can never be free. And here in Harare, at last, we had come back home.

Leaders of governments and the thousands of participants and volunteers agreed unanimously at the summit to adopt the Harare Declaration. All agreed to return home and organize summit follow-up committees to assure that the Harare Declaration would be supported and implemented throughout the United States, the Caribbean, and other nations of the world. Because of its historic importance I include it here.

HARARE DECLARATION
FOURTH AFRICAN–AFRICAN AMERICAN SUMMIT

We, the Heads of State and of Government and Heads of Delegations representing the participating African countries,

We, Heads of the Delegation of the Government of the United States of America,

We, the Representatives of the African American Community headed by the Reverend Dr. Leon H. Sullivan and

We, the Friends of Africa,

Meeting at the Fourth African–African American Summit in Harare, Zimbabwe, from the 21st through the 25th of July, 1997, reconfirm our solemn commitment to implement the Declaration of Principles and Actions adopted during the First Summit held in Abidjan, Côte d'Ivoire, hosted by His Excellency Felix Houphouet-Boigny in 1991, the Second Summit held in Libreville, Gabon, hosted by His Excellency El Hadji Omar Bongo in 1993 and the Third Summit held in Dakar, Senegal, hosted by His Excellency Abdou Diouf in 1995, whose objectives were to strengthen the relations of friendship and solidarity established between Africans and African Americans by history, culture and common destiny and to find the ways and means likely to help accelerate the African development process in a cooperative and consultative framework, and in the spirit of the contemporary evolution of the world towards the beginning of the new millennium.

We acknowledge that the Harare Summit is of historic importance; and by virtue of our contacts, discussions, reflections and resolutions, the Summit did assume an empirical dimension commensurate with planned goals. The Fourth Summit was held in a significant and hopeful era for Africa with regard to world progress.

We acknowledge with appreciation the achievements of the first three

Summits, which also contributed to a substantial debt restructuring program for sub-Saharan Africa undertaken in coordination with the United States, France, Germany, Italy, Paris Club, World Bank, International Monetary Fund and the United Nations; a Best-and-Brightest African Bankers Training Program has already trained two hundred and fifty mid-level bankers throughout sub-Saharan Africa; new investments of over a half billion dollars have been made, including the construction of factories and the creation of thousands of new jobs; skills training centers have been expanded; a Thousand Teachers for Africa Program has been launched with four hundred and fifty teachers already helping to upgrade the educational systems in ten African countries; a Thousand Schools for Africa Program has been initiated; a partnership with the World Bank is making possible the digging of fifty thousand tubewells; large quantities of education supplies have been shipped to Africa; and clinics and extensive health programs, including cardiac surgery initiatives, have been launched. Large scale river blindness projects are underway impacting thousands of affected people. Plans have been made for the initiation of a continent-wide HIV/AIDS containment program.

We, the Heads of State/Government and of Delegations, the representatives of the African American community and Friends of Africa participating in the Fourth African–African American Summit in Harare, would like to underscore a continuation of these objectives and stress particular achievements of these Summits.

We renew an unequivocal will to establish and implement the conditions and programs allowing for African economic recovery and growth in a democratic environment, including:

- Our commitment to intensify African economic integration in order to identify viable, stable and reliable markets for foreign investments and the industrialization of our countries within the framework of the Sullivan Plan for Africa.

We reaffirm our efforts to broaden basic education and eradicate adult illiteracy through:

- Bonding of international ties, beginning with an unprecedented Aide Memoire signed during the Harare Summit involving OAU, UNESCO and IFESH which is designed to assist, in a massive manner, to rehabilitate its educational system (in both the formal and the non-formal sectors) as an important contribution to the on-going process of peace building, capacity enhancement, civil society empowerment and the overall socio-economic and political development of the continent;

- The continued reduction and writing off of Africa's debt tied to education and other essential development needs;

- Appropriate progressive national policies on staff training and education.

The Summit appreciates the commitment of African Americans and Friends of Africa to expand support for African development, particularly in the building of productive partnerships to achieve food security; in promoting human resources for a more effective management of African enterprises and for the judicious utilization of raw material, mineral, and energy resources; and in planning, as well as implementing, a comprehensive program to support the strategic goals and objectives to enhance the quality of life, especially among the grassroots population. In this regard, we reaffirm:

- The design and implementation of health and environmental policies with a major Africa-wide focus on the containment of HIV/AIDS, and which protect in dynamic reciprocity man and nature; and

- The development of appropriate modalities to encourage the restoration and repatriation of historic African artifacts.

We recognize the potential of future African generations to compete and prosper in the 21st century by urgent integration of Africa into the information superhighway networks and finding ways to acquire other new technologies.

The recommendations from the sector workshops and assemblies will be reviewed and prioritized by the Summit Ambassadorial Planning Committee. In this regard, we entrust the Committee, under the leadership of the Summit Convener, with the monitoring and the implementation of this Declaration. We instruct the Committee to examine a proposal for the creation of a Permanent Secretariat to follow up the Summit recommendations and decisions and a proposal to alternate the Summit venue between Africa and the United States. We further instruct the Committee to ensure the widest possible dissemination of this Declaration and to sensitize the international community, and American and indeed world public opinion, corporations and companies, in particular, to its contents.

We are encouraged by the spirit in which the International Forum on Business, Investments and Private Sector Cooperation was conducted. The Forum opened new perspectives for a more dynamic, more pragmatic and more balanced approach to North-South and South-South socio-economic and political relations in the areas of trade, technology transfer, business development, health, education, democracy, human rights, transparency, environment, population, women, and children.

We have already, in this regard, defined the conditions and mechanisms for the development of the private sector by African Governments and by their partners in development. This orientation offers to thousands of American, European, Asian and African investors and entrepreneurs an appropriate framework within which to broaden their investments and to enhance and accelerate the transfer of technology to African countries.

We are pleased to acknowledge the participation of over three hundred American companies and corporations, as well as the United States' Government Departments and Agencies in the Summit. We urge each of them to find ways to expand their investments or to begin to invest in African economies. In an effort to ensure the participation of Africans and African Americans in these enterprises, American companies are encouraged to enter into joint ventures with small and medium-size companies in Africa. We note and welcome the new trade and investment policies recently announced by the President of the United States, as well as urge passage of the proposed Congressional legislation designed to create an enabling environment in the facilitation of business investments in Africa. In this context, we stress that official assistance for poverty eradication and infrastructure development in Africa remain relevant and will continue to be needed for some time to come.

We also note with appreciation the presence and encouragement expressed by the representatives of the supporting governments (France, Germany, the Netherlands, United Kingdom and the United States of America) and supporting international bodies (OAU, UNESCO, African Development Bank, World Bank, World Health Organization, and the United Nations Development Program). We urge them to continue to collaborate with the Summit leadership in its quest to help improve the quality of life in Africa.

We acknowledge with deep appreciation, the outstanding contributions that the Reverend Dr. Leon H. Sullivan has made to sub-Saharan African countries during the past twenty years as a builder of human bridges and as an advocate and implementor of programs of self-help, education and the transfer of technology. We commend him for providing the leadership which has resulted in the African–African American Summit movement, which has focused on the creation of pragmatic and positive strategies to help deal with the development of Africa, to create closer cooperation between Africans and African Americans, and to better American and African relationships for the support of Africa. We also express our deepest gratitude to the Reverend Dr. Leon H. Sullivan for apprising the world community of the Summit activities through the worldwide media and by personally visiting several countries and meeting with national and international leaders, including Heads of State and Government, and we ask that he continue in his role as Convener and the guiding light of Summit activities.

We, the Heads of State/Government representing participating African countries; we, the members of the Official Delegation representing the African American Community; we, the Delegation of the Government of the United States of America; and we, the Friends of Africa, meeting at the Fourth African–African American Summit in Harare, Zimbabwe, express our sincere gratitude to His Excellency President Robert G. Mugabe, his Government and the people of Zimbabwe for their warm and generous hospitality and for hosting this historic event. This Summit is another milestone in the distinguished, dedicated and illustrious commitment of President Mugabe to serve the cause of Africa and that of humanity. We enthusiastically applaud President Mugabe's leadership and the goodwill which he has generated during the Fourth African–African American Summit. Finally, in expressing our heartfelt thanks, we wish President Mugabe and the people of Zimbabwe continued success, peace, prosperity and happiness.

The Conference
Harare, Zimbabwe
July 25, 1997

The goals adopted by the summit were ambitious. They are, by 2002:

- to increase debt relief from $60 billion to $100 billion, tied to education and accountability by the heads of the nations, to make sure they did not enrich themselves, as had often been done by many in the past at the expense of their nations and the children;

- to recruit and place in posts throughout sub-Saharan Africa two thousand master teachers from the United States and the world, to provide retraining for one hundred thousand African teachers, who would be teaching ten million children a year;

- to increase the number of Best-and-Brightest bankers from 250 to 500, young men and women who would be leaders of their banks and play leading roles in taking over the banking and financial institutions and the treasuries and reserve banks of African countries, taking the place of expatriates from abroad who had been running the banks in African countries for three hundred years;

- to build one thousand schools, mostly in African rural areas where schools had never existed, with a future objective to increase the number of new schools built in the poorest rural areas to ten thousand in ten years;

- to equip thousands of schools in urban and rural areas with supplies such as books, pencils, pens, rulers, erasers, typewriters, faxes, and computers, looking forward in ten years to providing help to every school in sub-Saharan Africa;

- to quadruple the number of medical clinics in every country and in every urban and rural area in the next ten years so that clinics and health care are available to every child in sub-Saharan Africa;

- to see that regional hospitals are effectively strengthened, equipped, and built and to see that in ten years a major hospital is established and adequately equipped in every country in sub-Saharan Africa;

- to see that, all across Africa, programs will be effectively started for halting the spread of HIV/AIDS, with nationwide models put in place in at least four sub-Saharan countries and with the view that in five more years HIV/AIDS will effectively be contained and controlled in every country in the sub-Saharan African region;

- to expand new investments in sub-Saharan African countries from $500 million to $2 billion in five years and to see that in the next ten years new investments would grow to $20 billion dollars annually, creating two million new jobs on the African continent and two hundred thousand new jobs in the U.S. and other supporting developed countries;

- to increase the number of new businesses by Africans, African Americans, and friends of Africa in sub-Saharan African countries to ten thousand in five years and to see that in fifteen years the number would increase to one hundred thousand, especially with training and jobs for former combatants and helping thousands with owning new businesses;

- to develop and initiate as models in several sub-Saharan countries relevant curricula to teach schoolchildren at the earliest ages the concepts and values and workings of democracy, human rights, respect for others, and the culture of peace and to see that in ten years these studies are taught in the early years in schools in every sub-Saharan country;

- to establish education and training programs for the handicapped in every summit-participating sub-Saharan African country with the objective to have in place in every nation in the next ten years a supported project to assist with problems and needs of the disabled and handicapped, especially with training and jobs for disabled former combatants;

- to raise interest in sub-Saharan Africa in the United States and around the world, among the governments and people, and to see that in the next ten years a positive knowledge of Africa is included in all textbooks used in primary and secondary schools in the United States and in every developed country in the world;

- to assure the possibility of dual citizenship for African Americans and others seeking dual citizenship in every summit-participating sub-Saharan country and to see that in ten years dual-citizenship opportunities for African Americans and other friends of Africa are fully recognized and accepted in nations throughout sub-Saharan Africa;

- to see that Global Sullivan Principles for Corporate Responsibility in Africa are implemented by all multinational firms operating in sub-Saharan African countries and to see that in ten years Global Sullivan Principles calling for a living wage, equal pay for equal work, training, and the elevation of those formerly excluded to better jobs are implemented in large numbers by all companies having operations in all sub-Saharan nations, with sufficient monitoring and with the backing of investors, consumers, and governments from America and the world;

- to begin exchange programs of visitations between Africans and African Americans to help close the gaps between Africans and African Americans in churches, schools, organizations, and homes and in ten years to have created a climate of close cooperation between the continents;

- to operate a summit secretariat, with offices in the United States and in Africa, to coordinate and follow up on all summit actions and activities, supported by African nations, African Americans, and multinational bodies along with other friends of Africa;

- to introduce science and technology, beginning at preprimary levels, so that the very young are familiar with advances in science and technology and are able to compete in future years with youth from Asia, America, and Europe and to see that in ten years science and technology are an ongoing part of education programs in every sub-Saharan African nation at all levels;

- to establish one hundred Opportunities Industrialization Centers (OIC) at all levels in African nations in five years and to establish 250 OICs in ten years, training one million unskilled Africans a year for jobs;

- to establish vast programs of education for women, helping with family planning, literacy, and education and with health assistance for families, especially the young;

- to reach millions through existing schools and new ones, which would be used during the day by the young and at night by mothers for education and training in the areas of health and business development, in recognition that children and mothers are the backbone of the future of Africa.

Some of the greatest accomplishments of the Harare Summit are evident in the words of the many who attended from the United States, Africa, and other parts of the world. The following statements help to tell the story of what the summit meant to many:

The brainless honeybee honors the law of regeneration and drops pollen where it picks up nectar. It feeds the flower that it robs. That's why there are no homeless honeybees. That's why there are no slum honeybee hives. That's why honeybees are not pulling coup d'états on each other because there is a fair distribution of resources and security....

The corporations that drill oil, mine ore, sell products, must likewise adhere to a policy of reinvestment. Chevron, Texaco, Gulf, Shell, all the manufacturers, telecommunications, must have an eye toward partnership, and the key to partnership is mutuality of interest.

Reverend Leon Sullivan intends to build a thousand schools at $10,000 each. We support him in his laudable effort. There are many African individuals, brokers of airplanes and oil and minerals, that can do this themselves, if it is their will to do so as part of a government policy of reinvestment.   (Rev. Jesse Jackson)

It became very clear to me that there is a new wind blowing throughout this continent: a wind that heralds the coming of opportunity, that arises from a sense of self-reliance among the countries and leaders of this continent. It's a wind of change and progress that invites companies like my own (Procter & Gamble) to play a greater role in the continent's growth.

(John Pepper, CEO, Procter & Gamble Worldwide)

Like Rev. Sullivan, I believe that American business in particular must play a critically important role in promoting economic development in Africa, and I think the Sullivan Principles have provided a workable context for American operations doing business in Africa.

(Coretta Scott King)

African–African American summits are first and foremost meetings where are intermingled the past and present, emotion and memories, giving way to new hopes. This is certainly what led Rev. Sullivan at the third summit in Dakar to declare in front of thousands of participants: "I can foresee a bridge between America and Africa that one day my black children, brothers, and sisters will walk on freely in both directions."

...I would like to say how happy I am with the significant achievements and the progress which have been obtained. Africa is seen more and more as a continent of the future, an important place in international politics, despite the existence of areas experiencing crises which we are to resolve with our partners and through the framework of the OAU and the UN.

(His Excellency Abdou Diouf, president of the Republic of Senegal)

A vibrant Africa, with strong political and economic ties to the global community, is a continent of greater stability and expanding markets. A vibrant Africa is a region of strong partners for America, to work for peace and against tyranny, fight disease, and protect the environment; to make our economies grow and provide for our people. What is good for Africa [is] good for America.

Africa is marching proudly into a brighter future...a future made possible by those of courage, vision, and vigilance.

(Rodney Slater, U.S. secretary of transportation)

The success of the process of a biennial dialogue Rev. Sullivan sought would not have become a reality if he had not been received and welcomed by African leaders. It is...imperative that we get to know one another even better than before in order to fully appreciate the various circumstances under which we live. Africans and African Americans need each other. I am, therefore, pleased to note that Rev. Sullivan has brought to this year's summit a most topical theme: Investment and Business Opportunities in Africa.... This theme lays a very appropriate emphasis on the need to do business with one another, which will provide the much-needed substance to our relationship.

(His Excellency Robert G. Mugabe, president of Zimbabwe)

It is a great honor to be speaking at the Fourth African–African American Summit, as it was an honor Sunday evening in Pretoria to be able to meet President Nelson Mandela and so many other distinguished African and African American leaders. This summit truly marks the first week of the twenty-first century for Africa and U.S.-Africa relations.

...In order for people to flourish and prosper, they must be free. The most important tool for building and developing any economy is freedom — not only market freedom but civil and religious freedom as well.

(Jack Kemp)

These partnerships are not meant just to benefit our lives today or to achieve immediate goals of our companies. It's far more important to unify our interests and make and fulfill commitments that will bene-fit our children, grandchildren, and generations to come. As part of a responsible and faithful partnership, Chevron has invested billions of dollars in this continent.

We are a part of this great continent, and we intend to stay. With our African partners, we've built a bridge with sturdy foundations, and it's one that many others can cross.   (Ken Derr, CEO, Chevron)

A new day has come to Africa. We are joining hands as peoples of African heritage from around the world, and I believe it is a bond that will never be broken again.

(His Majesty Mswati III, King of Swaziland)

We are embarking upon a great journey in one of the most exciting mo-ments in history. All the way from Latin America, to Eastern Europe, and now in Africa to the Pacific Rim, the time of freedom is ringing. And the pace of change is quickening.

Country after country is discarding old dogmas and looking to the light of liberty to guide them along a new and better road. Those who stubbornly cling to the old ways will be left behind by millions of people who, for the first time in their lives, are going to be free to follow their dreams with minimal interference from the state.

(William E. Simon, former U.S. secretary of the treasury)

There is a change taking place in the way companies manage opera-tions around the world. Companies that traditionally staffed operations with expatriates now seek to staff with local personnel and managers that know the country's culture. They quickly develop local talent to staff the most skilled positions and the customer relations responsibili-ties. At Owens-Corning we are recruiting and developing leaders who can function across cultures.   (Glen Hiner, CEO, Owens-Corning)

It is the most spiritual and enlightening event I have ever attended in my life! I LEARNED!   (Judy Tabron, Detroit, Michigan)

I enjoyed it; my family enjoyed it; we learned a lot, met a lot of wonderful people.   (Dr. Hazel Harper, Bishop, Kentucky)

I believe in and strongly support Rev. Sullivan's vision for Africans and African Americans.   (Virginia Bishop, Philadelphia, Pennsylvania)

I enjoyed the culture and the country. It also allowed me to gain some insight on African economic issues.   (Michail Smith, Bryan, Texas)

I set out to the African–African American Summit to seek advice, to acquire perspective, to do this project right. Instead, I found nectar for a thirsty soul, and I acquired a voracious appetite for knowledge about who I am. My impressions are as extraordinary as they are intrinsic. Africa is far from "dark." It is God's window, unparalleled in natural beauty. I found drama, sophistication, color, and spirit.

I cannot express my admiration and pride for Rev. Leon Sullivan. I thank him for giving us all the rich opportunity to connect with Africa. I will be forever grateful to him for crushing "apartheid" with his "Sullivan Principles," his knowledge, his courage, and his persistence. I thank him for his freedom of pursuit, his undying faith in God, his dedication to education, for freedom is education. I thank him for giving me a new "why" in my life.

(Joni Sledge, member of the vocal group Sister Sledge)

Beyond my preaching, in my ministry have been three main goals:

- to train black and other poor youth in America for jobs for self-sufficiency and to help America;

- to end apartheid;

- to get America and the world to pay attention to Africa and to help Africa's development.

The first two goals have been achieved. The third goal of Africa's advancement as a region is beginning to happen with the summits, which have raised the consciousness in America about Africa that never existed before.

In March 1998, President Bill Clinton made a twelve-day trip to

Africa, the longest time any sitting president has ever spent on African soil. When I heard of the impending journey, I thought of the time in July 1993 when President Clinton and I were together welcoming Nelson Mandela to America prior to his election as president of South Africa. I asked the president to go to Africa so Africans could see him and know that America cares about Africa. I continued to urge such a visit with the president and his advisors because I knew how important the visit to Africa would be. It was a joy for me to see him make the trip. When I learned about it, I spoke on the *Voice of America* and said to the world, "Go, Bill, go," with the understanding that the historic journey of the president would be not a sideshow but a main event.

Later in 1998 I met with Hillary Clinton, who has great interest in Africa, and impressed on her how important the follow-up to their African journey would be, and we agreed to work together with African leaders, African Americans, and friends of Africa to help with education, business and investments, and democracy for the advancement of the continent. In past months President Clinton, Hillary, and others such as Secretary of State Madeleine Albright and former Secretary of State Lawrence Eagleburger have worked with me to secure support for our work in Africa from other nations of the world, such as Japan, China, Malaysia, Taiwan, and Saudi Arabia, for the building of thousands of schools, the opening of hundreds of skills training centers, and the sending of thousands of master teachers to help Africa move ahead.

Also in 1998, I met at the United Nations with Secretary General Kofi Annan. I have received his full support. In a letter written to me after the January visit, he stressed that he would work with me in any way he could with the summits and our other efforts in Africa.

The Fifth African–African American Summit, called the "Summit of Summits," will convene in Accra, Ghana, on May 17, 1999, attracting more than eight thousand delegates and other participants, whose numbers are expected to far exceed attendance at any previous summit. Large delegations from the United States, the Caribbean, South America, Europe, and Asia are prepared to attend. More than five hundred companies — small businesses, medium-sized companies, and large corporations — will be sending representatives; among them will be a large number of chief executive officers from America, Africa, and other parts of the world. These representatives from America will be meeting with five hundred African business leaders from companies of all sizes. A high-level delegation representing the United States will be sent from the White House. The Summit of Summits will establish the summit movement as one of the most important gatherings to be found anywhere in the world assisting the development of a continent.

With the help of Almighty God, seemingly impossible things can be done, and mountains can be moved.

Chapter 20

Seeing No Alps

M Y CLOSING ADDRESS to the 1997 Harare Summit spoke of my broader vision for Africa, African Americans, and the black diaspora, telling of the work we still must do.

WE SEE NO ALPS

This week here in Harare, in this country so brilliantly led by President Robert Mugabe, who led a mighty revolt against colonial rule in this country and who has done such a remarkable job in placing Zimbabwe on a scale equal to any other developing country in the world, past views of Africa are being obliterated. A new Africa is being born as an emerging and spreading cadre of new African leaders, nation by nation, are pushing aside the old and introducing the new.

Something new is happening in Africa today that has never happened before! Africa is rising. The children and the leaders are learning, human rights and justice for the people are growing, and interest from African Americans and from the black diaspora is mounting and expanding. We are here in Harare this week in the thousands, and what we see is only the beginning. These summits are bringing a new spirit of unity among black people around the world in a solidarity in support of Africa that has never, never existed before. We are building together a bridge of unity to help the children of Africa. And we want the world to know that as a result of these summits and other efforts by the OAU, the United Nations, OIC International, AFRICARE, and others in the United States, this is a new day for Africa. And in the future, the world will have a new Africa to deal with like it has never seen before.

What we have started in Côte d'Ivoire, in Gabon, in Senegal, and now in Harare will build and grow, and the results from these efforts for the development and future of Africa because of what we do will last for centuries to come.

In the future it will be proven that, in no uncertain terms, Africa can do what others have done in this modern world; Africa can and will do, too. What Malaysia and Singapore and Korea have done, going from dirt roads and thatched roofs and wooden shacks, we can do, too. So here in Harare, we say to the world, "Watch out because a new Africa is on the way." Something new is happening here educationally, economically, politically, and democratically that soon will astound the world. Africa is on the move. It will take time, but nothing can stop her now. The train is on the track. America, Europe, Asia, and the world can get on board, but the new African train is going anyway. And Africa will have to be contended with by companies and governments as has never been before.

And to African Americans I say, "Get on board." It is time to help the motherland. It is time to help home. It is time now that African Americans stop just talking about black pride and black power and shaking our fists. It is time for African Americans to begin to help ourselves and to put something back into the land from which we have come. We complain too much about what others are doing to us, and we do precious little to help our own. This is a call for African Americans to stand up and reach out to help Africa. As the Polish help Poland, as the Irish help Ireland, and as the Jews help Israel, it is time that African Americans helped Africa. Our destinies and future are tied together. So today, at the conclusion of this summit, I am encouraging African Americans to wake up and to strengthen our ties to Africa. Every people needs a base to build upon to have a future, and Africa is our base.

God has blessed us in America. He has taken us from slave ships to where we are today. African Americans are the most privileged and blessed black population in the world, and it is time that we give something back to help the homeland. It is not right that we, as African Americans, have so much and our black brothers and sisters have so little. It is not right that we have our schools and colleges and universities and education available for all of our children and two-thirds of the children of Africa have no schools at all — not even books, pencils, pens, or anything to learn with. It is not right that we have our running water and all the comforts of a modern world and most of the children and people of Africa have to go to the streams and the rivers for water to drink, to clean their bodies, to wash their clothes, and to help with the most basic hygiene needs. It is not right that many African Americans in the United States have two cars in their garages, and sometimes three...Buicks, Cadillacs, Mercedes, and BMWs and the vast majority of the people of Africa have to walk miles and miles wherever they go and most of the children have no shoes to wear. It is not right that we have incomes of $30,000, $50,000, and $100,000 a year and the average per capita income for every boy and girl, man and woman, in sub-Saharan Africa is less than $300 a year, and I could go on and on. It is not right that in America we have so much and in Africa our brothers and sisters and children have so little and we do nothing to help them. The time has come that every African American in the United States should begin to think of ways that we can help and put something back to help the advancement and the children of Africa. For this reason, when we return to the United States, we are going to organize follow-up summit committees in a hundred cities to help with teachers, nurses, schools, pens, pencils, paper, and also with investments so that we can take some of the money some of us have hidden in our mattresses and put it in self-help investment programs like the SHIPs we are organizing to help ourselves in America and to help mother Africa.

So I say to black Americans, let us get ready to put something back to help our own in the motherland, and let us begin at last to stand up and to speak out for Africa as the Polish speak out for Poland and as the Irish speak out for Ireland and as the Jews speak out for Israel. I say the day has come for black Americans to speak up and out for Africa. We must speak up to our congressmen, speak up to our senators, speak up to our president for a bigger piece of the pie for Africa. We do not get more than we do for Africa because as black Americans, we do not speak up and we do not stand up for Africa. And the time has come for us to stand up, stand up, stand up ... all across America, for Africa.

Also this day, at the close of this summit, I call on African leaders to do more to help their own people and to practice good governance and democracy and to stop lining their own pockets. The needs of the children of Africa must take precedence over anything else that the leaders might gain for themselves. The children of Africa must come first. They are the future. And there must be an end to corruption in Africa.

But again, we ask and implore our African leaders to do your part! Practice democracy, good governance, justice, and human rights and help educate the children. And help put an end to corruption, lining your own pockets, and stop thinking just of yourselves, and in thirty years, Africa will be a new superpower in the world.

And in Africa there must be an end to tribal hatred and conflicts, and the culture of peace must begin to be taught in every city, town, and village on the African continent, from the preprimary to the primary and secondary levels so that somehow there can emerge a culture of peace all across the continent for the progress of Africa. Peace must prevail! A peace tied to development with education and the teaching of unity, science, and technology. Peace in Africa must prevail if there is to be progress.

There must be improvement of health among the people who are dying too soon, especially from AIDS. We have to work on stopping the spread of AIDS because if the spread of AIDS is not stopped, it will wipe out entire populations in the future. Therefore, here in Harare we announce today a war on the spread of AIDS in Africa. We cannot solve the problem of AIDS, but together with the cooperation of these heads of nations and multinational organizations such as the World Health Organization, the OAU, the United Nations, the European community, and especially America, we can help stop the spread. And, we will need all the help in this fight against AIDS from the world that we can get, as well as from the people living inside the countries.

So today, we draw a line against the spread of AIDS in Africa. We call on everyone everywhere to help because what we do affects everyone: America, Europe, Asia...everyone. If the world does not stop AIDS here and elsewhere, like the wind, it will join up with the spread of AIDS everywhere. Perhaps, in stopping the spread of AIDS in Africa, we can set an example and help the world.

Also today, we call on all multinational companies doing business in Africa to practice the Sullivan Principles of human rights and to provide a living wage and to support economic, social, and political justice. As the Sullivan Principles worked in South Africa, they can work in every country in Africa and throughout the world to help workers and the people with jobs, better pay, advancement, justice, human rights, humanity, and peace!

Finally, there must be the laying of a twenty-first-century cornerstone for the future of Africa. Yesterday, we announced the laying of a cornerstone of education for all the children of Africa in the next decade. Without education, none of the things I have mentioned today can be achieved. Therefore, we announced a recently new and unprecedented agreement for massive education in Africa. The Organization of African Unity, the United Nations Educational, Scientific, and Cultural Organization, and the International Foundation for Education and Self-Help have agreed to work together, in the next five years, to help with education for millions, including school-leavers, school dropouts, and the unemployed with trained hands and minds to help with the building of their nations: plumbers, carpenters, bricklayers, electricians, farmers, entrepreneurs, computer operators, machinists, and medical technicians, training from the bottom up so that people at the bottom can help with the building of their countries. This is not for the shirts and ties but for the training of the hands from the bottom up.

Together, we have agreed that, in the next ten years, OAU, UNESCO, and IFESH will work for the building of ten thousand schools in the rural areas of African nations where schools do not exist. In these schools, millions of children will be trained from the preprimary years on up in literacy, mathematics, science, technology, democracy, and the culture of peace. We have agreed to send an army of twenty-five hundred master teachers to help upgrade the skills of five hundred thousand African teachers in ten years, benefiting millions of children a year.

Here in Harare, we have agreed to a revolution of education spreading through every country in Africa. And in this revolution we want the donor community of the world to help. And we want every individual and organization and institution in America to help. We ask Europe and Asia to help with money, schools, books, teachers, pencils, pens, paper, maps, chalk, typewriters, and computers; and with soap, bandages, antibiotics, and any way they can help. And every dollar given by donor nations or multinational organizations we want to see matched with help from ordinary people from the United States, Europe, and Asia and especially African Americans. We call on help from churches and organizations and institutions from the United States and from around the world. And we will be calling on multinational organizations and countries of the developed world to help Africans.

For four hundred years, America and Europe took everything they could of value out of Africa, and it is time that the United States and Europe put something of value back into Africa. Our first call is for education.

For this revolution of this "Education for Africa" campaign, we ask the support of the world — governments and businesses. We want America, Europe, and all of Asia — men, women, boys, and girls everywhere — to find a way to help. It is a revolution of education. If you can't read, you can't lead. But help the children of Africa to read and count and to develop their hands and minds, and they will do anything anyone else can do. And in time, they will do it better than anyone else. This is a revolution of education for the children of Africa we present today.

And we call on African Americans in the United States at last to help Africa. The time has come for African Americans to help Africa. We cannot ask others to do what we refuse to do for ourselves. We will work to see that we do all we can as African Americans in the United States and to push America and the world to do more to help Africa. This pledge I make to you. And we must find ways as a people with our friends to use collective investments to help Africa. Of this you will hear more from me in the days ahead.

The challenges ahead are ominous, and the obstacles will be great. But whatever the obstacles, let us not let anything, anything, turn us around or get in our way. When we leave from this place today, go and do something to help Africa. And when we meet opposition ahead, don't stop and don't turn around. Just trust in God and Allah, and together let us keep going and climbing over the opposition.

The story is told of Hannibal, the black Carthaginian general, who lived two hundred years before Christ and who, with forty thousand soldiers and a caravan of elephants, went forth to engage the armies of Rome. Hannibal's soldiers thought that he would lead them eastward, but Hannibal led them westward up through the straits of Gibraltar and northward through Spain until they came to the foot of the mighty Alps, mountains that had never been crossed by armies or so many animals before. Astride his trusty horse, Hannibal looked back and cried back to his troops, "Behold the Alps." And forty thousand soldiers returned the words, "Behold the Alps." A second time Hannibal called back, "Behold the Alps," and the soldiers replied, "Behold the Alps." Then a third time Hannibal shouted back to his troops, "Behold the Alps!" and a third time the legions, forty thousand strong, responded, "Behold the Alps." Then Hannibal, the story goes, removed his sword from its sheaf, pointed it forward, the steel shining in the sun, and cried back to his men, "Forward march! We see no Alps!" And Hannibal, with forty thousand men, a caravan of elephants, and hundreds of horses, climbed the mighty Alps with ice and snow and rain and sleet and stormed the gates of Rome.

As we leave the summit in Harare, there will be many obstacles we will face on the way. There will be the Alps of some who will not believe in what we are trying to do. There will be the Alps of skeptics and doubters, and many who want to see us fail. There will be the Alps of division and dissension among some who will want to see things done another way. There will be the Alps of those who want to cause disruption because they cannot have their way. There will be the Alps of white people and black people who will not want us to succeed, and the Alps of many who will create discord, saying they are our friends. Yes, as we leave Harare, there will be Alps here and Alps there. But I say to you, "Do not let the Alps stop you." The mountains are high, but they do not reach the stars. Delegates and participants, I say to you today, "Forward march! We see no Alps!" There will be obstacles. Forward march! There will be opposition. Forward march! However great the problems ahead, forward march! God is with us. Forward march; forward march! The summit at Harare, forward march! Until we meet again, let us together continue to build the bridge to help the children of Africa! Let nothing stop us! Forward march! We see no Alps!

At the close of the summit in Harare, there came immediate action. Follow-up committees were organized in one hundred American cities involving city councils, fraternities and sororities, public schools, colleges and universities, and hundreds of community organizations working with the young and the old. The stage was being set for an even greater participation in the next summit, scheduled for 1999.

Following Harare, the Schools for Africa Program got underway for the purpose of building hundreds of schools in rural areas of sub-Saharan Africa for children who never before had a school to attend. The program got a great boost from well-known philanthropist George Soros, who gave $1 million, to be matched by others, for the construction of one hundred schools in South Africa.

Afterwards I traveled to South Africa and met with the business leaders of companies that had been a part of the Sullivan Principles. Their companies pledged to triple the Soros gift. The added support of the South African government that matched the Soros and company contributions and commitments increased the initial gift four to one, making it possible for us to build four hundred schools in South Africa. During that visit on October 9, 1997, I flew with Dr. Wright, my loyal and amazing executive director of IFESH, in a helicopter over hills and mountains to remote sections of South Africa to dedicate the first schools that had been completed with the self-help and labor provided by the people in the communities. Hundreds attended the opening of the first schools. Mothers wept because, as one of the mothers said to me, "This will be the first time our children ever had a school to go to, and now maybe my children can amount to something." The

Helping Others Help Themselves

View of the opening ceremony of the OIC in Philadelphia, January 26, 1964. It was attended by 10,000 people.

Progress Plaza, 1962, the first shopping center built by blacks in the United States through a Sullivan project.

Site of the beginning of OIC, January 26, 1964, in Philadelphia. Now there are OICs all over the world.

The first million-dollar garden apartment building built in 1964 by Sullivan and his Zion nonprofit organization.

Progress Human Services Center, 1966, the largest of its kind completely run by blacks in Philadelphia.

An annual OIC industry dinner attracted 4,000 participants in Philadelphia in 1972.

Sullivan greets a trainee at an American Indian OIC in Minnesota. The OIC serves thousands of Native Americans daily throughout the United States.

Milwaukee, Wisc. One of thousands of new homes being built across the United States through Sullivan's programs.

Several Opportunities Towers constructed through Sullivan's efforts for handicapped and aged citizens of Philadelphia accommodate hundreds of residents.

Several thousand homes were renovated or built by OIC in Philadelphia and throughout the United States through OIC housing programs.

Sullivan speaking at a ball park about OIC.

Training class at OIC in Phoenix, Arizona, where more than 25,000 people have been trained.

OIC home for homeless in Philadelphia. Built by trainees and homeless people.

One of the OIC training centers in Carlisle, Pennsylvania, is among 100 such centers in the United States.

OIC training class in Menlo Park, California, where more than 50,000 people have been trained.

Graduation exercises of OIC in Philadelphia in 1982.

Sullivan meeting with the corporate advisory council for OIC, consisting of leading industrialists in America.

Support from High Places

Sullivan meeting with Pope John Paul II at St. Peters in 1984 to discuss the Sullivan Principles in an effort to urge greater efforts to end apartheid.

Senator Robert Kennedy meeting with Sullivan in 1968 at an OIC in Philadelphia and committing his support.

Richard Nixon meets with Sullivan at Progress Plaza in Philadelphia, while running for the presidency, and pledges his support for Sullivan's minority business efforts.

President Lyndon Johnson meets with Sullivan in 1964 at the old jailhouse, home of the first OIC in Philadelphia, stating that this is "one of the best days" of his presidency and announcing support for Sullivan's training programs in the United States.

Presidential candidate and great friend of Sullivan, Hubert Humphrey, addresses the OIC annual convocation in 1970.

Sullivan and President Gerald Ford discuss a plan to train 100,000 workers for better jobs in the United States.

Rev. and Mrs. Sullivan at a White House dinner with President Gerald Ford and the emperor of Japan.

Leon Sullivan meets with Henry Kissinger at the State Department in 1976 to discuss the Sullivan Principles in South Africa.

Sullivan meeting with President Jimmy Carter to discuss jobs for inner-city people in America and plans for Africa.

Sullivan and President Ronald Reagan agree on a program to support expansion of OICs of America and call on his cabinet to work with Sullivan for the creation of jobs.

Sullivan meeting with Secretary of State George Schultz to discuss the Sullivan Principles and greater support from the U.S. government to help end apartheid.

Sullivan and General Colin Powell meet in 1990 to discuss the need for jobs in the United States and Sullivan's self-help efforts in Africa.

Sullivan meeting at the Russian embassy with Mikhail Gorbachev, President of Russia, and discussing Russia's support for the Sullivan Principles in South Africa.

Rev. Sullivan with Grace Sullivan and President and Mrs. George Bush as Sullivan receives the Presidential Medal of Freedom in 1992. It is the highest civilian honor given to an American citizen for beneficial service to America.

Leon and Grace Sullivan meet with President Bill Clinton at a dinner in Washington, D.C. that recognized Sullivan's efforts in Africa to help the poor.

Sullivan with President George Bush in 1991 at the Oval Office as they discuss the Sullivan Principles and sanctions against South Africa to end apartheid.

Sullivan meeting with Secretary of State Madeleine Albright in 1997 to discuss U.S. support for African and the African–African American Summits.

May 1998, Rev. Sullivan and Dr. C. T. Wright meet with Hillary Clinton who gave her support for Sullivan's programs in Africa.

Sullivan with President Nelson Mandela in South Africa at the Fourth African–African American Summit in July 1997.

Working to End Apartheid

Leeds Castle in England where corporate executives from around the world gathered for private and unpublicized meetings at the call of Rev. Sullivan to plan and work for the end of apartheid in South Africa. There were three such meetings held at the castle in 1985, 1986, and 1987. (See castle surrounded by a moat.)

General Motors Board in 1974. Leon Sullivan is in the 3rd row, 2nd from the right.

Sullivan at the announcement of his membership on the Board of General Motors in 1971. He was the first black director of a major corporation, from which he launched his Sullivan Principles in 1977.

Sullivan delivering the commencement address at Dropsie University in 1980. The address emphasized the importance of the Sullivan Principles to end apartheid.

Rebuilding Africa

Leon and Grace Sullivan in Ghana in 1970 visiting the marketplace.

Sullivan's Ethiopian visit in 1977 with some of the country's leaders.

The OIC in KwaZulu, South Africa.

Visiting the OIC in Lagos, Nigeria.

Rev. Sullivan with farm trainees at the OIC in Togo.

OIC Cote d'Ivoire farm center.

Cote d'Ivoire OIC Business Development Center.

Receiving flowers from a Liberian OIC trainee who was formerly a combatant.

Opening a farm in Gambia.

Participating in the opening of the OIC in Liberia.

One of the first schools of a hundred being constructed in rural areas of South Africa by Sullivan's IFESH program.

One of a thousand new schools being built in sub-Saharan Africa.

A class of the Best & Brightest African Bankers Training Program, numbering 250, trained in the United States for leadership with banks in Africa.

Witnessing the building of an OIC in Ghana.

Left to right: Dr. C. T. Wright, Executive Director of IFESH; Rev. Leon Sullivan, President of IFESH; C. L. Mannings, President of OIC International; H. Art Taylor, President, OIC of America.

Sullivan with African American children in 1996 at the Liberty Bell at the signing of an agreement with UNESCO to support education in Africa.

August 1998. The latest group of master teachers sent to Africa, now totaling over 500 master teachers since 1991. Master teachers have already trained 25,000 African teachers who are helping millions of African children.

March 1998, Sullivan signing a $15 million grant from USAID to IFESH for training and other education projects in African countries. Signing with Sullivan (left to right) are Senator Arlen Specter (R-PA), USAID administrator J. Brian Atwood, and Congresswoman Nancy Pelosi (D-CA).

June 1998, Sullivan receiving a contribution from the Links Foundation to build schools in Africa, at the first biannual Summit fundraising dinner. Held in Washington, D.C. the dinner announced Summit results and was attended by 1,000 people from across America and Africa.

Awards and Honors

Sullivan receiving an award from A. Philip Randolph for service to blacks and other disadvantaged persons. At age 22, Sullivan was appointed president of the March on Washington Movement by A. Philip Randolph, who was a labor leader, father of civil rights in America, and mentor to Rev. Sullivan.

Sullivan is made Paramount Chief in Sierra Leone in 1974.

Sullivan receiving a doctorate at St. Peters College.

Sullivan receiving a doctorate at Virginia Commonwealth University.

Sullivan receiving an honorary doctorate at DePaul University in 1987.

Sullivan receiving a Doctor of Divinity degree at Northeastern University in 1983.

Embraced by a Faithful Family and Congregation

Sullivan speaking to the Zion Baptist Church congregation totaling 6,000 members in 1985.

Zion Baptist Church. Rebuilt by Rev. Sullivan and his congregation in 1971 after a fire, Zion is one of the largest multimillion-dollar churches constructed by blacks in Philadelphia history.

Leon and Grace Sullivan in Ghana in 1970 during one of their first visits to Africa. A castle built for slaves during the slave trade is in the background. Ghana would later be the site for the Fifth African–African American Summit.

Sullivan at Zion Baptist Church in 1989.

Leon and Grace Sullivan at the OIC convocation in San Antonio, Texas, in 1997.

The Sullivan family, 1998. Left to right: Leon, Hope, Grace, Julie, Howard.

building of a thousand schools throughout sub-Saharan Africa was well underway.

Also following the Harare Summit, we moved forward with an unprecedented and exciting Education for Africa movement, beyond anything that had existed before. The agreement reached by OAU, UNESCO, and me to help in a massive way with education for Africa began to become a reality. The joint program was a necessity for help-ing to deal with a growing problem of illiteracy among the young and the old and to help with vocational education for the hundreds of thousands of unemployed youth in sub-Saharan Africa who were roaming the streets without education, skills, or jobs.

We have plans to call a donors conference in 1999 to be attended by people from the United States, various European nations, Japan, Taiwan, Saudi Arabia, Malaysia, and other countries who, we hope, will make commitments of millions of dollars to support the tripar-tite agreement reached at the Harare Summit by OAU, UNESCO, and me to develop, in the next ten years, 250 OIC skills training centers, to build ten thousand new schools in rural areas, and to help send twenty-five hundred new master teachers to upgrade the instructional skills of teachers in sub-Saharan African nations. The objective, within the next decade, is to help with the education of children, as well as mothers, numbering in the millions throughout sub-Saharan Africa. This tripartite agreement marked the beginning of a revolution of education in Africa that will in time reach across the continent.

We have also focused on increasing debt relief for African na-tions. Following the Harare Summit, I continued my contacts with the leaders of developed nations — the United States, France, Ger-many, the United Kingdom, and Japan, along with the World Bank, the International Monetary Fund, and the Paris Club in France — to increase debt relief for sub-Saharan African nations from the $60 billion already attained to $100 billion by the year 2002.

Harare Summit follow-up committees have been formed in every state in the United States and are in varying stages of organization. They are being put together mainly by members of state legislatures who attended the summit and who are now seeking the support of state governments throughout America to help with the economic and commercial development of sub-Saharan African countries. It is our plan for the 1999 summit to have participation from all state legislatures and from several governors. State representatives will focus on questions and issues related to commerce and trade for their states.

On July 10, 1998, we convened a meeting of thirty mayors of large and small cities in the United States, led by forward-looking Mayor Wellington Webb of Denver. These participants organized mayoral follow-up committees in their cities to have a hundred mayors at the upcoming Summit in Ghana, to advance commerce and business opportunities in Africa, and to help create new jobs for their American cities. In addition, summit follow-up committees were organized at several black colleges and universities and at Big Ten and other universities in the United States, including Ohio State, Michigan State, Indiana University, Penn State, University of Chicago, Howard University, Tulane, South Florida University, Florida A&M, Tuskegee University, Arizona State University, and other historically black colleges and universities. Among their commitments is to help develop exchange programs with their schools of professors, curriculum development specialists, and students. And they will work with chancellors of African schools for the development and improvement of colleges and universities on the African continent.

We met with Madeleine Albright, the U.S. secretary of state and a great friend to our work, who in addition to helping me with contacts for support from other countries asked us to help with the clearing of land mines in Africa that were killing or crippling thousands, a problem that was so movingly addressed by Princess Diana of England prior to her untimely accident and death. Plans were immediately put into place to help the African countries beset with this terrible, life-threatening problem.

On October 8, 1997, U.S. secretary of transportation Rodney Slater convened a roundtable meeting of government and business leaders and others in Washington, D.C., to organize greater support for future initiatives of the African–African American Summit and our work in Africa. President Bill Clinton sent a letter encouraging cooperation with Secretary Slater's efforts for summit actions, and he pledged his full support. More than five hundred top-level government officials and business and community organization leaders attended the conference, creating a whole new level of assistance for Africa within the United States government and also among others.

On October 31, 1997, a number of top business executives led by

Frank Fountain, highly regarded vice president of Chrysler, met with me in Arizona to help plan for the next summit in 1999, the objective being to get cooperation and support from every major industry in the United States. We want more and more U.S. corporations to launch new investments and joint ventures of American companies with African businesses with the understanding that all companies from the United States operating in Africa will, in the future, follow Global Sullivan Principles to ensure support for education, affirmative action, human rights, and economic and political justice in the countries where they do business and to help with the culture of peace.

American sororities such as the AKAs, one of the largest women's sororities in America, rallied thousands of members to help the SOS campaign for children and schools with needed supplies, including literally millions of pencils and pens. LINKS, one of the most recognized service organizations of African American women in America, sent a team of one hundred to South Africa in December 1997 to start building schools and to dedicate the first school built by LINKS in South Africa. LINKS has followed up with contributions and plans to build many more schools in South Africa by the year 2000. Also, colleges, communities, businesses, churches, and individuals have joined in the campaign to build hundreds of schools in sub-Saharan Africa. I can see my plan for building a thousand schools in sub-Saharan Africa will be realized in the next decade.

Also as a part of the summit follow-up effort, hundreds of church organizations and scores of conventions have pledged their cooperation to help Africa. This includes thousands of African American organizations and churches, among them the Lott Cary Missionary Convention. One of the largest black missionary organizations helping Africa, Lott Cary started an extensive nationwide campaign to collect shoes, tons of clothing, books, and other needed items for African children for a special effort directed towards the rehabilitation of Liberia. The Lott Cary Missionary Convention has named it the "Liberia 100 Campaign," meaning one hundred pairs of shoes for the children and one hundred sets of apparel for children, men, and women to be collected by each of their thousands of churches and shipped to Liberia. The churches of the Lott Cary Missionary Convention alone collected tons of clothing and school supplies to help thousands. Also, the Church of Jesus Christ of Latter-day Saints has collected warehouses full of items for the SOS appeal for Africa, with financial help, and various other religious bodies have continued with their great support of our work, especially in Liberia, contributing millions of books, school items, clothes, and medical equipment and supplies.

Also, large-scale programs were being planned to help with the containment of HIV/AIDS, which was spreading rapidly through sub-Saharan Africa.

As a result of these and many other efforts, including news reports all across America on the success of the summit, communities large and small in the United States have begun to show an unprecedented interest in Africa. Our aim to build bridges of cooperation from America to Africa has taken hold, and I can see both by sight and by faith that in twenty-first-century America, African Americans and the world will see Africa in a new light. All Africa has needed is encouragement, education, and the tools to move ahead. The rest they can do themselves, especially if African leaders will end corruption, make children a priority, and stand up for democracy.

Also as a result of Harare, African nations began to introduce legislation making possible dual citizenship for African Americans and friends of Africa who want to maintain their citizenship in the United States while having a more definite, lasting, and supporting role in the developing frontier on the African continent. African Americans will increasingly discover their roots and will join in the effort for building a new Africa.

Chapter 21

Rebuilding Liberia

T HE MOST IMMEDIATE, challenging, and difficult of all our Harare
Summit commitments was the decision to assist with nation
building by helping with the reconstruction of a troubled Liberia, a
country in which I had been very active prior to Harare. In 1990,
after decades of division and strife in Liberia, rival factions entered
into warfare after a deadly coup that wracked Liberia and left a million
of its own citizens homeless in the capital city of Monrovia, along with
a million others, mostly children, who were refugees from neighboring
nations. In seven years two hundred thousand people were left dead in
the streets, and hundreds of thousands more had been wounded, their
lives decimated in a country that had no law. Were it not for the efforts of Nigeria, which took the leadership in marshaling a peace force
to bring order to the country, atrocities would have been even greater.

I decided in 1996, before the Harare Summit, to go to Liberia myself to see what the conditions were on the ground and to determine
if it was even possible for us to help. I had something in Liberia to
build on, which was something few others could claim. I had a successful, thriving and dynamic Opportunities Industrialization Center
(OIC) in Monrovia and several other centers in other parts of the
country. When the strife broke out, virtually all aid groups from other
nations fled. The OIC stayed. This was the case mainly because the
leaders, including the workers, teachers, and administrators of the
OIC in Liberia, were all Liberians. Thus, while others fled to their
home nations, the Liberians from the OICs were already home and
had no place else to go short of becoming refugees. When the fighting finished in the streets and in rural parts of the country, the OIC
leaders and followers, whose trainees numbered more than twenty
thousand, immediately returned to restore the OICs that had been
all but destroyed. They began providing assistance to the poor, needy,
and dying.

I am extremely proud of the work of the OICs in Liberia, for their resilience has been remarkable, thanks in large part to capable leaders. When I entered Liberia, that leadership was behind me. These people believed in God and in self-help, and they had faith that Liberia could and would be rebuilt. It was also tremendously helpful that the political leaders in Liberia, including the newly elected president of the country, Charles Taylor, knew of the work of OIC and IFESH (International Foundation for Education and Self-Help) and were all prepared to work with us.

At the summit, we had promised to help Liberia, though many considered it a hopeless situation. Helping to transform a country almost totally destroyed by a protracted series of crises was a mighty challenge for the government and people of Liberia, the international community, including the United States, and the summit movement. The plan for Liberia revolved around development efforts tied to peace, for the two are inseparably related. Development assistance was necessary if the country was to succeed in developing lasting peace. But without peace, there can be no successful development.

The ultimate goal was to create sustainable growth and thus to improve the standard of living for the people. Among the problems to be addressed by the Liberian government and the international community were food security, water management, health conditions, demobilized soldiers, displaced individuals and refugees, education, microenterprise training and employment, agricultural needs, transportation facilities, and the rebuilding of industries, just to mention a few. IFESH and OIC found themselves at the center of the pursuit of these goals.

I traveled throughout Europe seeking support for Liberia. We found sympathetic ears, especially in the Netherlands, where the minister of development cooperation, Dr. Jan Pronk, listened to my request to help Liberia and in a meeting in December 1996 committed $2 million to help with education and other needs. This was contingent upon the peace holding in Liberia and on elections that would give the country a democratically elected government. I immediately returned to Liberia and spoke to the nation, appealing to the people by radio to keep the peace and to work for a democratically elected government and head of state. I met with the former faction leaders, and they committed their cooperation, along with the military leaders of ECOWAS, the security force from various African countries led by

Nigeria that was doing a truly remarkable job for security and order in the country. Minister Pronk's commitment of support was also based on the condition that I secure a significant grant from the United States government and from other donors for our efforts in Liberia. Within two months, I had secured $2 million in a matching grant from the United States to support the OICs and IFESH. I also secured a commitment of $5 million from the European Union in Brussels, Belgium.

The elections were held in Liberia in August 1997, during the time of the summit. As soon as I returned to America, I sent IFESH representatives from the United States to Liberia. Right away we began to lay plans for large-scale programs to help the people, especially the children, with training, jobs, and everyday practical needs such as clothing, shoes, medicine, food, reconstruction of houses, and the building of schools. We also sent master teachers to help upgrade the training of those Liberian teachers who had not fled the country so the children could be educated as quickly as possible. Schools had been closed for eight years during the turmoil, and there was no formal teaching at all during that time.

Our Liberian plan of development-tied-to-peace is now well under way. As of this writing, hundreds of projects and programs are being organized throughout the country. Our efforts have taken hold as a result of remarkable cooperation among the people, the new government, the OICs, and the hundreds of nongovernmental organizations (NGOs) in the country who rallied to the cause, along with support from Europe, the United States, and other parts of the world. There has also been a lot of prayer and hard work toward the goal of helping the "New Liberia" become a reality.

OICs are being established in every region of Liberia. Hundreds of schools and clinics are being built. Farms are being developed, and bridges and roads are being built by large numbers of volunteers from Liberia, the rest of Africa, the United States, and other nations who have joined the campaign. I am encouraged by what I have seen and heard, for I have pulled out all the proverbial stops on behalf of Liberia. At the time of the writing of this book, it is my number one challenge. I have appealed to the United States and the developed world, along with the stronger countries in Africa, to join the rehabilitation effort. And there has been tremendous cooperation from the Organization of African Unity, without whose support the things we are doing to help Liberia could not be successful. The OAU is the greatest hope for peace in a united Africa.

I have put so much energy into Liberia because success there will determine what we are able to do later in Rwanda and other troubled nations on the continent. If the model of development-tied-to-peace works in Liberia, it can work anywhere. Similar assistance is sorely needed in Somalia, Angola, Rwanda, Mozambique, and the Congo. So a lot is at stake in Liberia, and many have been working overtime to make sure our efforts do not fail. All this is not to say, however, that my efforts have been limited to Liberia. We have been promised support from the Belgian government for designing training and education plans for the people, especially the children, of Rwanda, which in 1994 experienced a massive genocide that left more than a half-million Rwandans dead. In Rwanda in 1995, traveling by helicopter, Dr. Wright, who has been with me in the most difficult of situations, and I visited mass grave sites. In one, thirty thousand people had been buried together. Thousands of human skulls — heads that had been cut off in terrible tribal conflict — lined the sides of the pit. We saw thousands of children sitting around the mass grave stunned and grieving, looking down at the graves of their mothers, fathers, brothers, sisters, cousins, and friends. I had seen many things in my life but never anything so depressingly tragic as what I saw that day. The sight will remain with me the rest of my life, and it will motivate me as I put every ounce of energy I can to working toward building an Africa where peace prevails.

If peace is to win out over war, the nations of the world must do more than send guns and tanks to such places as Liberia, Rwanda, Somalia, and the Congo. To the extent that Europe and America have done that, they participated in Africa's strife and tragedies. In fact, over the last four centuries, Europe and America have taken tens of millions of people and an untold amount of resources out of Africa, much of it during one hundred years of colonial rule. All this and more helped bring African nations to where they are today. The world has taken everything it could out of Africa. Now the time has come for the world to put something back. The leaders of African nations must also do their part by stopping the lining of their own pockets and by working for reconciliation and the ending of tribal hatreds and border conflicts. Compromise is a better choice than violence. Happily, I can see more and more new African leaders emerging all across the continent who care deeply about unity, democracy, humanity, peace, and, most importantly, about carrying out the will of God, who clearly desires peace. I believe with the help of God, even with all the problems and challenges that lie ahead, their efforts will succeed. I for one will continue to call on America and the world to do their part to help move Africa ahead to its rightful place in the sun.

Chapter 22

Rediscovering the Mother Continent

During the twenty-first century, rapid transportation and communication will start a revolution in the movement of people throughout the world. A journey from New York to Africa will be as commonplace as a trip from New York City to Los Angeles. Africa will be as near as a noonday hop, one an ever-growing number of people will take advantage of.

I expect that thousands upon thousands of African Americans will make the trip, largely as a result of the African–African American summits, which have brought discussions about Africa in the United States to the fore. When they see Africa for the first time, they will find that it is different from the continent they imagined. Hundreds of tourist businesses with trips from the United States to Africa have already begun to form. The gaming parks of Kenya, Tanzania, and Uganda will be known and visited by African Americans as never before, just as in past years they have been frequented by affluent European and American white tourists. Tourists from colonial nations and America have been traveling to Africa all along — hunting, bird watching, going on safaris, and climbing mountains such as Kilimanjaro. Following the summits and the new awareness they have brought, African Americans will do the same, and they will discover for themselves the natural wonders and beauties of their mother continent, a continent rich in beauty, resources, and opportunity. Most importantly, they will realize that what they see in some sense belongs to them.

The experience will be new for black Americans, most of whom up to now have known Africa only as a dark continent of danger, jungles, and former slaves. In fact, the Tarzan movies are about as much as many blacks — and whites, too, for that matter — have known about Africa. In fact, most blacks in America had until recently shut Africa out of their thinking. They were simply not interested in hearing or learning about the land from which their ancestors had come. The biennial summits have helped revolutionize these attitudes and to erase the ignorance. Africa is increasingly being discussed in the black community in a more positive light.

By the time of the Harare Summit in 1997, a "going home mania" was evident in many African American churches, organizations, and communities. A month before the summit, the summit office was besieged with phone calls from blacks who wanted to make the trip, but the planes were full and all the hotel space was taken. They will all go eventually. They want to see Africa for themselves, if only for a few days. They want to return home, thus affirming President Felix Houphouet-Boigny's statement at the First African–African American Summit in 1991, "They will return to the tree one day, and when they do, we will be here waiting to receive them."

The Harare Summit had a mighty impact on the United States. Throughout America, parents made requests — even demands — for community leaders to put studies of black heritage in the schools of America, from preprimary through the high-school years. Blacks in large numbers in the United States began to learn about Cush, Sheba, and Timbuktu; Shaka and the mighty Ashant; and the great kingdoms and civilizations of ancient equatorial Africa. They learned that Africa was the birthplace of civilization. They learned of how African influences helped shape what became known as the developed world. They learned that centuries before slavery, what we now call the Congo, with all its present troubles, was a center of art, industry, and advanced government long before there was a Portugal, a France, or an England.

As a result of the summits and other efforts, black boys and girls growing up in the United States who previously disparaged their African heritage will for the first time begin to develop pride in who they are. Up to now, black Americans have silently looked down upon their African brethren, their own heritage. Our goal with the African–African American summit movement was not just to help Africa but to help black youth in America and around the world learn to respect and appreciate themselves. I long for the day — and it will come — when every black person in the United States will be proud to say, "I am an African American." This new awareness will help advance genuine black pride in the United States, as black Americans and Africans give one another the love and respect they desire and deserve.

As a result of the influence of the summits, blacks in the United States will begin to call for and demand greater and greater support for Africa from the United States government, as Jews in America call for support of Israel. By the mid-twenty-first century, I predict thousands of blacks in America will request dual citizenships to make Africa their second home. Many will break their ties completely with America and become full African citizens. These will perhaps mostly be artisans, professionals, and younger people, who instead of "looking west" will begin to look southward to Africa. The summits in the future will continue to help Africa, but they will also help black Americans, and they will help supply jobs for American businesses searching for new markets and employee pools. In fact, the development of Africa will create tens of thousands of new jobs in America and add to the economic strength of the United States, just as the Marshall Plan for the rebuilding of Europe meant an economic boom for the United States.

Calculations made for the Sullivan Plan for the Development of Sub-Saharan Africa (which is found in Appendix C) reveal that the rehabilitation and development of Africa — its cities, its farms, its infrastructures, and its industrial needs — would create two hundred thousand new jobs in the United States each year for generations to come. This is not to mention the thousands of jobs that will be created in Europe or the millions of new jobs in Africa. As the strengthening of Africa contributes to the strengthening of America's economy, racial tensions in the United States will wane, even though we have a long way to go on that score.

The summits and the new developing Africa will bring about the reversal of the African "brain drain" to America. In 1945, following World War II, thousands of Africans came to the United States to attend schools of higher education, as good schools in Africa were few. Most did not return. By 1990, there were more African college graduates in the United States than there were in Africa, but at the same time, easily one-half of all the taxi drivers in New York City and Washington, D.C., were from Africa or the Caribbean. Many of them were highly trained in education, engineering, business, or the arts. However, because of continuing race segregation and restrictive employment practices in the United States, they could not use their training, so they worked wherever they could. Many sent money back home to help their families, but with Africa as it was, they saw little

incentive to return. With the coming of the new Africa and a return to democratic governments, following the demise of Communism,
Africans in America will increasingly look towards home.

My purpose is not to start a "Back to Africa" movement among
African Americans. We have found a place for work and home in the
United States. Despite America's prejudices, African Americans have
become full citizens of the United States. Most will stay, and they
should. This is our home, and America would not be what it is without
us. Nevertheless, Africa is our historical home. And as we discover
our mother continent, self-esteem will increase and crime rates will
fall. More black youth will be in schools of higher learning, and fewer
will occupy prison cells.

Africa's place in our history assures Africa's place in our future.
When I arrived in Harare, Zimbabwe, in 1997 with a thousand Americans, I opened the Fourth African–African American Summit with a
speech that articulates my hopes for Africa and my vision for the future. I include it here because it captures my feelings about how we
should embrace Africa as our mother continent.

CLIMBING THE TALLEST TREE

To all who are here in Harare, from all levels and stations of life, from
governments, businesses, education, and every other sector of human development, we want to thank you for your presence. This Harare Summit
will go down in history as one of the truly important milestones in the
progress of sub-Saharan Africa and the entire African continent.

Six years ago, when the First African–African American Summit was
launched, we were not given half a chance to succeed. Something like
this had been thought about but never tried before. But, with the help
of God and Allah, although many said it could not be done, we are here.
We are here from around the world by the thousands: Africans, African
Americans, and friends of Africa. We are here!

By the providence of God and Allah, we have been able to reverse
the fates of history. Who would have believed it would ever happen? But
God moves in mysterious ways, and this is one of the ways he has moved
in the affairs of people. Three hundred years ago they took us away in
boats, but we have come back in airplanes. We have come back from
the United States and from the Caribbean and from the United Kingdom
and from all around the world of the black diaspora, and we are here

in Harare today united and indivisible as one, and we want the world to know that we will never be separated again.

And we have returned as sons and daughters of Africa with our friends with something to give back to the motherland. We left in chains, but we have returned as free people. We have returned with strength and with skills and with money and with resources and with political power. We have returned to help Africa, and we want the world to know that it will never do to Africa or black people what it has done before. We are just not going to take it anymore.

What is happening here today is wonderful to observe. For the first time in history on this scale, we see black people coming together with our friends to work for the advancement of sub-Saharan Africa in education, in business, in health, in agriculture, and in democracy and peace. And because of what we do here and because of what we have been able to do during the past three summits and because of what we will be able to accomplish from this summit in Harare in the future, the day will come when the nations of sub-Saharan Africa will stand shoulder to shoulder with every other developing part of the globe.

Together, we are laying the groundwork for an African renaissance that will propel Africa in future years to her rightful place in the sun. The Bible has said that the day will come when Ethiopia will stretch forth her hands unto God, and today, here in Harare, we are seeing Africa stretch forth her hands unto God. And new freedoms and equality and economic progress will happen in the next century in sub-Saharan Africa on a scale never envisioned before, for what others have done in development and advancement Africa can do, too. What Malaysia and Indonesia and Singapore have done in the past thirty years Africa can do, too. All Africa needs is the education and the technology and the investments and the support of the rest of the world, and in the next three decades Africa will be able to match any other developing country anywhere in the world. All Africa needs is the education and the technology and the chance and the support to prove what it can do.

After the first three summits, already we have seen things happen that have astounded observers. All of the goals set by the former summits are being realized. It is hard to believe that so much could be done in such a short period of time.

Debt relief has been called "an albatross around the necks of African countries," but as a result of these summits and our working with the Paris Club in Paris, France, and the leaders of developed nations such as Germany, France, and the United States, agreements have been made making it possible for $60 billion of debt to be lifted from poorer African nations. And now, we are continuing to work with the Paris Club and the leaders of the G-7 nations and the World Bank and the International Monetary Fund to see that in the next few years debt relief for sub-Saharan Africa will amount to no less than $100 billion.

When we began these efforts for debt relief, many said this could not be done. But from the first African Debt Relief Session we secured at the United Nations in 1991, following the first summit in Côte d'Ivoire, this massive relief of debt for African nations has been realized. And we shall continue on, even beyond the $100 billion until 90 percent of the debt, both bilateral and multilateral, has been forgiven with a plan to convert portions of the remaining debt into schools, into training centers, into education, then clinics, and hospitals and wells and farms as a part of the African renaissance that I am speaking about today.

As a result of the last summits, great strides have already been made in business and investments in sub-Saharan Africa where it did not exist before. In the last six years as a result of these summits, $500 million has been invested by American companies in sub-Saharan Africa, and within the next few years, we want to see to it that these new investments in African businesses will exceed $2 billion. It can and will be done.

And in health—because we know 75 percent of the illnesses in Africa result from the lack of clean and fresh water, already as a result of these summits fifty thousand wells are being dug in cooperation with the World Bank, and in the next several years, we want to see that number increase to a hundred thousand, and then to hundreds of thousands more. We want the day to come when no child in Africa will have to walk more than a mile for clean and fresh water. And from this summit, we intend to work together with the leaders of the nations of Africa and all the health organizations of the world to see to it that the spread of AIDS in Africa is brought to a halt.

And with education — at the past summits we set goals to improve literacy and skills for African children. As a result, five hundred master teachers from the United States have already been sent to African countries, including Ethiopia, Benin, Côte d'Ivoire, Gabon, and others, upgrading the skills of fifty thousand teachers who are teaching more than two million children a day. And we have just begun. In future years we will send hundreds and thousands of teachers more. The cooperation from the African nations and leaders in support of this Teachers Program has been phenomenal. Nations who are experiencing the success of these teacher efforts are reaching out to make certain that the program continues and expands. Even when there are times when funds are cut off from the United States, they are saying to us, "Let this program go on because it is helping our children in a way we have not seen before, and we are ready to do whatever is necessary as nations to see that it continues."

And, we have seen a need for schools, especially in the rural areas where half of the children in Africa have no schools at all. Therefore, we have begun a Schools for Africa program that is building at this very moment a thousand schools in sub-Saharan Africa—small two-room schools in places like Sierra Leone, South Africa, and here in Zimbabwe, where the first of these schools in this country was unveiled just yesterday during this summit. And from the thousand schools that we will build in the next several years in countries throughout sub-Saharan Africa in the countries of all the leaders who are represented here today, we will build thousands more and thousands more, until the day comes when every child in Africa will have a school to go to, a desk to sit at, a book to read from, a pen or pencil to write with, and a pad of paper to write on. And during this massive effort to improve education in sub-Saharan Africa in the next decade, not only will we teach children to read and to write and to count; we will also teach them about science and technologies so that they too will know something about Mars because the day will come when the little black children that we teach today in Africa will be walking on the surface of Mars. And out of these schools a new leadership for sub-Saharan Africa will emerge with new skills and leadership capabilities that will make good governance and the practice of democracy in Africa an envy to the rest of the world. For education is the key to progress for sub-Saharan Africa and any nation, for if you can't read, you can't lead. And out of these summits we intend to teach the children to read so they can lead, and also how to love because an educated mind without an educated heart will still not give Africa what it needs to work with to move ahead. Our children must learn in Africa and in America and throughout the world not only how to read but also how to love. That is what peace is all about. Money is not the answer to the problems of Africa or anywhere else in the world, but humanity and love are the answer.

On and on I could go about the African renaissance that is ahead because of these summits and the cooperation and the work of these great leaders of African nations who are here with us today and the help of the other leading and powerful nations of this world, whom we will be calling upon to help far more than they have for the advancement of this great continent. For let it be known that the economic advancement of Africa also helps with the economic advancement of the world. Help develop Africa with business and jobs and development, and the jobs and the development in Africa will help with jobs and development in America and the rest of the world.

It is high time at last for the world to wake up and to do more for Africa. The fact is that most of the problems in Africa are a result of what the world has done. In the past, this world has taken everything out of Africa it could — its people, its resources, its heritage, and its pride — and it is time that the world put something back into Africa for its development with businesses and investments and loans and grants and its support, especially for the children, who have nothing to do with the problems they see every day all around them.

And here, make no mistake about it, I am speaking to the rich nations of the world because they have a responsibility to do more. Historically, what has been taken out of Africa for four hundred years has helped to make these great and powerful nations rich: its slaves, its gold, its diamonds, and everything else with value that could be taken away. So today in Harare I am calling on Europe to do more for Africa. I am calling on the United Kingdom and France and Germany and Portugal and Belgium and Holland and every other leading nation to do more for Africa. I make no excuses for it. I am like Robin Hood. I take from the rich and give to the poor. And I am especially calling on the United States to do more for Africa. because America would not be what it is today without the African Americans. And when I go back home I will personally be calling on the president of the United States, Bill Clinton, to do more and the Congress of the United States to do more and the people of America to do more and especially the African Americans to do more, who do more talking about helping Africa than they are helping to do themselves. As a matter of fact, too often African Americans criticize what others are doing to them and to Africa without doing their part to help Africa and themselves.

I am pleased with what the summits have accomplished thus far. And we want to thank everyone from the nations of Africa and the great leaders of Africa and especially those leaders who are with us today. And we want to thank the friends of Africa and our friends in business and education from the United States and from around the world, and especially once again we want to thank this official delegation that is representing our government and the president of the United States. We want to thank everyone that has had anything to do in making these great summits so successful. And I want to thank all of those in Africa, America, and every place who have helped me with this work I hold so dear to help the children and our people.

The question has been asked why I do what I do. I am not a politician, I am not running for anything, and there is certainly no money in it for me for what I do. Well, I do what I do, *first*, because I am an American but, *most of all*, because I am an African American, and I am dedicating my time and my life in the United States and Africa to help our people. And finally, I do what I do because God wants me to do it. For it is God's work, and God helps me do what I do. I am not standing here alone. God is standing here with me.

I once heard it said, "Climb the tallest tree in the forest, and if you fall, at least you will land on the tops of shorter trees." Here in Harare, we are climbing the tallest tree in the forest of the world, on a continent that has been neglected and ravaged and looked down upon for centuries by the rest of the world. We are trying to climb this tall tree with these summits, with education, and with business and with jobs and with health and with food and with schools and with teachers and with clean water and with ways to halt the spread of AIDS. We are trying to climb this tallest tree in the forest today in the world. And I know we may not climb as high as we want to climb. We may not be able to accomplish all the things we want to accomplish. We may even now have gone as far as we can climb; but if we fall... at least the world will know that we tried, and Africa will know we tried, and God will know we tried, and we will land on the tops of shorter trees.

My vision and hope for Africa rest on children and their education. In Harare, a tripartite agreement between the Organization of African Unity (OAU), the United Nations Educational, Scientific, and Cultural Organization (UNESCO), and the Sullivan entities comprising Opportunities Industrialization Centers (OICs), the International Foundation for Education and Self-Help (IFESH), and the Progress Movement, whose aim is to develop the capacities of grassroots individuals and institutions in all the nations of Africa, launched a revolutionary program of support for educational rehabilitation in Africa. The agreement is known as the New Grand Partnership for Education.[1] A profile for the program, called the "Program of Support to Educational Rehabilitation in Africa" (PROSERA), was based on the Sullivan training and educational models that were operating in half of the countries of Africa. PROSERA has a dual purpose of grass-roots development of education in Africa and the promotion of the culture of peace on the African continent.

The tripartite agreement was presented with the great help and inspiration of Salim Salim at the OAU summit meeting in Harare, Zimbabwe, held the first week in June 1997, at which time President Robert Mugabe was made OAU chair. It was later presented to the African–African American Summit also in Harare in July of the same year. Both bodies unanimously and enthusiastically approved the partnership's plans for action.

The justification for PROSERA emerges from the simple recognition of education's vital role in the addressing of Africa's many needs: "Africa needs to be assisted in a massive manner to rehabilitate its educational system (both the formal and the informal structures) as an important contribution to the ongoing process of peace building, capacity reinforcement, and civil society empowerment as the overall socioeconomic and political development of the African continent." The history of Africa's educational system over the past forty years is telling: "Far-reaching educational reforms have taken place since the 1960s, but serious problems still remain without appropriate solutions, due to lack of resources, political instability in a number of places, and largely because of the economic problems of the 1980s, the 1990s, and, more particularly, the debt burden on African countries."

The formal tripartite agreement signed by IFESH, UNESCO, and OAU "should be seen in the context of a massive attack on some of the key educational problems of our times." Two major areas warrant the concerted efforts of all involved:

1. The development of useful and salable skills (in dropouts, illiterates, semiliterates, displaced persons, demobilized soldiers, all classes of out-of-school youth, etc.) as a solution to the problem of unemployment and as a means of meeting some of the inadequacies of existing technical-vocational education programs

2. Massive production of physical facilities (school buildings, basic school furnishings, etc.) to replace facilities destroyed by wars and civil strife and to provide schools for large numbers of young persons needing formation education

PROSERA's efforts complement, rather than replace, ongoing efforts by governments, nongovernmental organizations (NGOs), funding agencies, and humanitarian bodies to ensure the socioeconomic recovery of Africa in general and the rehabilitation of educational systems and structures in particular. More specific aims include providing societally useful, cost-effective vocational skills that should enable beneficiaries to go straight from learning to socioeconomic application (in the form of self-employment or jobs) and mobilizing local communities to own their own educational infrastructures and facilities by being fully in charge of decisions and actions concerning choice of sites and designs, construction work, furnishings, management, maintenance, and every other need associated with the continent-wide effort.

Unprecedented in Africa and possibly in the world, PROSERA is an agreement among a private individual, leaders of the nations of a continent, and the best-known United Nations organization for education and human development, UNESCO. The agreement has been enthusiastically received throughout Africa and with organizations around the globe interested in Africa's education and advancement.

PROSERA represents the first time an effort of this kind and scope for education for Africa has been agreed upon. From the summit in Ghana and then during future summits, reports on programs with PROSERA will be made. I have no doubt that in the next ten years results from this agreement will affect tens of millions of lives, especially youth across Africa.

Note

1. All quotations regarding PROSERA are from the New Grand Partnership For Education agreement.

Chapter 23

A Journey of Faith

THERE IS ALWAYS a cost to be paid for leadership. Sometimes the cost is all you have. I believe that justice and freedom are not just worth fighting for; they are worth dying for. So far at least, that has not been part of God's plan for me, but through the years there have been many difficult and lonely times.

I felt alone, and often frustrated, especially when I did not receive the support I was seeking, as happened many times during the early years of the Sullivan Principles. I recall one meeting in December 1985 at which several university representatives were present to discuss whether to pull their stock investments from certain South African interests in order to meet the full requirements of the Sullivan Principles. The majority complied, but Harvard was a notable exception. In fact, Harvard did not support the Principles at some critical junctures.

Later in 1985, Harvard University offered me their Harvard Award for my work in South Africa. Because of the position Harvard was taking toward the Principles, I turned down the honor. I later learned that I was the first person ever to turn down this prestigious award, one that had been bestowed upon presidents, kings, leaders of nations, and other notable people for their exemplary and distinguishing achievements. Yes, it would be gratifying to have that Harvard Award hanging in my office, but life has shown me that some things, especially principles, are more important than awards.

By faith, I always believed my ultimate mission would be accomplished, but again the road has often been difficult and painstaking. For the better part of ten years I worked against the grain. Nearly everywhere I went in America and Europe, I encountered opposition to my approach. Some of it came from my closest ministerial friends, many of whom had worked with me in the civil rights movement through the years. I continued, sometimes alone with God in knowing what my next step would be.

While I had many opponents, I also had many incredibly faithful supporters, some of whom I have mentioned in these pages and will also mention here. Whenever I asked Roger Smith, chairman of General Motors, for anything related to my cause, he never let me down. Not only did he work hard to elevate blacks within General Motors, but he personally met with government leaders on a number of occasions in South Africa and with captains of South African industry to push for the goals of the Sullivan Principles. He continues to help me with our work in sub-Saharan Africa. Other supporters include Mike Rosholt, who as chairman of Barlow Rand in South Africa, in the 1980s the largest South African employer of blacks in the country, brought a delegation of high-ranking businesspeople from South Africa to the meetings at Leeds Castle.

I am blessed to have had great people such as Dr. C. T. Wright, an extraordinary man, helping me. Like me, he was born poor. In fact, he says if he had been born one day earlier he would have been born quite literally in the cotton fields of Georgia. But Wright obtained the best education available to him, and after serving as a provost and as a president in several universities, he came to work with me. Without him as executive director of the International Foundation for Education and Self-Help (IFESH) and without his brilliant and indefatigable help, I doubt if I could have pulled together the summits and begun the various development projects so important to Africa today.

Then there is Dr. C. L. Mannings, the remarkable leader of OIC (Opportunities Industrialization Centers) International. At one point, I had sent Dr. Mannings to a country in western Africa to start an OIC. He managed to get a letter back to me saying, "I am trapped beneath a truck in Africa in the middle of a revolution... bullets are flying all around me. I want you to know that if I never see you again, I thank you and God for giving me this opportunity to help our people in Africa."

In previous pages I have called attention to the steadfast support I received from "Great Zion" in Philadelphia: Zion Baptist Church. Even though my commitments to South Africa often took me away from day-to-day pastoral duties, my church placed its full support — prayers, money, and time — behind me. My wife, "Amazing Grace," whom I could never credit or thank enough, shared my vision and my struggles, walking with me every step of the way. As a mother, wife, and helper, she has no equal, which is why this book is dedicated to her. For all important things achieved in the world, there are those who pay a special price, and this is true of Grace Sullivan. No one will ever know the sacrifices she made in standing by me and helping me with all the things I have attempted to do. As I zigzagged across America and the world it was Grace who maintained a home, cared for the children, and in untold ways made it possible for me to continue on. Grace is a remarkable woman; prepared for exceptional achievement in her own right, she gave it all up. Neither I nor the world will ever be able to repay the debt we owe to Grace Sullivan. Without her, the things we were able to achieve would never have been done. And most important of all, I give credit to the God I have trusted since childhood who has given me strength and guidance for this awesome journey.

On one occasion, during one of my many visits to Europe calling on the companies of Europe to take a stronger stand against apartheid, I met with the head of the Baptist Association of Churches of England. He noticed I was traveling alone, as I usually did, and he asked, "Aren't you afraid? You are alone and are dealing with diamonds and gold and billions of dollars of profits, and I guess you know there are those who do not want you around." And I replied, "No, I am not afraid . . . and I am not alone. This is God's work, and what happens happens. I know God is with me."

God was always with me, and sometimes God intervened. For example, once, during a period when I was banned from South Africa, I was flying in a small, single-prop plane from Swaziland to Lesotho, a small independent kingdom surrounded by South Africa. In order to take a flight into Lesotho, I had to be flown over South Africa because I had not been granted a visa to land in the country. The pilot had decided not to refuel when he took off from Swaziland on the way to Lesotho. The plane flew into a head wind, using up the fuel far more quickly than the pilot anticipated. As the plane flew over one of the tall mountains that divides Lesotho from the rest of South Africa, the pilot informed me that his little plane had run out of gasoline. Having just reached the other side of the mountain that separated the two countries, the pilot and I looked around for a place we could land. I saw what appeared to be a cow field below, and I told him to land there. By the time the wheels touched and landed in the field, the fuel gauge was on zero, and the propeller had stopped turning. The little plane bounced and bounced along until it came to a halt in a ditch. The pilot's face had turned white as snow. I looked up and said, "Thank you, Jesus." I was praying all the time the plane was going down, and God reached down and saved us.

On another flight from Anchorage, Alaska, to a very remote little village occupied by Eskimos where we were going to establish an OIC program, I was once again in a small, single-prop plane. (Small planes tend to give God opportunities to display his faithfulness!) We had to fly over a tall mountain, called Resurrection Pass, where just a few months before an Alaskan congressman had gone down in a little plane. The wreckage of that plane was still visible as we flew over a snow-capped peak. Suddenly, there was a great squall, which picked up the little plane, turned it around, and seemed about to tear it apart. The hair on the pilot's head stood straight up in the air. His face was as red as fire. He looked at me and shook his head, and I began to pray. Once again, God reached down and saved us. Somehow, the little plane straightened out and, on its own, headed back to Anchorage. I wanted to keep on going toward our destination, but the pilot said, "No way! I'm going back home." We never reached the village of the Eskimos to establish the OIC, but I believe God was testing me again and making me stronger in my faith for the future work he had for me to do in taking the OIC movement into the most difficult parts of the world. God has a way of testing us and preparing us to be stronger for the work he has for us to do.

I know that anything I have accomplished is ultimately God's work. I and many others have been vessels. I hope that the work we have done and continue to do will develop and grow, that its fruits will be visible for many years to come. That work will go on without me. There will be those coming along who will take my place and who will go on to do far greater things. Realizing this humbles me and helps me understand that, in all we attempt, nothing is more important than faith. With faith, what seems like nothing becomes something. My faith is a faith that includes action. It is a faith that says if you believe in something and work for it, it will be accomplished.

All I have written about in this book is inseparably tied to my faith. My work is the result of my faith. Faith sparks determination and a plan, always a plan, to make the vision become real. This was true at each step of the way — from the OIC movement to the development of community investment cooperatives to the writing of the Sullivan

Principles to the organizing of the African–African American summits. Many will say that such faith does not apply to them because they are just ordinary people, not a Moses or an Abraham or a Mahatma Gandhi, Rosa Parks, Mother Teresa, Martin Luther King, or Nelson Mandela. To them I say that every word I have written actually applies only to ordinary people. The people I have mentioned are ultimately ordinary people. They have become "famous" only when others have chosen to view them that way. Most wanted to be seen as just ordinary people. Ordinary people are the ones God uses most. They identify most with the needs and the aspirations of the masses and the poor. And ordinary people are with us always.

I have heard it said that all professors have but one lesson, all politicians have but one speech, and all preachers have but one sermon. Is this saying true? Well, my sermon for more than fifty years has been, "Use what you have in your hands." Following is a summary of that sermon, which I believe applies to everyone.

USE WHAT YOU HAVE IN YOUR HANDS

And the LORD said unto him, What is that in thine hand? And he said, A rod. (Exodus 4:2, KJV)

Remember Abraham was a shepherd man when God called him to take his family and turn to a place unknown to begin the establishment of a nation. Moses was the child of a slave woman, placed in a basket in the bulrushes of the Nile to be found by the daughter of Pharaoh and raised as a part of the royal family. Remember Jesus was considered an illegitimate child, his father still unknown, who, to our knowledge, never went to school a day in his life and whose only writing about which we know was some scribbling in the sand. With all he had done and all he had said to inspire and help the people, he was turned upon by his own, many of whom cheered when he was crucified.

Remember Rosa Parks was a seamstress when she refused to sit in the back of the bus in Montgomery, Alabama, and gave the spark to the civil rights movement in the United States. Remember that Martin Luther King, as he grew up, was considered by many as having little promise. As the story goes, on one occasion young Martin Luther King ran across the campus of Morehouse with his coattail sticking out. One of the professors seeing him run by said, "See that boy Martin? He is not going to amount to anything. When he gets older, he will become a preacher somewhere in some little town, and he will never be heard of again."

God finds greatness in ordinary and unknown people, and as a part of the script that God has for us in our lives, he helps us become what we can be. Every boy and girl in the poorest towns and cities of America and in the most remote places of the world are the new Abrahams, Moseses, Mohammeds, Sojourner Truths, Martin Luther Kings, and Nelson Mandelas. And wherever we are in any place, small or large, whatever our beginning or circumstances, God can take us and use us to become leaders and shapers of the lives of people. We need but develop our faith, our belief in God, and find a determination and will to work to make our dreams come true and our visions realities.

Use what you have in your hands, wherever you are. Those who do this are the makers of a better America, a better world of human rights and justice and peace. Saints are derived from ordinary people. Keep your mind open to the advice and counsel of others, for God speaks to us in often strange and unusual ways. We do not make ourselves. Through events and through views of others and the guidance of God, the best in us can be realized. Our work goes on. We look back at what has been done and what can be done tomorrow.

And God uses what is in his hands. Having been born in the hill country of West Virginia, I could never have imagined the life I would, by God's grace and guidance, go on to lead. Not many black men get a chance to serve on the board of a major corporation. Few of any color can pick up the phone and call a senator or president. Never in my youth did I dream of having access to world leaders, some of whom I have been privileged to call friends, or of hopping around the globe, traipsing off to Africa or Europe like it was a trip to the hardware store.

Some might say I have done what I have done because I am still trying to get out of that alley in West Virginia and help others get out of their alleys, too. Or maybe I can still see myself as an eight-year-old boy with a nickel in hand to buy a Coca-Cola and can still hear that man at the soft-drink counter saying to me, "Stand on your feet, black boy, you can't sit down here." I have been standing on my feet against prejudice and segregation all my life. And I will continue to do so till the day I die.

As for me, I cannot help but view my life in terms of God's plan,

God's script for my life. Ultimately, everything I have done or tried to do has sprung forth from a straightforward and simple faith. As a child I experienced poverty firsthand. I saw people all about me living in need. For as long as I can remember, the desire to respond to such need has been at the center of who I am. My faith has revolved around the belief, supported by Scripture, that God cares about the poor, about peace, and about justice. And part of our mission as Christians is to care for the needy and to work for justice and for peace.

With the help of my wonderful wife, who through the years has kept my feet on the ground where they belong, I have tried to remain humble, remembering that God is ultimately responsible for all the good I am able to accomplish. Thus, I have never been distracted by the temptation to run for political office or to make a lot of money and live a life of luxury, though I am taking things a bit easier in my senior years. My simple faith has revolved around helping the poor and the underprivileged peoples of America and the world, and I have no plans for changing that now.

Of all the ways I have attempted to help the underprivileged, the most important one is my steady and constant preaching of a philosophy of self-help. My simple faith is an active faith. It does not wait around for others to do whatever they will. Rather, it takes action. Every project or movement I have started has revolved around the conviction that men and women must do all they can to bring justice, freedom, and peace both to themselves and to others. "Use what you have in your hands" is Sullivan principle number one.

Moses used what he had in his hands. One day while Moses was on Mount Horeb minding the sheep of his father-in-law, Jethro, God told him to go down to Egypt and tell Pharaoh, "Let my people go." He had no following, no army. Moses took with him a simple rod. He returned to Egypt and commanded Pharaoh to let God's people go. God took care of the rest.

The history of achievement is in many cases the history of men and women who faced seemingly impossible odds and who overcame because they trusted God and used what they had in their hands. Frederick Douglass was a runaway slave who took a pencil in his hand and wrote "My Bondage and My Freedom." Harriet Beecher Stowe wrote *Uncle Tom's Cabin*, which helped turn the Western world against slavery. George Washington Carver took a peanut into his hand on his way to becoming one of the world's most acclaimed scientists.

Dr. Charles Drew, with a test tube in his hand, assisted in a discovery of blood plasma that would save millions of lives around the world. Unable to see or hear, Helen Keller learned to read, listen, and speak with her hands, providing inspiration and hope to millions of other blind and deaf people.

Marian Anderson took a hymnbook in her hands and learned to thrill the world with her voice. Jackie Robinson took a baseball bat in his hands and proceeded to hit and run his way into the Hall of Fame. For André Watts, it was a piano. For Michael Jordan, it was a basketball. For Tiger Woods, a golf club. Barbara Jordan overcame the odds against her to become one of the nation's most respected political voices. Dr. Andrew Brimmer left the cotton fields and went on to become the premier black economist in America and the first African American to be a member of the Federal Reserve Bank. The whole world knows what became of the prediction that Martin Luther King Jr. would never amount to anything. The pages of history are laden with accounts of blacks, Hispanics, whites, and others who, in spite of obstacle after obstacle, succeeded through faith and determination.

We must use what we have in our hands. For as witnessed to by the landmark 1996 legislation in this country, the day for welfare is coming to an end around the world. In the future we will all have to stand on our own feet. The common goal of the OIC movement, the 10–36 Program, SHIP, and IFESH is to do just that.[1] The emphasis on self-help, however, must be supplemented with efforts to create opportunities for people and to enhance their sense of confidence and self-respect. That being the case, the OIC programs are as relevant today as when they were launched over three decades ago. In the feeder program today, black women are taught that it is not necessary to be blond to be beautiful, and black men are taught that it is not necessary to be white to be smart. Students learn to be proud of their heritage. They read about Aesop, the black writer of fables; Hannibal, the black Carthaginian military genius; the glories of King Tutankhamen of Egypt; the writings of Pushkin, the black Russian poet; and Benjamin Banneker, the great black American astronomer and mathematician.

Trainees learn the histories of other minority groups as well: the Irish, the Italian, the German, the Jew, the Asian, the Native American, and the white Appalachian. The goal is not just to develop black pride but to build an appreciation for America as an amalgam of people from all over the earth. We are a nation of minority groups, all of whom are equal in the eyes of God and all of whom have contributed to the growth and development of this great country.

The OIC feeder program teaches consumer education to alert trainees to unethical and unfair practices in the business world and to help them evaluate what they buy. They are taught how to tell a fresh loaf of bread from a stale one by the markings on a wrapper, how to tell when a can of tuna fish was canned, how to tell a fresh chicken from a spoiled one, how to tell a good piece of cloth from a bad piece by the texture and the weaving, and how to stretch a dollar to make it go further.

All feeder program centers are spacious and bright. The use of pastel colors helps to overcome the effects of the drab and gloomy environments from which many trainees come. Posters and displays abound, as do symbols and single-word slogans such as Cleanliness, Time, Think, Work, and Togetherness.

English as a second language has become a popular extracurricular course designed to meet the needs of trainees who have come to America from non-English-speaking countries. OICs in the United States have trainees from virtually every Latin American country, from Europe, Asia, the Caribbean, and Africa. Many trainees are reluctant to leave the feeder program for skills training centers because, for the first time in their lives, they have found someone who cares about them. Visitors have commented that the spirit among the trainees is almost religious. Indeed, there is an amazing cohesiveness among these adult learners. Nothing brings people together more than mutual aspirations to reach common goals. These individuals have become a part of a great wave that is moving ahead like a sea tide. Even the administrators, counselors, and teachers are caught up in it. When teachers relax from their best efforts, students, by the effort of their desire to learn, push them on like a wind moving the arms of a windmill, like a stream pushing the wheels of a waterwheel round and round. The OIC movement is driven by the will of the people to become more than they have been, more than they and others thought they could be.

I am pleased and proud that the OIC model lies at the center of Africa's rebirth. This model recognizes first and foremost that the mind of a child in the deepest bush country in Africa is more important than a thousand computers. Plans call for OIC training centers to be put in place in every nation on the African continent, creating vocational skills for countries and for regions within countries that previously had no access to training. The OIC model fully supports the Harare Summit's emphasis on education as being the key to unlocking Africa's brighter future. Monumental efforts must be made for Africa to catch up technologically with the rest of the world, but these efforts must begin with the basics.

It is estimated that half of the youth of Africa, 115 million, are illiterate. The percentage of illiterate adults is roughly the same. This should come as no surprise, given that as late as 1900, with the exception of a special few, blacks living in tropical Africa could not read or write. At Harare we determined, "If you can't read, you can't lead." Thus, teaching every child in sub-Saharan Africa to read, write, and count has become the goal. We will move on from there to teach people how to be electricians, plumbers, carpenters, bricklayers, mechanics, computer operators, modernized farmers, and entrepreneurs. Many will go on to become scientists and teachers or doctors or ministers.

I close with the following messages to various groups of people:

To ministers, I say that for these times, a minister must be geared toward and trained not just in "Thus saith the Lord." He or she must also help to get it done. Without action, ministry is like a stool with one leg. It will not hold up. The prophets of old acted in concrete terms, combining theology with action. It is my conviction that the whole spectrum of theological education must undergo a complete process of reformation, with a new focus on meeting needs and guiding others to do the same.

The wearing of a long black robe and calling oneself "Reverend" does not mean one whit to God. So to those who aspire to be ministers, I say, "Either be prepared to help and lift the people or leave the ministry alone." That was the approach that enabled four hundred "colored preachers" in Philadelphia to turn the city upside down in terms of providing job opportunities for thousands and thousands of black youth where doors had previously been closed. These four hundred ministers left their denominations at the door and prayed and worked together for a common goal. Our preaching to the church must express a commitment to bringing both hope and practical relief to the poor and needy, especially the children. People will not need milk and honey in heaven. Many do need ham and eggs on earth.

To the world's corporations, I call attention to an enduring lesson from Communism. The human needs that gave rise to Communism remain. Either corporations within a capitalistic, democratic, free enterprise system will find ways to help ordinary people earn a fair living wage in the context of humane and just working conditions, or the system will collapse. I hope that corporations, on their own initiative, will examine the Global Sullivan Principles and make changes accordingly.

I urge my fellow African Americans never to limit yourselves. Stand on your feet as tall as you can and reach up as high as you can. You may not reach the stars, but you will get closer to them than you were before.

Don't tell me you are black and poor. Tell it to somebody else, but not to me. I've been around too long to fall for that line. I know from experience that you can take your blackness and be proud of you are. And you can work with others and use what you have in your hands to make something for yourselves.

You have more potential influence than you may realize. In 1997, the annual purchasing power of blacks in the United States was $650 billion, or 10 percent of the national domestic sales. We read in the Old Testament that Pharaoh sent his army to bring the Hebrew children back after they had left Egypt. Old Pharaoh had learned pretty quickly that the Egyptian economy was in trouble without the purchasing power and the labor of the Hebrew people. Not only did they number in millions, but the Hebrews also contributed to the Egyptian economy by working in homes, quarries, and fields. They may have been slaves, but they were slaves with resources who helped Egypt thrive. In the same way, if black people would suddenly disappear from America, the economy would fall into immediate disarray. In the future our purchasing power will continue to grow.

You do not have to tell me that the laws are sometimes unjust for racial reasons. You do not have to tell me that racial prejudice still runs rampant in the social realm. I know these things. But what I say to you is that these are not the primary reasons that our country's prisons are so filled with black youth. They are in jail also because something has been missing in the teaching of values such as self-esteem and respect for others and their property.

Too many times, the problems faced by African Americans continue, not because of a lack of opportunity, but because of the failure to take advantage of opportunities. I remember on one occasion appealing to fellow members of the General Motors board, who were themselves leaders of companies, to put black people on their own boards. A year later, one of my closest associates on the board said to me, "Leon, I did what you asked and put a black man on my board, but he just sits there and never says anything. He is a fine man and I like him very much, but the only thing he does is vote on the motions." I'm sure this fine man who says nothing is far from alone, not only in corporate America but in other institutions. I say to blacks and others representing constituent groups in these kinds of corporate positions to say something, do something, raise some questions. Do your part to help make companies more sensitive and responsive to the recognition and the needs of those who historically have been underrepresented and unheard in high places.

I especially urge black youth in the United States and Africa and those of the black diaspora to study hard and work hard. Ask questions and take risks. Explore and take advantage of your opportunities. Although I surely support affirmative action, I know that affirmative action will only go so far, but excellence cannot be contained.

In closing, I say to all people one last time that nothing and no one can help people who do not want to help themselves. Even a limitless supply of money will fall short if the will to help oneself is lacking. But the good news is that the miracle of change is right here before us. We hold it in our own hands. God has given us the ability and the power, and it lies within ourselves. Our minds and our feelings, our collective will and our commitments, are sufficient to accomplish the tasks at hand.

You may not think that you have the ability or the wisdom that others seem to have. You may feel you are not the right color or don't have the right education or the right background or enough money. You may feel you are not good-looking or that you cannot command the respect or recognition that others seem to be able to command. I say to you that many of those "better off" people feel the same as you do. If only you will use what God has given to you, work with it and develop it, be proud of who you are and what you have, God will do the rest. It will not help to sulk over what you don't have or to begrudge others for what they have. Rather, be thankful for what God has given to you. And if there is something you want in life, don't give up and say it can't be done.

What I'm talking about is not about color or culture; it's not about being black or being white or being Asian. It's about all of us being human. The only question is whether we will use what we have in our hands. I say we can. I say we must. And I believe that even the lofty goal of freedom and peace for the world is ours to grasp or turn away. I stake that claim, not as an idealist, but as a person of simple faith, faith in God who has proved time and again through my life that he is capable of moving mountains.

Note

1. The 10–36 Program, which I started with members in Zion Baptist Church, was a collective investment plan in which four thousand African Americans in Philadelphia invested $10 a month for thirty-six months, putting enough money together to build shopping centers, housing developments, and other enterprises that were valued in 1998 at $75 million. In fifty years, it will be worth $1 billion. I later used the same basic idea in another way to start SHIP (Self-Help Investment Programs), which as of 1998 were being formed in many cities and towns throughout America helping blacks and others with business development and housing in their communities. See Appendix D for more information on SHIP.

Appendix A

Sullivan Principles for U.S. Firms Operating in South Africa

*The Sullivan Statement of Principles — 1987
(with amplifications July 1978, May 1979,
November 1982, November 1984)*

Principle 1. Nonsegregation of the races in all eating, comfort, and work facilities.

Each signatory of the Statement of Principles will proceed immediately to:

- Eliminate all vestiges of racial discrimination.

- Remove all race-designation signs.

- Desegregate all eating, comfort, and work facilities.

Principle 2. Equal and fair employment practices for all employees.

Each signatory of the Statement of Principles will proceed immediately to:

- Implement equal and fair terms and conditions of employment.

- Provide nondiscriminatory eligibility for benefit plans.

- Establish an appropriate and comprehensive procedure for handling and resolving individual employee complaints.

- Support the elimination of all industrial racial discriminatory laws which impede the implementation of equal and fair terms and conditions of employment, such as abolition of job reservations, job fragmentation, and apprenticeship restrictions for blacks and other nonwhites.

- Support the elimination of discrimination against the rights of blacks to form or belong to government registered and unregistered unions and

193

acknowledge generally the rights of blacks to form their own unions or be represented by trade unions which already exist.

- Secure rights of black workers to the freedom of association and assure protection against victimization while pursuing and after attaining these rights.

- Involve black workers or their representatives in the development of programs that address their educational and other needs and those of their dependents and the local community.

Principle 3. Equal pay for all employees doing equal or comparable work (or the same period of time.)

Each signatory of the Statement of Principles will proceed immediately to:

- Design and implement a wage and salary administration plan which is applied equally to all employees, regardless of race, who are performing equal or comparable work.

- Ensure an equitable system of job classifications, including a review of the distinction between hourly and salaried classifications.

- Determine the extent upgrading of personnel and/or jobs in the upper echelons is needed, and accordingly implement programs to accomplish this objective in representative numbers, ensuring the employment of blacks and other nonwhites at all levels of company operations.

- Assign equitable wage and salary ranges, the minimum of these to be well above the appropriate local minimum economic living level.

Principle 4. Initiation and development of training programs that will prepare, in substantial numbers, blacks and other nonwhites for supervisory, administrative, clerical, and technical jobs.

Each signatory of the Statement of Principles will proceed immediately to:

- Determine employee training needs and capabilities, and identify employees with potential for further advancement.

- Take advantage of existing outside training resources and activities, such as exchange programs, technical colleges, and similar institutions or programs.

- Support the development of outside training facilities, individually or collectively — including technical centers, professional training exposure, correspondence and extension courses, as appropriate, for extensive training outreach.

- Initiate and expand inside training programs and facilities.

Principle 5. Increasing the number of blacks and other nonwhites in management and supervisory positions.

Each signatory of the Statement of Principles will proceed immediately to:

- Identify, actively recruit, train, and develop a sufficient and significant number of blacks and other nonwhites to assure that as quickly as possible there will be appropriate representation of blacks and other nonwhites in the management group of each company at all levels of operations.

- Establish management development programs for blacks and other nonwhites, as needed, and improve existing programs and facilities for developing management skills of blacks and other nonwhites.

- Identify and channel high management potential blacks and other nonwhite employees into management development programs.

Principle 6. Improving the quality of employees' lives outside the work environment in such areas as housing, transportation, schooling, recreation, and health facilities.

Each signatory of the Statement of Principles will proceed immediately to:

- Develop programs or evaluate existing programs, as appropriate, to address the specific needs of black and other nonwhite employees in the areas of housing, health care, transportation, and recreation.

- Evaluate methods for utilizing existing, expanded, or newly established in-house medical facilities or other medical programs to improve medical care for all nonwhites and their dependents.

- Participate in the development of programs that address the educational needs of employees, their dependents, and the local community. Both individual and collective programs should be considered, in addition to technical education, including such activities as literacy education, business training, direct assistance to local schools, contributions, and scholarships.

- Support changes in influx control laws to provide for the right of black migrant workers to normal family life.

- Increase utilization of and assist in the development of black and other nonwhite owned and operated business enterprises including distributors, suppliers of goods and services, and manufacturers.

Principle 7. **Working to eliminate laws and customs which impede social, economic, and political justice.** (This was originally known as the "fourth amplification.")

Each signatory of the Statement of Principles must proceed immediately to:

- Press for a single education system common to all races.

- Use influence and support the unrestricted rights of black businesses to locate in the urban areas of the nation.

- Influence other companies in South Africa to follow the standards of equal rights principles.

- Support the freedom of mobility of black workers, including those from so-called independent homelands, to seek employment opportunities wherever they exist, and make possible provisions for adequate housing for families of employees within the proximity of workers' employment.

- Use financial and legal resources to assist blacks, coloreds, and Asians in their efforts to achieve equal access to all health facilities, educational institutions, transportation, housing, beaches, parks, and all other accommodations normally reserved for whites.

- Oppose adherence to all apartheid laws and regulations.

- Support the ending of all apartheid laws, practices, and customs.

- Support full and equal participation of blacks, coloreds, and Asians in the political process.

With all the foregoing in mind, it is the objective of the companies to involve and assist in the education and training of large and telling numbers of blacks and other nonwhites as quickly as possible. The ultimate impact of this effort is intended to be of massive proportion, reaching and helping millions.

Periodic Reporting

The Signatory Companies of the Statement of Principles will proceed immediately to:

- Report progress on an annual basis to the independent administrative unit Reverend Sullivan established.

- Have all areas specified by Reverend Sullivan audited by a certified public accounting firm.

- Inform all employees of the company's annual periodic report rating and invite their input on ways to improve the rating.

The Sullivan Principles in South Africa were intended to help dismantle and end apartheid and to help with opportunities and freedom for the millions of blacks and others of the nonwhite population.

The Role of Multinational Corporations in the Republic of South Africa: Where Is the World!

Once to every man and nation comes the moment to decide....
— JAMES RUSSELL LOWELL

I first want to express my appreciation to the Institute of Race Relations for the invitation to be the Hoernle Memorial Lecturer this year. I have carefully read the program and policies of the institute and have read of your high ideals and activities. You deserve the highest commendation for your efforts. I particularly like the setting of this great hall because it is representative of this noble university that has lit a candle, rather than cursed the darkness, by upholding the policy that all who wish to learn, regardless of race or color, are welcome through its doors.

I want to also acknowledge the presence of so many of my black and nonwhite brothers and sisters. I pray God my coming, in some way, will help in some small measure at least to lighten your burdens. I particularly want to thank those black leaders without whose willingness I would not have accepted this invitation to be here today.

This evening, I come to your country as a black man with an appeal. It is an appeal for equality and for justice and for freedom for the black and other nonwhite population of South Africa. I come though not just for them but for all the people of your nation, white and nonwhite alike, because your destinies are tied together. For, "the laws of sacred justice bind oppressor to oppressed; and close as sin and suffering joined we march to fate abreast."

The Hoernle Memorial Lecture for the Institute of Race Relations was delivered at the University of Witwatersrand in South Africa on September 4, 1980.

I ask you, therefore, as I speak to you here and to your nation, to find the national will to save your beloved country before it is too late and to provide full human rights and individual freedom to all your people and to let South Africa become South Africa, equally, for everyone. Above all things else, the need in South Africa today is for individual freedom and the recognition of the universal and inalienable rights of man. The notion must be confronted and dispelled that a white person is superior to a black person or a black person inferior to a white person or a person of any color inferior to another just because of the color of their skin.

I emphasize individual freedom because nothing will be more important to the future of your country than this. Without individual freedom for your black and other dark-skinned people, there will be no future peace in your land: the individual freedom to work where a person wants to work on the basis of one's ability and willingness to learn; the individual freedom to live where a person wants to live according to one's desire and circumstances to do so; the individual freedom to attend a school with equal access, without restriction because of color or race or tribe; the individual freedom to take equal part in choosing one's government and decide who shall make laws and govern lives, as well as to be part of those who govern; the individual freedom to move about without hindrance because of racial characteristics or identity; the individual freedom to speak as you please without fear; the individual freedom to be what you want to be and to work and to strive and to save and to own, as all others, for the benefit of your person, your family, your community, and your nation.

It must be sounded from your pulpits, taught in your classrooms, interpreted in your laws, and practiced in your nation. It must be realized here, as elsewhere, that if a nation is to be truly democratic, the fundamental premise of the equality of all people before God and man must prevail. Whatever other measures are attempted to assist with your racial conditions, such as the Principles, these efforts can and will only go so far until nationally and constitutionally and in practice your racial segregation ends and individual freedom for all your people becomes a reality.

Already unrest and disorder grow and will continue to grow and mount until you change your outlook and your ways of dealing with your nonwhite population. Unless you change, your country will be engulfed with turmoil, and your cities and towns and countrysides paralyzed with revolt and destruction. Unless you change, nothing you do will stop the devastation that lies ahead — neither your secret service or your police or your military. Unless economically, socially, and politically you change and there is individual freedom for all, one day the tides of revolution will sweep over you and destroy everything you have built.

While there is still time, in the name of justice and in the name of God, accord your nonwhite population, through the actions of your parliament, your councils, your institutions, your churches, and your businesses, their status as full citizens, with human dignity and all the rights and opportunities it provides. Do it before it is too late. It is time for South Africa to change with the times.

Racial discrimination has been with you a long time. Since 1660, less than a decade after the Dutch settled here, when a wild almond hedge was planted on a hill above Capetown and a pole fence was extended from it beyond which no black was to venture, South Africa has had its color bar. Since then black people have been constantly subjugated, and their labor exploited. David Livingstone wrote of inland South Africa in the 1840s and the widespread use of unpaid labor for the white farmers on the premise that "The people should work for us, in consideration of allowing them to live in our country."

These kinds of attitudes and practices have continued through the years, but racism took its worst and most dehumanizing form when, in 1948, South Africa structurally and officially adopted apartheid and made segregation the law of the land: enacting statute upon statute and piling indignity upon indignity upon its black and other nonwhite people. Apartheid and its policies of separate development, and all the laws and regulations that have followed, have made South Africa, in the eyes of the world, the most oppressive government dealing with human beings on the globe today:

- Black labor has been bureaucratically controlled and exploited for the growth of a white-owned and -dominated economy.

- Black and other nonwhites have been legally, systematically, and arbitrarily relegated to racially concentrated areas.

- Blacks and other nonwhites have no power politically and are used economically.

- The gap between white and black wages defies description. Families in vast numbers have been broken as influx control laws have restricted family life.

- Medical and natal care is so poor in black reserves, half the children born that live die before they are five years of age.

- Schools, where they exist, are glaring symbols of inequality.

- The despised passbook continues to be used, restricting freedom to work, live, or play.

- For nonwhites there is no due process of law. A person is assumed guilty until proof of innocence is provided, but indefinite detention for suspects or potential witnesses is permitted.

- One-half million people are received into prison each year, and in proportion to its size, South Africa has the highest prison population in the world and has recorded half of the world's judicial executions.

- Protests against segregation and discrimination and apartheid have been systematically and brutally crushed; leaders and supporters, suppressed, banned, jailed, exiled, and, in cases, believed to have been killed.

And there is so much more.

The roots of three hundred years of racism go down so deep one wonders if the only answer to it all might have to be a military one in the end. I hope not. In the spirit of that hope, I stand here today, reaching out, along with others, for another answer. A means must be found for all to live together in this beautiful country in harmony and peace.

There is a need to find a way to build a bridge between your white and nonwhite population before havoc overtakes you all. It is to help build that bridge, if possible, by peaceful means that the Principles of Equal Rights for United States Firms in the Republic of South Africa was conceived and initiated. The Principles must be viewed as a humanitarian and economic effort, using companies of America, combined with companies of the world, to help build that bridge and to help right the wrongs and injustices against blacks and other nonwhite people in South Africa before it is too late.

Before I speak further of the Principles and how they came about and how they continue to evolve, you should know something about me. All of my life I have been engaged in the struggle for equal rights and opportunities for black and other oppressed people in America.

From the time as a boy, in the town where I was born, when I was told to stand on my feet at a lunch counter by a prejudiced white man because I was black, I have been standing on my feet against race discrimination. Since my youth, I have fought race prejudice in America. My past has been constant in the struggle for justice and freedom.

I am also a minister of God and a Baptist preacher. I am pastor of the Zion Baptist Church in Philadelphia, one of the largest congregations in America, but I am a minister who believes that his mission is to help people to live on earth as well as in heaven, and I believe in the word of Jesus when he said, "I am come that men might have life, and they that they might have it more abundantly." I believe that God wants us "to preach good tidings unto the meek, to bind up the broken hearted, to proclaim liberty to the captive and to open the prison to them that are bound." I cannot emphasize enough that I am a minister and a Baptist preacher, not a politician, not an educator, not a philosopher, not an economist, and not a businessman. I am a minister and a Baptist preacher, and I have gotten into this effort trying to meet challenges as they have arisen, as you will find later, step-by-step.

Also, I am a black man. There are eight hundred million of us in the world along with three billion other people of color, and we cannot permit a system that legally divides and segregates and degrades people simply because of the color of their skin, such as apartheid, to continue in the world today. Apartheid must come to an end, one way or another, and I intend to help bring it to an end if I can, hopefully, by peaceful means. My main personal objective is to help end apartheid. I want to see apartheid eliminated from the face of the earth. And the world must help make it happen.

Hurricanes are not deterred by national boundaries. Epidemics do not select persons because they are black, brown, yellow, white, or red. The seas indiscriminately wash many shores, and pollution from one nation can easily reach the shores of another. In a world such as ours where the few can dominate the many, no one knows what direction history will take. We must never forget Fascism and what happened because no one dared to stop it before it was too late. We must recognize there is a racial pollution here in South Africa that must be stopped; and it must be stopped now.

I know the question will be asked, "You have enough to do at home. Why aren't you in America dealing with your problems there?" And

I can only reply, "I am busy dealing with the problems there." In 150 cities I have established programs to help deal with the problems there with training and education, but to the extent that I can, it is my responsibility as a preacher and a black man to do what I can also to help deal with the problems that blacks and other nonwhites face here, for our fates are tied together. Wherever people suffer indignities anywhere because of the color of their skin, we all suffer and we must strive to help remove these indignities. That is what I am trying to do.

My involvement with Africa is not new. I have made many journeys to Africa in the establishment of training centers to help school-leavers and school dropouts and people who are unemployed to secure skills so they might be able to perform useful work and to add to the technical development and capabilities of themselves and their nations. Hundreds of thousands of previously unskilled and unemployed people have benefited from these programs in America, and thousands, in Africa. These programs are now operational in nine African nations, including your own neighboring Lesotho, and there are further plans for their development in many other parts of the continent. They are the most successful community-based training programs in Africa.

I have made a commitment to do what I can to help black people not only in America but also in Africa because I believe in the future of Africa, and I want to see every section of Africa independent, trained, prosperous, and free. I want it clearly known that I am proud of my African heritage. I am proud to be an African American.

My active involvement with South Africa parallels my active participation with General Motors. In 1971, I accepted an invitation to become a member of the board of General Motors because I believed in that capacity, along with other things, I could help blacks and others in America and other countries to secure equality and a better way of life. My relationship with General Motors has been a productive one.

My first public reaction regarding the Republic of South Africa occurred in 1971 at the annual General Motors stockholders' meeting. At that meeting I stated my views that General Motors Company should withdraw from the Republic of South Africa until apartheid was ended. To my knowledge, I was the only board member in America or in the world to take such a public position on a stockholders' meeting floor. I held that position until the summer of 1975 when I stopped over in Johannesburg, and stayed at the Holiday Inn, during a trip to Lesotho to establish an OIC training program there.

While there, I was met by a number of blacks, coloreds, labor leaders, and other private individuals, many of whom learned I was there through stories that appeared in the local papers reporting a statement I made on arrival condemning apartheid. During those meetings that lasted all through the night, I was asked, over and over again, to make an attempt to see if it was possible to get American companies and other companies to become a real force for change in South Africa by taking a stand against racial segregation, beginning with their own operations. I was told that although a few companies had done a few things, the effort had never really been tried.

Upon returning home, I continued to think about it and prayed to God and was directed to initiate this effort among companies, starting in America, with the hope it would spread around the world to direct the power and strength of multinational corporations against the evils of race discrimination that exist here and to find out, once and for all, conclusively if the influences of companies could, indeed, be organized sufficiently in America, and hopefully around the world, to become a major force in ending the discriminatory conditions in South Africa. My approach was to be a peaceful one because my efforts against injustices have always been in the direction of peaceful means: even in America, when I organized and led great economic boycotts against companies that discriminated against black people there, until the companies changed their policies.

I am aware conditions in America cannot be compared with conditions in South Africa. Here racism is so deep and so entangled in centuries of traditions and customs and practices that one wonders if it can ever be ended without warfare; still, I believe in South Africa that peaceful means, if given a chance, with the help of almighty God, and the persistence of people who believe in the ideals of freedom, can prevail. Also, I know that a violent answer in South Africa will, inevitably, mean the loss of untold numbers of lives, perhaps in the millions, and most of them will undoubtedly be black. So, I proceeded on, still not certain my plan would work, and still at this moment not certain how far it can go, but willing to give it a try. This endeavor took the form of what has come to be known as the "Sullivan Principles."

In March 1977, the plan was initiated with twelve companies. It became the first united effort of its kind on behalf of companies ever attempted in South Africa. From the beginning I saw the Principles as an evolving process. From the start I knew that other steps would be required and additional phases would have to be initiated if the desired goals were ever to be realized and that, in time, it would have to become worldwide.

At the outset the resistance of many companies was very strong, but I decided to start where I was and with what I had, even with the initial wording, and to work to where I wanted to go. As a result, since the first announcement, the Principles have been amplified and expanded several times, including such things as the right of black workers to organize and belong to trade unions and support for changes to influx control laws and to allow for the right of family life for black workers, which is now denied. There are still steps ahead that will have to be taken, as well as other phases to be initiated, as the program evolves, strengthens, and unfolds.

For the benefit of some who might not know what the American Principles and their guidelines really are, I will give highlights of them at this time, as well as an idea of the process that has been developed with the companies for implementing and carrying them out.

Principle 1: Nonsegregation of the races in all eating, comfort, and work facilities.

Each signatory of the Statement of Principles will proceed immediately to:

- Eliminate all vestiges of racial discrimination.
- Remove all race-designation signs.
- Desegregate all eating, comfort, and work facilities.

Principle 2: Equal and fair employment practices for all employees.

Each signatory of the Statement of Principles will proceed immediately to:

- Support the elimination of all industrial racial discriminatory laws which impede the implementation of equal and fair terms and conditions of employment, such as abolish job reservations, job fragmentation, and apprenticeship restrictions for blacks and other nonwhites.

- Support the elimination of discrimination against the rights of blacks to form or belong to government registered unions and acknowledge, generally, the right of black workers to form their own union or be represented by trade unions, where unions already exist.

Principle 3: Equal pay for all employees doing equal or comparable work for the same period of time.

Each signatory of the Statement of Principles will proceed immediately to:

- Design and implement a wage and salary administration plan which is applied equally to all employees, regardless of race, who are performing equal or comparable work.

- Assign equitable wages and salary ranges, the minimum of these to be well above the appropriate local minimum economic living level.

Principle 4: Initiation of and development of training programs that will prepare, in substantial numbers, blacks and other nonwhites for supervisory, administrative, clerical, and technical jobs.

Principle 5: Increasing the number of blacks and other nonwhites in management and supervisory positions.

Each signatory of the Statement of Principles will proceed immediately to:

- Identify, actively recruit, train, and develop a sufficient and significant number of blacks and other nonwhites to assure that as quickly as possible there will be appropriate representation of blacks and other nonwhites in the management group of each company at all levels of operations.

Principle 6: Improving the quality of life for blacks and other nonwhites outside the work environment in such areas as housing, transportation, school, recreation, and health facilities.

Each signatory of the Statement of Principles will proceed immediately to:

- Participate in the development of programs that address the educational needs of employees, their dependents, and the local community. Both individual and collective programs should be considered, including such activities as literacy education, business training, direct assistance to local schools, contributions, and scholarships.

- Increase utilization of and assist in the development of black and non-white owned and operated business enterprises including distributors, suppliers of goods and services, and manufacturers.

- With all the foregoing in mind, it is the objective of the companies to involve themselves in every possible way and assist in the education and training of large and telling numbers of blacks and other nonwhites as quickly as possible. The ultimate impact of this effort is intended to be of massive proportion, reaching millions.

Recently several expansions have been made, consistent with the evolving nature of the Principles. They include:

- Requiring all companies to work towards the upgrading of blacks and other nonwhites to all levels of the company's employment.

- Requiring all companies to hold periodic meetings with representative black and other nonwhite workers to determine the extent to which the Principles are being fully implemented.

The Principles represent one of the most detailed and comprehensive industrial fair-employment charters ever voluntarily developed and activated in a united way by companies anywhere against racial discrimination in the world. If the Principles were followed and implemented by multinational companies in the Third World countries they would become a major force in the elimination of workers' inequities, widespread poverty, and pervasive ignorance and illiteracy in those countries.

As part of the process that has been developed in the planning and implementation of the Principles, every effort has been made to involve the companies on a close and continuing basis. All signatory companies, through their representatives, meet regularly through the year to exchange ideas, to summarize efforts, to discuss reports, to receive directions, and to plan future actions. Each company, through its representative, is assigned to at least one task group, representing each of the six Principles, to assure close, ongoing participation. A seventh task group of company representatives deals specifically with periodic reporting and nonwhite business development.

Each American-based task group has a counterpart task group in South Africa, designated to work in cooperation with the American group on plans and objectives. In the future, American task groups will strive for closer collaboration with South African representatives. This is essential because the work that really counts will be done here in South Africa and not in America or some other part of the world. Too, I have found already, since being here, the great need for closer coordination, and I want to commend and encourage the South African task-force group representatives for the work they have done.

Also, task groups have been asked to work towards the greatest possible involvement of blacks and other nonwhites in all projects and programs. The significant involvement of blacks and others must be emphasized. Blacks must be a vital part of everything that is attempted in the improvement of South Africa, not only with the Principles but also with the codes and with everything else that relates to the future. Otherwise, success in all things will be limited, as the companies will be helping to create a new paternalism that will be totally destructive to everything the Principles are trying to accomplish.

Each company is expected to fill out a questionnaire, two times during the year, describing the efforts of the company in implementing the Principles. The cumulative information is placed in a report prepared by an organization of outstanding creditability, the Arthur D. Little Company, and the report is made available on a semiannual basis to the public. For these reports, the data and information is gathered of the most exacting kind and maintained to help with the most accurate measurements of the company's efforts. An annual rating is given each company for its performance. The reporting requirements for the Statement of Principles for American companies are substantially more stringent than those for any other codes. The companies and their ratings are made public.

Next month in America, great interest will be centered on the next company "report card," as more and more stockholders and large investors and organizations will be making investment, divestment, and consumer judgments on the basis of the companies' ratings on the implementation of the Principles. It can be expected that growing numbers of selective divestment campaigns will be initiated against nonparticipating companies and companies that fail to implement the Principles in an acceptable way. In the near future, I will be meeting with presidents from a hundred colleges and universities that have endowment funds amounting to billions of dollars, as well as state treasurers, pension and insurance company heads, and leaders of other fiduciary institutions, to discuss their investment policies regarding signatory and nonsignatory companies.

In America, of the approximately 300 multinational corporations doing business in South Africa, 140 have signed the Principles; they employ 80 percent of the American companies' South African–based workforce. The remaining 160 companies have not as yet become signatories. Strong efforts will be undertaken to persuade all remaining companies to become signatories to the Principles.

A voluntary on-site monitoring plan is being completed for much needed on-site inspection of American company activities, in addition to the semiannual progress reports, to ascertain visual compliance with the Principles in word and spirit. On-site monitoring is one of the most essential present needs for the success of this effort and hopefully will be fully underway within the coming year.

Never before in American industrial history has there been such a concentration and mobilization of companies around a volunteer transnational corporate activity. All things considered, though, the biggest question is that of "results" and what the Principles have actually accomplished.

According to reports I have received, there has, thus far, been measurable progress in both effect and substance. It is clear the Principles have had an effect on industrial thinking and activity in South Africa. The fact that I have been asked to deliver this annual lecture is some evidence of that, but also there is little question the Principles have made an impact on the thinking of multinational companies operating here, as well as on South African companies. The Principles have established, as never before, a new worldwide sensitivity to the humanitarian role companies can, and must, play in South Africa. The Principles have become a catalyst for change.

In the past thirty-six months since the Principles, more has happened in South Africa, as far as equal opportunity for black and other nonwhite workers is concerned, than has happened in the past one hundred years. The Principles have, also, become an impetus for increasing and widening desegregation efforts in private and public places throughout the nation. The Principles have their own momentum, and they will continue to change conditions.

One of the most encouraging developments in the past year has been efforts of a number of your largest South African companies with a voluntary commitment to support the Principles and to improve employment practices in their respective companies. These companies employ more than 750,000 workers, most of them black and nonwhite.

This participation of South African companies with the Principles in the improvement of employment practices is one of the most hopeful signs of recent occurrences. We hope to collaborate with these companies to the fullest extent possible because the most important and lasting progress that can be made in South Africa will come from those who live here and not from those who live across the seas. I am hopeful that, in time, many other South African companies will support fair employment practices and end all racial discrimination.

It should be noted at least thirteen fair-employment codes from other nations have been developed as a result of the Principles. Although the American companies employ less than 2 percent of the South African workforce (and less than 1 percent of black workers), the Principles are already impacting the lives of hundreds of thousands of workers, and it can be expected to be in the millions. It is also the aim of the Principles to help the poor and the masses outside the workplace and to assist them at the "grass roots."

In addition, the American companies have shown some important results in measurable substance. According to information received from Arthur D. Little reports, as of October 1979, more than 75 percent of signatory companies had fully desegregated their workplaces and facilities. Walls have been torn out, and new facilities have been constructed to end segregation, in spite of laws that said it could not be done, and many companies were moving towards the implementation of the other objectives and goals of the Principles, such as equal pay for equal work and the upgrading of blacks and other nonwhites to supervisory and other jobs.

A further interim report of June 1980 has shown hopeful progress being made in other areas to improve conditions of life outside the workplace, particularly in education. A paramount aim of the American Principles is the improvement of education. It is believed that the development of an educational infrastructure is essential for the future of the black and nonwhite population and, whatever happens in South Africa, the people will need to be educated. The American companies are proceeding in this regard with timetables and goals. Already, hundreds of scholarships have been given, and there will be thousands; schools are being adopted, and there will be hundreds; literacy programs have been initiated, and they will reach hundreds of thousands. Management training programs have been started, and they will train tens of thousands; skills training programs and technical schools have been opened and are being developed, and there will be scores of them, reaching tens of thousands of students.

Some evidences of educational benefits as of April 1, 1980, as a direct result of the Principles by American signatory companies are as follows:

1. The number of scholarships provided for blacks and other nonwhites: 655 in universities in South Africa and overseas, with a projected goal of 1,000 by the end of 1980 and 5,000 by the end of 1984.

2. Adopt-a-school programs (companies sponsoring elementary and secondary schools as *interim efforts* only until essential and nonsegregated equality of educational opportunities is available for all): 70 schools now adopted, serving 50,000, with a projected goal of 100,000 by the end of 1980 and serving at least 1,000,000 by 1984.

3. Company teaching-staff contribution of hours to job training programs: 70,000 hours, with a projected goal of 200,000 hours by the end of 1980 and in the millions by 1984.

4. Management training for blacks and other nonwhites: presently 1,000 in professional, supervisory, and managerial training, with a projected goal of 1,500 by the end of 1980 and tens of thousands by 1984.

5. Skills training programs (in-house and external): 7,000 presently enrolled (4,000 being technicians and artisans), with a projected goal of 10,000 by the end of 1980 and 100,000 by 1984.

The interim report cited also showed increasing efforts by companies in the improvement of housing, health benefits, and health-care services; black and nonwhite business development; and the initiation of other kinds community and human development programs.

Whatever might be said, it is clear that there has been some movement and some progress in South Africa as a result of the Principles. Therefore, I am encouraged but still very much dissatisfied because in relation to the need, it has all fallen far, far short of my desires and progress is far, far too slow. Conditions in South Africa are of such that the greatest urgency is required if the Principles and codes are to be effective enough to meet the needs at hand. Although there has been movement, the companies are not moving fast enough; in spite of the positive things that have been happening, the companies, over-all, simply are moving too slow. The companies must be pushed more, for greater results. They are moving at the pace of a possum, when they should be moving at the speed of a hare. The companies are like a possum crossing a road, "taking their own good time." This includes American companies and other companies of the world as well.

To be sure, I am pleased by the leadership role the American companies have taken thus far in this progress, and I am pleased the Principles have been an important catalyst for change, and I am pleased for the recognition they have received, but I am far, far from being satisfied. They must do more to end discrimination, upgrade their workers, and promote equal opportunities outside the workplace. I acknowledge that some American companies are trying hard and doing encouraging things, but overall American companies must do more, and they must do them faster.

So, I will be returning to America and turning screws, more and more. I will be pushing all the companies, harder and harder to implement the Principles faster and faster, because the needs of black people in South Africa today are beyond description, and massive efforts are needed to eliminate their problems and to help them get rid of their oppression. Most whites don't know what is going on where the black people and nonwhites live. Most of you live in your modern protected cities, and you never see where the people live. It is beyond description, and their oppression and humiliation are constant: bannings, beatings, jailings, exiles, suppressions, killings. And any American companies that do not do their part to improve those conditions and to help alleviate that oppression simply have no moral justification for remaining in this country, and as far as I am concerned, they should pick up, pack up, and get out.

So, I will be supporting selective divestments against American companies that do not cooperate with the Principles and who fail to favorably comply with their implementation. I will, also, be "calling for" and urging strong United States government action against them, including tax penalties, sanctions, and the loss of government contracts. And, if change still does not come fast enough, I will consider stronger measures, including total divestment and, ultimately, a total embargo on all American exports and imports to and from South Africa.

In the past, companies have made excessive profits off of cheap labor, lack of workers' rights, and segregated employment practices. We are just not going to stand for it anymore. So...I will be doing all I can to get the American companies to do more and to move faster to help in a definite way to improve the conditions of black and other nonwhites here. And, let it be heard in the corporate boardrooms of America that either their affiliates in South Africa must shape up, or they should ship out. If there has ever been any question in any of your minds about my independence, you can forget about it now. I am here to help black people and to help end this terrible system of apartheid. I may fail — but the world will know I tried! What you see is what you have, and no one tells me what to do...no congressmen, no group of companies, no one but God...and my wife!

And I am, also, particularly concerned about the efforts of European companies and other companies in complying with their fair-employment codes and promoting equal opportunity outside of their plants and businesses. European companies and other companies are lagging far behind the American companies. More *pressure, pressure, pressure,* must be put on them, too, for results.

Several years ago, when I first initiated the Principles, I made a trip to Europe to secure cooperation and participation of European companies behind the Principles. I was told they preferred to develop a code of their own. Later, the European Economic Code for South Africa was initiated. I was encouraged by this development and hoped that the companies from these countries would back up their codes because we are aware that 65 percent of foreign investment in South Africa is in European-based companies. Since then, I have been watchful for results, and I have been deeply concerned, distressed, and disappointed by the caution of their efforts. Out of prudence, I will not speak as sharply to them as I can and do of the American companies, but the European companies will have to become more vigorous behind their codes in South Africa and stop playing games with their codes, as must, also, companies from other nations with great influence in South Africa, as the Japanese, who have been far too silent on these matters. The Japanese and others are making money out of Africa. They ought to do more to change the conditions! Much, much more is required of all. Companies of the world simply are not doing enough.

And place not all the blame on the South African plant manager, or even altogether with the South African government, but also with the home offices where the decisions are made. It is time the home offices of multinationals took hold of their responsibilities in South Africa and make the decisions and the resources available to get a job done! Frankly, I have found there is more desire to improve conditions among some South African businessmen than among the foreigners.

Now, I am aware the companies cannot solve all the problems in South Africa by themselves. It is a mistake to think they can. The problems here are far too deep and complex for that. In order to end racial discrimination in South Africa, help is needed from many fronts: from churches, unions, schools, governments, the United Nations, and world public opinion, along with the companies. But companies have a major role to play because they have been among the chief beneficiaries of an unjust system, and they should be required to the utmost of their capabilities to help improve the conditions of the people and to help change that system.

It is my hope that the interested public in these European and other nations with interest in South Africa will use their investments and their consumer power and their influence with their governments to press these companies towards greater efforts. All companies should be required to implement their codes and to report their progress and be monitored, and there should be sanctions and penalties against them if they fail to do so. If they do not comply, I will publish the names of the defaulters.

The Principles and the codes were never intended, as far as I am concerned, to *appease* conditions, but they were meant to *change* conditions; some might have thought they were meant "to appease" and to provide a cover for the companies to hide behind, but No! No! They were not meant to appease or to cover up. They were meant to help change the discriminatory conditions here; otherwise, as far as I am concerned, they lose their purpose. If the companies of the world, with their Principles and their codes, fail to make a greater thrust inside and outside the workplace soon, and if they fail to use their power and influence to help persuade the South African government to end its racial and discriminatory laws soon, then we will have missed the mark, and we can all forget about our peaceful solutions. Time for peaceful change is running out.

In Europe, and elsewhere, the voices of protest against racial injustice have been muted. Let them be heard again. Where are the liberal churches? Where are they? Let them be heard again. Let them be heard from London; let them be heard from Paris; let them be heard from Milan; let them be heard from Berlin, Stockholm, Tokyo...let them be heard again. Where are you, Geneva, with your high-sounding platitudes on freedom? Where is the world? There is a tragedy here. Where are you?

I am making an appeal today to companies of the world to use their power and influence to help end racial discrimination in South Africa and to help end apartheid. I ask the companies of the world to stop using the Principles and codes as a camouflage and to realize they can no longer "do business as usual" in South Africa. I ask the companies of the world to demonstrate their commitment to change. You can, if you will, along with other thrusts help turn this system around.

Let the companies of the world in South Africa agree that within this next year every company and business in South Africa will take down all racial signs and end all racial segregation and discrimination in the workplace.

Let the companies of the world in South Africa agree that within this next year a plan of equal pay for equal work will be developed, and an action program, beginning now, for the upgrading of black and other nonwhite workers, be achieved so blacks won't all be at the bottom, but they will begin moving to the top. And don't say they are not qualified. They are as qualified as some of the white workers you have moving up. Clear the way and give them a chance, and in your plans work towards an adequate living wage for every worker.

Let the companies of the world in South Africa agree to face up to one of their greatest challenges and to insure the rights of black workers to association, to organize or belong to the union of their choice. Also, give them the right to be represented in collective bargaining. One of the greatest hopes for a peaceful solution in South Africa is cooperation "with" and "equality" of opportunity and benefits "for" the black and nonwhite workers. I implore you, don't suppress the workers. Let them organize if they choose, and work with them. To do less will be counterproductive. There has been more labor unrest in recent months by black workers in South Africa than since 1973. Give the workers their legal opportunity and rights to express themselves; otherwise, you invite expanding disruptions.

And with respect to the Principles, let it be clarified that when it says "to acknowledge, generally, the right of black workers to form their own union or be represented by trade unions, where trade unions already exist," it means if workers choose to organize, American signatory companies should recognize any representative registered or unregistered trade unions and should work with them to help improve the lot of the workers. It has been indicated to me that as a result of the Principles, something new is happening in South Africa. There has developed a "new workers' awareness" throughout the nation. Do not victimize those who are trying to organize. Work with them to your mutual advantage and give the black workers a bigger piece of the pie.

Also, let companies of the world agree to begin to expand their efforts outside the workplace, as described in statement 6 of the Principles. Let the companies of the world agree, beginning now, to assist in the initiation and the support of massive educational programs that will lead to the ending of illiteracy throughout South Africa and to the equalization of standards of education for every school and every child in the nation.

Let the companies of the world agree, beginning now, to assist with the development of training centers that will teach thousands and thousands of nonwhite youth with technical skills, as quickly as possible, and reach millions by the end of the decade.

Let the centers be planned and designed to meet the needs of unemployed and unskilled youth on an expansive scale — youth who are frustrated because they are idle, frustrated because they are neglected, frustrated because of discrimination and segregation — remember "frustration breeds destruction."

Let the centers be open to all, with the fullest support of the companies: their facilities, equipment, instructors, curriculum development, and operation funds.

Let the training be shaped to meet the needs of the trainee, with heavy emphasis on development of confidence, attitude, work habits, basic communication and computation and practical skills, that can help youngsters get a job or make a job for themselves: bricklaying, electrician, carpenter, plumber, automobile mechanic, radio and television technician, appliance repair, typist, keypunch operator, gardener, mechanical farming, electronic assembler, power machine operator, tile and carpet layer, medical assistants, and on and on. Begin with a few of these centers and develop them by the hundreds.

And in these centers teach the blacks and other nonwhites self-confidence. For three hundred years their self-confidence has been taken away from them with teachings of white superiority. But teach these black young people to believe in themselves and what they are capable of becoming (and give them equality), and they will help build this nation into one of the greatest for its size on this earth.

And let the companies of the world agree, beginning now, to set individual company goals in every community where their businesses operate, to assist in the development of health facilities, electrification projects, housing programs, and the array of needs that have grown and festered through generations and generations of continuous neglect.

And let each of the companies of the world agree individually, beginning now, to assist with the development of one or two or more nonwhite businesses they can use as suppliers or deliverers of services; let the companies assist in management support, technical know-how, loans, and financial aid, thereby strengthening and developing businesses within several years, by the thousands, with the expectation of some developing into major enterprises: shopping centers, department stores, factories, mines, banks, etc. The need for black and nonwhite economic empowerment in South Africa is critical, and the need for business know-how, urgent — particularly in black communities where up to 90 percent of all black income is spent in all-white areas and with all-white merchants.

Let the companies work in cooperation with the national African Chamber of Commerce and qualified multiracial educational institutions and management-training and business-support organizations.

And in all things attempted, let the companies of the world remember that a significant involvement of blacks must be emphasized in everything tried in South Africa; otherwise, it will surely fail. In this respect, the white attitudes must be changed. The attitudes must be changed that blacks cannot measure up to whites on committees and in organizations or in top jobs. Give them a chance; they will measure up. Put them into every committee or program that is organized. Open the door. Let my people in. They will measure up.

The kinds of things I have mentioned today will be costly to the companies, amounting to billions of rand in new programs and tens of billions of new wages in this decade, but it is a cost that will have to be paid if there is any chance at all for a peaceful solution to the racial problems here. And it is time the companies begin to put back into the lives of the people a portion of what they have taken out. There is nothing stopping the companies from doing these things. The companies of the world can make a coordinated thrust to see community improvement occur in urban and rural areas for blacks and others throughout this nation. And such a coordinated effort should be planned for as quickly as possible to set deadlines for the accomplishing of goals and to develop an international plan for monitoring. And it is my belief that if the companies of the world do not begin to mount these kinds of efforts in a coordinated thrust, inside and outside the workplace, of the kind and magnitude described here, the Principles and codes should be reassessed as to their value in helping to bring about desirable change in South Africa.

In addition, someone must speak up for the political rights of the people. Although there has been some limited progress in the economic sphere here in South Africa, there has yet to be realization of blacks participating in the political process of the South African nation. The true extent of progress in South Africa must be measured in terms of the full acceptance of blacks in any system of a political nature. Blacks must fully participate in the system, both economically and politically, or all other efforts fall short.

It is my hope there will develop a moral imperative within South Africa, among the forces of goodwill, for the ending of all racial laws and for the full inclusion of blacks in the political process of the country. This moral push must come. It must come from the churches; it must come from the white middle class; it must come from the students at this point of the wedge; and if they want to save their country, they must speak out, speak out, speak out, for the full political inclusion of blacks and nonwhites in the primary government process and for the end of separate development. Separate development is at the core of the South African problem. There can be no fundamental progress until separate development is ended. The elimination of so-called homelands is mandatory for a just and peaceful solution to the problems of South Africa. Deal with separate development, and solve the problem; evade it, and with all other improvements, the main problem of South Africa will still exist. The Principles can help put a crack in the wall. *But the wall must come down.*

And may the day come when chief executive officers from various nations, representative of the multinational companies of the world, will call on Pretoria and request an end to race discrimination, separate development, and the exclusion of blacks from the governmental process. For if the businesses of the world speak, the government will listen. The task ahead seems so great, but it can — and it must — be accomplished.

There are those who have come to the Republic of South Africa and have returned to America to declare there is no hope, that there is no way of escaping violence, bloodshed, warfare: a revolution in which a military revolt destroys thousands of lives and those who try to put down the revolt destroy lives. They say, "Sullivan, your idea is a good one, but it is too late. The power structure in South Africa will only eliminate apartheid over millions of dead bodies." To them I say, "Where there is life, there is hope." We must try. I have come to look and to see for myself; I have come to listen and to hear for myself. I say every possible effort must be made to turn around this trend to destruction. Every human effort possible must be made to demonstrate the historical necessity to eliminate apartheid without a racial war, which would engulf the entire Third World and, eventually, possibly the entire world. Every effort must be made by governments, by businesses, by religious leaders, by educators, by labor leaders, by grassroots community workers, in an age of nuclear annihilation, to win the minds of men and women among the oppressed and the oppressors, to work together, and, in spite of the doubts, to find a way. And that is what, with the help of God, I am trying to do — to find a way out. We must try.

Here I acknowledge and give a salute to the most courageous people in the world today: the black and nonwhite men and women of the Republic of South Africa. I admire your great fortitude and ask you to hold on a while longer because God is not dead and "the morning cometh." I acknowledge, too, your great leadership. The black leaders of South Africa I have met are among the most courageous and able I have seen anywhere in the world. To blacks I say, "Develop more of them and follow them." And to the white community I say, "Listen to them," because one of the greatest hopes for peaceful change in South Africa is for the white leadership to recognize the validity of the emerging black leadership and to deal with them on an equal basis.

And to my black and nonwhite brothers and sisters I make this special appeal: Do not permit the divisive forces and influences to divide you. People will divide you if they can and pit you against each other, tribe against tribe, leader against leader, spokesman against spokesman. They will divide you and control you. Do not let it happen to you. Have your different points of views and strategies, as do other people, but when it comes to the common good of the black and nonwhite masses of your nation...be together; be together; be together.

And use the power that you have. I know the system has taken away most of your power — but use the power that you have. Use your brainpower: do all that you can to further the preparation of your people. For as long as your enemy can keep you a slave in your mind, you will be a slave forever. So continue, however you can, to protest your inferior schools, and stand up for better and equal education because education is the key to your progress. And desegregation, without education, is more frustration.

And use your faith power. Remember that God still lives and he has not left you alone.

Use your purchasing power. Learn how to put your purchasing power together and use it. Among blacks and coloreds and Asians there is more than 10 billion rand in annual purchasing power, one-third of the annual wage income of the nation. Learn how to use it in the opening of jobs and in the breaking down of racial barriers, and it will be more powerful than you could ever believe.

Use your power of self-help. God helps those who help themselves. Use your resources to develop programs of self-help: self-help cooperatives, self-help credit unions, self-help buying clubs, self-help, self-help, self-help. You help yourselves — and you will be surprised at what you will be able to do. And I, and others like me, will support you on the other side.

Black and other nonwhite ministers, labor leaders, community workers, youth leaders in the forefront of a new South Africa, you are a great and brave people: I salute you.

As I look at your country, the promise for what you can be is so great. The Republic of South Africa has been blessed as no other place in the world with an abundance of natural resources. South Africa can be an economic and multiracial paradise...in which all will prosper. Share your benefits with all your people. There is more than enough for everyone. I have noticed commission recommendations; I have noticed statements regarding the importance of changes. There is a glance by your authorities in a different direction. I hope this glance can be translated into meaningful movement. Your nonwhite population comprises five-sixths of your people: make them five-sixths of your nation's progress, or they will become five-sixths of your nation's destruction. Join together in your nation's progress.

As I near the end of this lecture, I want to tell you of my personal position, beyond the Principles, concerning bank loans to your government and new investments so you will understand fully where I stand on these matters today, regarding bank loans: Until apartheid has ended and there is clear, tangible evidence and demonstration thereof, no bank in the United States shall make any further loans to the South African government or its agencies and will give consideration only to specific, privately sponsored projects or programs, developed in cooperation with blacks and other nonwhites, which contribute to their social and economic advancement and equality and that do not support apartheid.

And it should be known that when I speak of the ending of apartheid in the bank statement and "clear, tangible evidence and demonstration thereof," I mean such things as the ending of the passbook system, the end to racially motivated banning and detentions, the rights of blacks to buy and own property anywhere in the nation, the ending of so-called independent homelands, equal protection under the law, and full citizenship rights and full political participation for blacks and other nonwhites equal to that of all other citizens in the Republic of South Africa. I will be pursuing support for this position or its equivalent throughout America, with the help of thousands of churches and bank depositors.

And regarding "new investments," I am opposed to new investments, except for retooling to remain competitive or for programs and projects that promote equality and improved social conditions for the nonwhite population until there are concrete evidences that apartheid is ending, including official meetings of white government leaders with black and other nonwhite leaders, such as a national convention, and a timetable with "common agreement" for full inclusion of blacks and other nonwhites equally in the economic, social, and political life of the country. At such a meeting or national convention, there should be real spokesmen for the people within the nation, urban and rural, and leaders like those in exile, banned, and like Nelson Mandela. Nelson Mandela must be freed!

There is a question as to the extent continued investments in a racially segregated society such as South Africa will help the masses. A full investment tide may indeed lift all the boats, but it does not help those who have no boats to sail. So continued investments might even serve to create a wider economic disparity between blacks and whites. And remember that for me, economic persuasions, reason, and my faith in God are the only weapons I have to use, and I intend to use them to the greatest extent of my ability.

In conclusion: An addendum about the importance of efforts of companies in South Africa as they relate to the future of the free enterprise system. I believe that in the Republic of South Africa, to a large measure, the free enterprise system today is on trial. I think that the survival of free enterprise will be determined by the extent to which companies from the Western world, and other areas, are willing to exert their influence to help change conditions in South Africa and Third World nations.

Recent developments have demonstrated to all that rising tides of discontent among the disadvantaged can change the course and the character of economic, social, and political systems. Historically, we know the revolutions that have shaken the world have come from lack of economic and political equality for the masses and lack of justice for the disadvantaged. Even today, the free enterprise system and the multinational corporations are being regarded by the disadvantaged of the world as dispassionate and unconcerned with the needs of the poor so long as they make their profits. And, as I see it, multinational corporations have, historically, been unresponsive to the needs of the poor, and for the most part, they are still so today. They have disregarded the human and social needs in the communities and environments where their plants and businesses exist. The great majority of the companies have been more interested in the bottom line than in helping people out of breadlines.

Within Third World nations, often referred to as developing countries, the free enterprise system and multinational corporations are regarded as enemies of the people and obstacles to social and economic progress. This need not be the case. The multinational corporations, companies, and businesses have the resources and capabilities to improve the quality of life for millions of people and to play a vital role in upgrading the social and economic lives of individuals, wherever they exist. The Principles should be applied throughout the Third World. The current negative view of multinational corporations and Western companies and businesses is pervasive among the poor and must be changed if the free enterprise system is to survive.

The Republic of South Africa provides the setting where companies can make significant progress in answering their critics by demonstrating clear and humanistic concern for the poor and the unemployed. They can use their vast powers and massive resources to help millions of people who have been cut off from opportunities to gain equality and equitable benefits from their labors and a better way of life. It is apparent that such direction is overdue and needed.

America, as the rest of the Western world, has a great deal to learn in this direction. The following comment appeared in an editorial in one of our great American financial journals, not long ago:

> It seems to us that the policy of American businesses makes little difference in South Africa, one way or another...most United States businesses in South Africa are expounding the sensible view that we provide goods and services to our customers, and profits to our investors; we obey the local laws and try not to do anything beastly, and politics is the politicians' business.[1]

It is this kind of view that must be proven wrong and dispelled because providing goods and services to customers and profits to investors might, unfortunately, have been considered sensible at one time, but not now. And observing local laws and trying not to do anything beastly is a day long gone. Today, humanistic interest had better be the concern of companies if, under the banner of free enterprise, they expect to survive. The greatest enemy of capitalism is not communism but the selfishness and lack of humanity of capitalism.

The challenges of Sharpsville, Soweto, "Crossroads," the death of Steve Biko, the continuing bombings and bannings and jailings of the people, all rise before us to be met. The Principles, their guidelines and continuing evolvement, and the codes are attempts, along with other thrusts, that are necessary to meet this challenge. Perhaps we did start too late in this effort, but I still believe if we vigorously pursue, to the utmost, the implementation of the amplified Sullivan Principles and push to the fullest for the elimination of all vestiges of discrimination in company operations, and if American and other businesses from around the world will work to alleviate the plight and the terrible conditions not only in the workplace but also outside the workplace, in communities and areas where companies and their plants exist, and if companies will be willing to be voluntarily monitored on-site and take a stand against injustice and apartheid — I believe that the free enterprise system can and will find a bright new day in the world because it chose, in addition to making profits, to stand up for what was right and to serve the needs of disadvantaged people.

Just before the turn of the nineteenth century, W. E. B. Du Bois, a great black scholar and philosopher, warned, "The problem of the Twentieth Century is the problem of the color line — the relation of the darker to the lighter races of men in Asia and Africa."[2] Here in South Africa, today that problem is seen at its apex. If it can be solved here, it can be solved anywhere.

For the sake of South Africa...

For the sake of all your people...

For the sake of the world.... Let's all work to solve it.

That, by the grace of God, there might be found, in spite of the odds, a peaceful alternative to warfare in South Africa.

It can...it must be done.

South Africa, my black and white and other nonwhite brothers and sisters, may God Almighty bless you on the way and help you all in this struggle for freedom. Take each other's hands, and help build the new South Africa together, for everyone.

Thank you very much.

Notes

1. *Wall Street Journal*, 18 August 1978.

2. W. E. B. Du Bois, *Souls of Black Folk: Essays and Sketches* (Chicago: A. C. McClung, 1903).

Appendix C

Sullivan Plan for the Development of Sub-Saharan Africa (1996–2016)

Introduction

With a population of 600 million people and the expectation of an increase to a billion people by the first quarter of the twenty-first century, sub-Saharan Africa is the most neglected and forgotten part of the world. Either sub-Saharan Africa finds new ways to effectively deal with the mounting economic, social, and political problems, or the entire region will find itself more and more engulfed with increasing difficulties and stressed by mounting external debt, deteriorating educational systems, declining agricultural productivity, devastating political instability, rising unemployment, widespread abject poverty, recurrent hunger, spreading diseases, an increasing rural-urban migration, and ethnic armed conflicts. Without urgent and far-ranging solutions, any hopeful prospects for the future of sub-Saharan African countries are dim.

Living conditions of the majority of people in the region are unacceptable. Today, in sub-Saharan Africa, there is less funding to help the poor nations than what existed yesterday. Radical actions and solutions to African problems are required at all levels within and among nations before situations get massively and uncontrollably out of hand. Generally, most of the world does not care about Africa except when atrocities are reported, and even then help is fleeting. More and more, sub-Saharan Africa is left on its own to seek and find its own solutions. Great powers of the world like the United States and other former colonial powers such as France, England, Portugal, Germany, and Belgium can no longer be looked to by sub-Saharan Africa for foreign assistance except for emergency and humanitarian needs. The

The plan was written by Dr. Leon Sullivan, with the assistance of researchers for figures and data, in 1987–88.

spread of Communism that caused the Western powers and the Soviet Union to be interested in sub-Saharan Africa no longer exists. When the Berlin Wall fell, support for sub-Saharan Africa fell with it.

Black Africa must find new, reliable, and sustainable ways to strengthen itself, nation by nation and region by region, with any help it can get from dependable friends and nations and with the effective use of widespread economic and educational self-help. While still some support, although marginal, can be expected from the United States and other Western powers, a program on a great and monumental scale must be developed by sub-Saharan African leadership in cooperation and concurrence with others to strengthen sub-Saharan Africa's position and role in the world.

A broad and realistic plan is necessary on an unprecedented scale to economically, socially, and democratically position the region to become competitive with the rest of the world in the twenty-first century. What is needed for sub-Saharan Africa, therefore, is a sort of expanded Marshall Plan, which with financial assistance from the United States encouraged European nations after World War II to work together for their economic strength and recovery.

In June 1947, following the devastating war that ended in the death of more than fifty-eight million people, and which left one-half of Europe in shambles, the United States agreed to aid Western Europe if the countries would meet to decide what was needed. The original name of the plan was the European Recovery Program. It was later called the Marshall Plan because the idea for broad assistance to Western Europe was suggested in a Harvard commencement address by Secretary of State George C. Marshall. The major intent of the program was not only to assist with the reconstruction of Europe for economic and humanitarian reasons but primarily to stop the spread of Communism into Western Europe.

The plan essentially comprised grants and loans primarily from the United States along with equal utilization of accumulated local currencies from Germany, France, Poland, and other affected countries. Seventeen European nations benefited from the plan, and the United States spent $16 billion (the modern equivalent of $150 billion) in food, machinery, and other products to strengthen Europe. This amount was matched by participating European nations in local currencies that had lost their monetary value because of the war. Also, extensive beneficial use of the skills and labor of the people of the countries was widely brought into play. The program ended in 1952, and as a result of the recovery efforts, within four years Western Europe was on the way to economic recovery.

By contrast, fifty years after World War II and followed by economic recovery in Western Europe, millions of African children are dying of malnutrition, lack of adequate health care, and widespread preventable diseases. For example, the World Health Organization (WHO) has estimated the infant death rate in sub-Saharan Africa to be more than 700 deaths for every 100,000 live births, while it varies from 5 to 30 per 100,000 in developed countries. Some of the main causes of the high infant mortality rate in sub-Saharan Africa are infectious diseases, malnutrition, and the lack of clean drinking water. According to one author, the bombing of Hiroshima and Nagasaki directly killed approximately one hundred thousand persons. Nuclear weapons have not been exploded in anger since August 1945. Unfortunately, today the effects of poverty, preventable diseases, and hunger kill an average of 12.9 million Third World children every year. Poverty, therefore, kills Third World children at the rate of a Hiroshima and Nagasaki bombing every three days. In other words, the world at peace is suffering a high rate of child mortality that exceeds the death rate of World War II. Poverty has killed nearly seventy million Third World children in five and a half years, compared to fifty-eight million dead in World War II, and sub-Saharan Africa is the most severely affected region in the world.

This example is another way of showing that human needs in sub-Saharan Africa today are greater than those in Europe before reconstruction. The main contributing factors to the lack of basic human needs in sub-Saharan Africa are the lack of interest and support from foreign powers; the nonexistent educational, physical, and political infrastructure; and a lack of effective debt relief, education, skills, and business development, which make whatever efforts attempted in the development of sub-Saharan Africa far more difficult than in Western Europe.

The development of sub-Saharan Africa requires a broad scale of assistance with solidarity improvements, high self-esteem, self-help efforts, effective debt relief programs, educational development programs, an increase in primary health care, farm production, and industrialization, and the creation of jobs to an extent never before attempted in African history. Urgent solutions must be found to such problems as external debt burden, unchecked population growth, abject poverty, unemployment, illiteracy, diseases such as HIV/AIDS, and ethnic conflicts.

Perhaps more than any private effort existing today, the African–African American summit movement presents a singular opportunity to pragmatically and effectively assist sub-Saharan Africa in a long-term and sustainable way. The Declaration of Principles and Actions adopted at the Dakar Summit in May 1995 calls for the continuation of African debt relief efforts, the establishment of agro-financial institutions, the restoration of internal and external balance of trade, a recommitment to good governance and democracy, an exchange of teachers and students between educational institutions in the United States and Africa, the containment of widespread diseases and rapid population growth, and the encouragement of African Americans and American businesses to collaborate in the creation of an enabling environment to encourage investment, trade, and industrialization in sub-Saharan Africa. Additionally, participants at the Libreville and Dakar Summits supported a strategy to conduct a massive campaign to control and eradicate river blindness in sub-Saharan Africa by the year 2016.

This Sullivan Plan is extracted from previous ideas, along with the practical implementation of the Declarations of Principles and Actions and the Reports and Recommendations from the Abidjan (1991), Libreville (1993), and Dakar (1995) Summits, which are directed towards the economic, social, and political advancement of sub-Saharan Africa. The plan aspires to accomplish the following objectives before the year 2016:

- to encourage self-reliance through self-help efforts,

- to develop a core of African professionals who can act as agents for change within their countries and the region,

- to strengthen democratic reforms and the nation-building process,

- to promote a more open environment for trade and investments,

- to provide the educational opportunities and technical support to African individuals that will enhance the effectiveness of private and public sector institutions and promote the democratic process,

- to strengthen the educational capacities and alleviate the deterioration of formal educational systems (particularly the shortage of trained teachers and the lack of instructional facilities) in colleges and universities in sub-Saharan Africa,

- to provide literacy training tied to health care to at least twenty million nonliterate adults and school dropouts,

- to help with the containment of HIV/AIDS,

- to provide agricultural training to two million low-income farmers,

- to provide nonagricultural skills training to six million unemployed and underemployed workers,

- to raise the status of women across sub-Saharan Africa.

In addition, the Sullivan Plan will accomplish these objectives by building high self-esteem among African youth, relieving the external debt burden, alleviating the educational crisis, improving health-care facilities and services, reducing the high population growth rate, increasing food production, promoting business and industries, and promoting democracy in African countries.

This plan covers a fifteen-year period (1996–2011) at an estimated total cost of $500 billion in hard local currencies for program support: schools, teachers, hospitals, clinics, agricultural projects, skills training centers, and so on. Although the initiatives discussed in this plan can be viewed separately, they are part of the same mission and are financially intertwined. They are all in keeping with Sullivan's pragmatic philosophy and efforts to alleviate poverty through sustainable development in sub-Saharan Africa. Each component of this plan will serve to support the socioeconomic and political objectives already identified by African governments. The initiatives of other developmental organizations, such as the World Bank's initiatives for capacity building and sustainable development in sub-Saharan Africa, are also taken into consideration. A brief description of the Sullivan Plan now follows.

Building High Self-Esteem

Statement of the Problem

One of the major elements of need in the development process of sub-Saharan Africa is the promotion of self-esteem and the belief in the capabilities of individuals. Self-esteem is feeling good about yourself:

> These feelings are based on the belief that you are an individual of worth, with talents, skills and abilities of which you have taken advantage. Most individuals with a healthy self-esteem affirm their culture

and feel that they are productive and valued. Their source of strength lies within themselves, and they are not dependent upon how others view them for their own personal validation. If you do not feel valued, it will be evident in your behavior; how you walk and talk and how you treat yourself and others.[1]

No development plans can succeed without the widespread efforts to build high self-esteem among Africans and people of African descent.

Today, most blacks in Africa and in the African diaspora still hold themselves in low self-esteem due to many decades of cultural imperialism under the dominant culture of Western Europe. This cultural imperialism has been reinforced by many years of slavery, colonization, economic exploitation, negative stereotypes, racial discrimination, apartheid policies, and all forms of prejudice against Africans and Africans in the diaspora. Exacerbated by the negative African image portrayed by the media in the international community, black Africans are usually the most negatively evaluated group of people, which puts them at the bottom of the social, cultural, economic, and power hierarchy in the world.

For many centuries, African civilizations were distorted, disfigured, and destroyed in order to aid acculturation. Africans and people of African descent are susceptible to various negative stereotypes of barbarism and human degradation. To some racist individuals and groups, Africa was and is still regarded and described as a "dark continent" inhabited by "niggers," "jungle bunnies," and peoples without history.[2] Black Africa was once regarded as the haunt of savages, the white man's grave, a continent riddled with suspicions and superstitions, full of fanaticism, destined for contempt, and weighed down by the curse of God.[3] In 1884, at the Berlin Conference in Germany, Africa was subsequently partitioned by the colonial powers and brutally exploited for a century.

For many decades in this century, Africans and Africans in the diaspora were barred from voting; their social status was degraded; they were denied eligibility for citizenship, denied the opportunity to hold public offices, barred from participating in the military, legally prevented from residing and working wherever they wanted, and disallowed from marrying whomever they wanted; and their children were prevented from attending whatever schools they liked. As a result, some African youth have developed an inferiority complex and low self-esteem. Many centuries of negative stereotypes have enhanced feelings of self-contempt, low self-esteem, and resignation among many Africans on the continent and in the diaspora. Many blacks, as a result, have suffered lower achievement and self-image, apathy, a poor perception of the future, and other problems due to many years of living under slavery, colonialism, oppression, and cultural and economic imperialism.[4] People who have low self-esteem have a generally negative view of themselves as well as a tendency to rate themselves negatively. All this has led many Africans and people of African descent to have the lowest prestige and self-esteem. More than five centuries of dehumanization, slavery, colonization, oppression, exploitation of human and natural resources, and other debilitations worldwide have contributed to massive rejection of human value and loss of self-pride among many black people.

Planned Strategies

Because of this psychological problem, there is a massive need for dealing with attitudes and "self-belief" among African people that must be promoted and encouraged. African youth must be taught to believe in themselves and in their abilities to improve conditions of their lives and their countries. No program or plan for the development of sub-Saharan Africa can succeed without dealing with this reality. This reality requires the creation of vast systems of educational programs to train, inform, and motivate a large number of African people toward self-improvement. The following specific programs and activities will be implemented by the Sullivan Plan to alleviate low self-esteem problems.

Educational Programs

To deal with low self-esteem problems, every use of traditional, non-traditional, and modern educational and cultural programs must be brought to bear to counter these pervasive attitudinal rejections of "self" far too prevalent among Africans and people of African descent. In this plan, special programs will be designed to reach millions of people across sub-Saharan Africa in the shortest period of time to alleviate this problem. Electronic communication and master teaching in technologies will be devised to reach thousands of people in urban and rural areas utilizing the newest methods of communication. Community-based grassroots, heritage educational methods will be used in cities and villages to promote cultivation of high self-esteem among the youth. These methods will also make extensive use of modern technologies including electronic communications systems along with traditional educational, instructional, and counseling methods, including "sit down" sessions with children and adults in day and evening sessions in every section of each country.

Deployment of Trained Teachers and Counselors

For such teaching programs to become very effective, a large, indigenously trained corps of teachers and counselors will be mobilized with broad-scale assistance through the utilization of such programs as the successful Teachers for Africa program (TFA) and the International Fellows Program (IFP) sponsored by the International Foundation for Education and Self-Help (IFESH) in the United Sates. Thousands of recruits from America as well as other parts of the world will be utilized in such a massive effort. The participating teachers and fellows will be serving as volunteers in African countries, helping to provide quality and sustainable education to the less fortunate. American teacher volunteers, particularly from the minorities, will serve as models for African students and teachers to improve their self-esteem.

Revival of African Cultures and Education

To help motivate positive resolution of low self-esteem among African youth, African cultures and traditions that have been found to be very useful in the past must be retrieved and reintroduced into African societies. African history, traditions, and civilizations must be taught in schools. African youth must be taught about African arts, music, songs, belief systems, history, accomplishments, customs, leaders, heroes, and other products of African thoughts and philosophies. African educational curricula must include all they can about the richness of Africa. African children must be taught to be aware of African contributions in science and philosophy to world development. African youth must be taught to be proud of their cultures.

Promotion of Literacy Programs

To improve self-esteem in sub-Saharan African countries, illiteracy must be eliminated. To accomplish this, appropriate education and reading of literature are critical in improving self-esteem. Reading the right literature will open new ideas, new philosophies, new perspectives, and evaluative systems that may provide new pride and high self-esteem. This plan will encourage the production of African pamphlets, literature, poetry, songs, videos, and other educational materials locally produced and made available to help both rural and urban people realize the importance of Africa's past constructive role in the world and her positive contributions to the world's civilizations. The reading of Africa's literary heritage, written by Africans and people of African descent, is capable of opening a youth's mind that had once resigned itself to inferiority and will be encouraged to greater achievements.

For this plan, widespread utilization of teaching facilities must be made available through schools, churches, homes, temporary training centers, tents, and whatever else can be devised. These innovative educational and counseling programs of extraordinary proportions will be planned and implemented over a seventeen-year period, reaching millions of people in all sub-Saharan African countries. Also, the plan will intensify use of telecommunication systems capable of reaching adults and youth by the millions in farms and cities during days and evenings.

External Debt

Statement of the Problem

One of the most pressing problems of the Third World countries today is foreign debt. In their efforts to industrialize and to provide their rapidly growing population with modern social services, many countries in sub-Saharan Africa have incurred large foreign debts. While in 1970 and 1981 sub-Saharan Africa's total official debt (excluding South Africa and Namibia) was slightly more than $5 billion and $50 billion respectively, by 1990 it had risen to nearly $140 billion (see chart 1 on the following page). Total private debt, which was zero in 1970, was more than $20 billion in 1990. With other external loans, the total indebtedness of the region was more than $171 billion by 1990. Today, all of Africa owes more than $500 billion in external debt. In fact, Africa's total debt plus the debt-service bill is virtually equal to the continent's entire annual economic output. For example, the $25 billion debt-service bill in 1990 was greater than the total aid received by Africa in 1989, which was $21 billion. However, in a comparative analysis, this amount is small compared to about $600 billion

Africa's Mounting External Debt

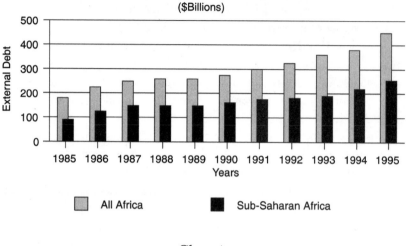

Chart 1

---

owed by Latin America. Brazil is today the leading debtor nation in the Third World, owing over $100 billion to international financial institutions. Nigeria is the most indebted country in sub-Saharan Africa with $40 billion, followed by Côte d'Ivoire's debt of about $25 billion. The main problem with sub-Saharan African debtors is their increasing inability to pay their debt.

Many factors contributed to the debt crisis in Africa. One of them is Africa's high dependence on the export of raw materials, which left sub-Saharan African economies vulnerable to the long decline of commodity prices that began in the late 1970s. The total value of sub-Saharan African agricultural exports has fallen dramatically since the 1970s. As a result, the burden of external debt has risen markedly for most countries in the region. Between 1980 and 1989, the total external debt rose from 27 percent to 97 percent of GNP and from 97 percent to 362 percent of exports (see chart 2).

Another factor contributing to the debt crisis in sub-Saharan Africa is the decline of foreign assistance from the rich countries to poor African countries. Review of literature on debt problems shows that between the period of 1984 and 1990, the flow of aid and investments from the developed countries to the developing countries,

Sub-Saharan Africa Profile

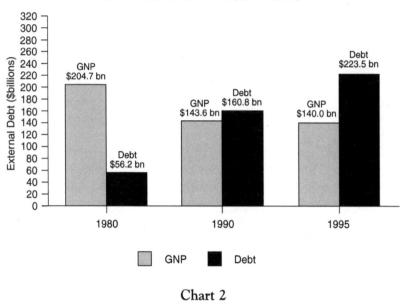

Chart 2

particularly to Africa, was reversed by the flow of interest and capital repayments by developing countries on their previously acquired debts (see chart 3). During this period of economic recession, the developing countries, particularly Africa, sustained the ailing economy of the developed countries. For example, the annual net transfer from Africa and other developing countries to developed countries, especially those in Europe, was $40 billion in 1990. In one author's estimate, this represented a transfer in real terms of about four Marshall Plans, given by the developing countries to the rich countries of the world. The Marshall Plan transferred $16 billion to Europe between 1948 and 1950.

As a result of heavy debt, most countries in sub-Saharan Africa have had to undergo major Structural Adjustment Programs (SAP). This has entailed a drastic compression of imports, sharp devaluation of national currencies, and the retrenchment of sizable portions of the large and salary-earning population. Consequently, the SAP has led to a deterioration of living conditions for most African people. It has contributed to the educational crisis, the increased unemployment rate,

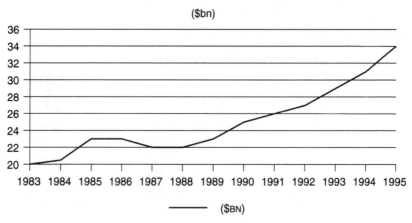

African Debt Service Payments

($bn)

1983 1984 1985 1986 1987 1988 1989 1990 1991 1992 1993 1994 1995

——— ($BN)

Source: Africa Recovery Based on World Bank data

Chart 3

and skyrocketing inflation in the prices of basic needs. It is now generally accepted in many African countries that the SAPs prescribed by the International Monetary Fund (IMF) and the World Bank are not the real solutions to the debt problems, particularly in Africa. For example, after five years of experimenting with IMF's Structural Adjustment Programs, Zambia has had to reconsider its commitments to the programs because of the adverse economic consequences on the citizenry.

Without a massive debt relief for sub-Saharan African countries, economic, social, and political development efforts for the nations are impossible. It is essential that there be a reexamination of debt policies affecting sub-Saharan African countries and the establishment of debt forgiveness programs. African leaders continue to be alarmed by the escalation of external debt resulting in the majority of the countries being unable to pay the interest or service charges, not to mention the principal loans, and thus making it impossible to provide basic services such as education, primary health care, and other vital needs to the people. As one of the leading African presidents in attendance at the First African–African American Summit

Two Scenarios of External Debt Relief

Strategies in Sub-Saharan Africa

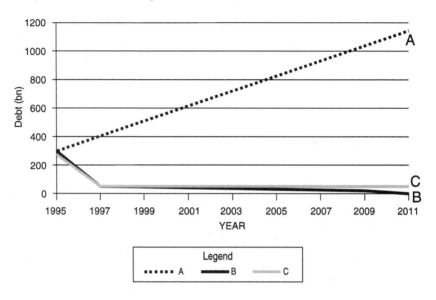

A represents: Scenario showing business as usual. African debt will rise from $300 billion in 1995 to over $1 trillion by the year 2001.

B represents: Scenario showing effective debt relief and reform programs as proposed by the Sullivan Plan. It proposes 90 percent debt conversion.

C represents: Scenario showing $30 billion repaid to the creditors over fifteen years.

Chart 4

has said, "The debt on us is like a millstone around our necks; without debt relief, most sub-Saharan African countries cannot possibly move ahead."

The estimated debt on sub-Saharan African countries today is about $300 billion and is growing in unpaid interest costs and unmet principal every day. If not removed or checked, the combined debt in the next fifteen years on sub-Saharan African countries will exceed $1 trillion (see chart 4). This is more than all the export revenues and taxes and domestic incomes of all the African nations combined. These mounting debts can never be repaid unless quick measures are taken to deal with debt problems. Most of the African countries will not be able to survive the ongoing rebellions, political chaos, and atrocities of wars in Rwanda, Somalia, Angola, Sierra Leone, Niger, Sudan, and Liberia unless something is done to support these countries economically. If Africa's external debt continues to rise as shown in scenario A in chart 4, living conditions in sub-Saharan African countries in the next twenty years will deteriorate. Much of Africa's financial resources will be diverted to pay interest on external debt. This also implies that there will be little or no financial resources left to support education, to provide primary health-care services to the needy, to provide infrastructural facilities, and to improve agriculture. Furthermore, there will be an increase in infant mortality rates and widespread political unrest on the continent. Alternatively, if urgent measures are taken to combat debt burden as proposed by the Sullivan Plan in scenario B in chart 4, then the debt will decrease in the next twenty years, which means improvement in the living conditions of the poor, in education, and in health services, a decline in infant mortality rates, less political instability, and economic growth. The pragmatic measures proposed by the Sullivan Plan to combat external debt for the next twenty years now follow.

Recovery Strategies

There is now universal agreement that urgent action needs to be taken to provide greater debt relief to African countries in light of the overwhelming constraints external debt poses on their development. Therefore, during the implementation of this plan, several strategies will be adopted to relieve Africa's external debt. Some of these strategies include the following:

Massive Campaign for Debt Cancellation

One notable feature of Africa's debt problem is its high proportion owed to multilateral institutions. This debt, which accounts for 30 percent of sub-Saharan Africa's total debt, cannot be rescheduled under current rules. The World Bank has warned that debt payments will continue to rise steeply in the 1990s and in the twenty-first century in the absence of significant debt cancellations. In the next twenty years, the Sullivan Plan will focus on the relief of external debt, which continues to pose major developmental obstacles to sub-Saharan Africa. The plan, among other things, will follow up on the successes that have already been accomplished by the African–African American summits on the cancellation of African debt. In 1991, a special meeting was convened at the United Nations and hosted by the United Nations' secretary general to deal with the African debt issue. Subsequent to consultations with the heads of state of several industrialized nations, including the United States, France, and Germany, the summit chairman and convener, the Reverend Leon Sullivan, developed a concept known as "debt relief tied to education and responsibility." As a result of this effort, and in collaboration with the Paris Club, it was announced on December 16, 1994, that over $30 billion in bilateral debt would be canceled for the poorest countries in Africa to help lift them out of poverty. According to the head of the Paris Club, this initiative will make it possible for these countries to have 60 percent of their debt written off, up from 50 percent. And with our continuing efforts, by the time of the Harare Summit in 1997, the total debt forgiveness had risen for sub-Saharan countries to $60 billion. The Sullivan Plan will continue to follow up on this new development in the next twenty years. Also, during the implementation of this plan, there will be a massive call for initiatives to help Africa resolve its external debt problems. The first five years of the implementation period will be used for getting approval and modality for debt relief for the countries of sub-Saharan Africa from the Paris Club, developed nations, the World Bank, the IMF, and the world's financial institutions.

During this period, about 90 percent (or $270 billion) of African external debt owed to multilateral and bilateral institutions and to the private sector will be asked to be forgiven, while the remaining 10 percent (or $30 billion) will remain on the books, with interest of 3 percent of the $30 billion remaining debt being converted annually into local currencies and used for education and human development. In other words, by 1998 the Sullivan Plan will aggressively persuade the Paris and London Clubs, the G-8 nations, bilateral donors such as the United States through the United States Agency for International Development (USAID), and multilateral donors such as the World Bank and the IMF to cancel up to $270 billion (90 percent) of the existing $300 billion external debt owed by sub-Saharan Africa. The remaining 10 percent ($30 billion) of the total debt will remain on the books of countries unamortized for seventeen years with interest paid annually in local currencies for education and human development.

As illustrated in chart 5, local currencies from participating African nations will be aided by grants and loans from donor countries, the World Bank, and the IMF. The Sullivan Plan will require fifteen years in order to have positive results.

To ensure the Sullivan Plan's success, African heads of state and governments will be asked to assure accountability and responsibility in the use of those funds for approved education and developmental needs and will be asked to take the lead aggressively, and with support from other summit leaders, especially the African Americans, to press for greater results of debt relief from the G-8 nations. Moreover, African governments will be encouraged to continue to broaden and deepen the necessary adjustments of their economies, for which popular participation is also needed in a democratic process of development.

Debt for Development Program

Debt for Development is an integrated program designed to address debt crisis in the Third World countries. As the name suggests, Debt for Development is about finding ways to convert debt to developmental purposes. IFESH has already proven, judging from its past experience, that the Debt for Development Program is an effective tool to reduce debt and to support human-resource development projects. This public-private sector initiative, commended by the United States Congress in 1993, is accepted by the United States banks inasmuch as it allows them to sell their debt, receive a tax credit, and remove the liability from the books. This process is especially attractive to certain private voluntary organizations (PVOs) since the debt is purchased at a discount and converted at face value, allowing the multiplier effects to be applied. Also, it is accepted by the debtor country since it is no longer obligated to use its foreign exchange hard currency to defray its indebtedness, but rather local currency over a period of years. IFESH has successfully implemented Debt for Human Development Projects in several developing countries, including Peru, Nigeria, Guinea, and Niger. Here are two models of the debt conversion programs in Peru and Nigeria:

The Peru Model: Blocked Asset Program: In 1991, American Express Bank Ltd. donated $5 million to IFESH to launch the first debt conversion program for a human-resource development program in the Republic of Peru. The Peruvian government converted the $5 million

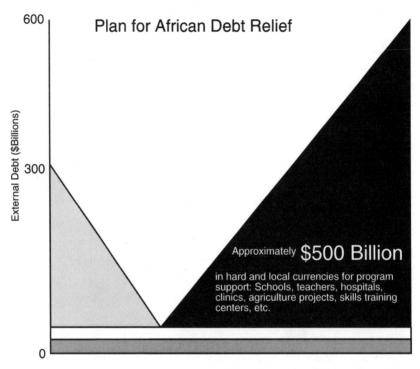

90 percent ($270bn) of the debt cancelled with 10 percent remaining on books for fifteen years.

Accumulated interest at 3 percent on remaining debt converted into local currency for education, health, and other human development purposes.

The 10 percent retained debt matched with grants and loans (new loans repaid with interest, annually, on a timely basis); also in-kind contributions and self-help after fifteen years of tax relief as described in the plan.

Retained $30 billion debt remaining on books of participating African nations, to be matched with hard currency support from loans, investments, grants, equipment, technical assistance, etc., from participating commercial institutions, banks, multinationals, and nations over a fifteen-year period, equaling $30 billion of added investment participation.

RESULTS: Will create 2 million new jobs in Africa and up to 200,000 new jobs for America, France, Germany, Japan, and other participating developing countries in needed machinery, equipment, materials, technical support, and other development requirements.

Chart 5

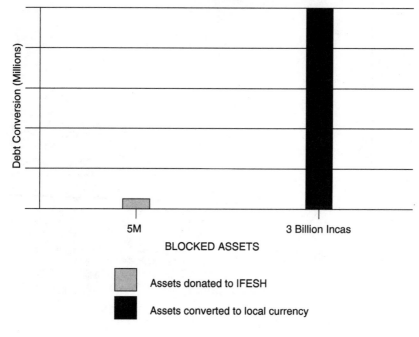

Peru Model: Blocked Asset
1991-1994

BLOCKED ASSETS

◻	Assets donated to IFESH
◼	Assets converted to local currency

Progress Results with Use of Converted Local Currency
1991–1996 (five years)

1. 20 skills training center: Training 5,000 Peruvians by the year 2000.
2. 6 work centers (factories): Employing 1,000 workers by the year 2000.
3. 4 orphanages: Accommodating 900 orphans by the year 2000.

Chart 6

in assets donated to IFESH into 3 billion incas (local currency). Since 1991, more than 3 billion incas has been paid to three local organizations in Peru for grassroots developmental programs. The organizations are (a) Makimama (Asociación Civil Makimama), (b) Foundation for the Children of Peru (Fundación por los Niños del Perú), and (c) Fe y Algería del Perú. Thousands of poor men, women, and children of Peru are now benefiting from these developmental programs. As a result of the conversion of the blocked assets and the development of these programs, it is projected that by the year 2000, about twenty skills

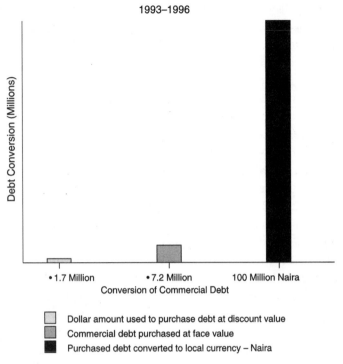

Nigerian Model: Debt for Development
1993–1996

Debt Conversion (Millions)

• 1.7 Million   • 7.2 Million   100 Million Naira
Conversion of Commercial Debt

☐ Dollar amount used to purchase debt at discount value
▨ Commercial debt purchased at face value
■ Purchased debt converted to local currency – Naira

Results

1. Developed 5 skills training centers serving 2,000 trainees per year.
2. Initiated River Blindness projects helping 150,000 beneficiaries prevent blindness.
3. In cooperation with World Bank counterpart funds dug 50,000 tubewells in Nigeria.

Chart 7

---

training centers will be established to train an additional five thousand Peruvians, and six work centers (factories) will be established, employing over one thousand workers (see the Peru Model).

The Nigerian Model: Debt for Development: In 1990, IFESH became the first American private voluntary organization to be awarded a grant from the USAID to promote and assist self-help developmental programs. Nigeria was one of several countries that participated in the program. In 1993, IFESH purchased Nigerian promissory notes with a face value of $7.2 million for $1.7 million. The $7.2 million was then converted into local currency, amounting to about 100 million naira (Nigerian local currency). Proceeds from the conversion of the promissory notes to local currency were used to fund six self-help initiatives in agricultural training, literacy training tied to health care, microenterprise, and community development programs. Specifically, proceeds from the debt conversion have (*a*) helped develop five skills training centers serving two thousand trainees per year, (*b*) initiated river blindness projects, keeping 150,000 beneficiaries from going blind, and (*c*) in conjunction with the World Bank, financed the digging of fifty thousand tube wells in northern Nigeria, which will not only be used to irrigate thousands of acres of dry farmland but also to contain the spread of the Saharan desert into the northern part of Nigeria (see the Nigerian Model). Recognizing the importance of this program and remaining conscious of the long-term effect that it will have on the economic and social development of the countries in sub-Saharan Africa, the Sullivan Plan will replicate this program in most African countries during the implementation period.

In an effort to address some of the business and economic problems in sub-Saharan Africa, the Sullivan Plan will convert $30 billion of the remaining debt on the books to local developmental purposes. Under this plan, the billions of bilateral and multilateral debt owed by African countries to the United States and European banks and companies will be purchased and converted into African local currencies for carrying out human-resource development projects. The local currency will be used primarily to support the following human-resource development projects:

- agricultural and health training projects, literacy tied to health care, and skills training projects;

- small-scale business projects to empower women and rural people;

- reduction in environmental pollution and rapid population growth;

- support of schools and other educational and literacy programs;

- containment of HIV-AIDS in sub-Saharan Africa

- in-country administrative supports for the Sullivan Plan such as stipends, salaries, and office operating expenses.

According to this plan, local currency proceeds from the debt conversion will be allocated to support developmental projects in the following areas: skills training with an emphasis on training for women in the workplace; health care with an emphasis on providing assistance to a comprehensive health program, including reproductive health and social services; agricultural training with an emphasis on increasing food productivity; basic literacy skills for adults; and microenterprise projects with an emphasis on entrepreneurial training for the rural population. These projects will be implemented by several development agencies including the Opportunities Industrialization Centers (OIC) International, AFRICARE, and effective women's, youth, and other local indigenous organizations. IFESH has successfully used the same Debt for Development Program to convert over $15 million in commercial debt from Nigeria, Guinea, Niger, and Peru to local currencies for funding developmental projects in those countries. IFESH will replicate these successful programs in many sub-Saharan countries in the next fifteen years.

Job Creation Programs

The creation of jobs for millions of unemployed people in Africa and the United States will be a major priority of the Sullivan Plan in the next twenty years. Without adequate availability of jobs for most Africans, Africans cannot realize freedom from poverty. By the year 2011, the Sullivan Plan will create two million jobs in sub-Saharan African countries. Jobs will be created in different sectors including the manufacturing, agriculture, self-employment, microenterprises, and skills training areas. Many developmental organizations that specialize in job training programs, such as the OICs located in seventeen African countries and the United States, will be asked to play a prominent role in job creation in both the United States and Africa.

To make this plan successful, vocational training programs will be designed to provide gainful employment opportunities to Africans by providing appropriate skills training, orientation, and counseling, as well as job creation, job development, and job placement for school dropouts and the disadvantaged. Most importantly, the plan will encourage job training in agricultural skills by organizing workshops and seminars on short-term and long-term bases. Thousands of new training centers will be established for upgrading skills. The plan will also encourage the development, improvement, and expansion of the existing services through staff training and expansion of facilities. The Sullivan Plan will also encourage the provision of technical, financial, and management assistance necessary to ensure that an infrastructure is developed within each program that will allow it to adjust to the changing needs of the community.

In addition to creating jobs in Africa with the hard currencies obtained from the United States and other cooperating developed nations to match local currencies for developmental projects in sub-Saharan Africa, the Sullivan Plan will be able to create over 200,000 jobs in the United States and other participating countries during its implementation period. With the provision of hard currency in forms of loans and grants to African countries coupled with local currencies, the plan will be able to create 200,000 new jobs in the United States and other countries through the export of equipment, machinery, technical support, and sales of goods to Africa. Estimated benefits for added workers' wages in the United States will total $6 billion in annual incomes from new jobs and add $120 billion in new wages for American workers during the fifteen-year plan.

Provision of Grants and Loans

Sub-Saharan African countries may still find themselves in serious economic hardship if the G-8 nations do not continue to provide them with loans and grants for developmental programs in the next twenty years. Provision of hard currencies to sub-Saharan African countries will greatly assist Africans to embark on self-help programs. The Sullivan Plan will make sure that grants and loans in a continuous assistance from the World Bank and the IMF are made available to sub-Saharan African countries during this period. The 10 percent retained debt will be matched with grants, loans, in-kind contributions, and self-help initiatives for fifteen years. New loans will be repaid annually with interest on a timely basis. The loans and grants will be used to supplement the developmental projects being carried out under the Debt for Development Program.

Education

Statement of the Problem

Scholarly studies have confirmed the significant role of education in promoting economic growth, nation building, and social change. In a study conducted by the World Bank in 1980, Dr. Norman Hicks found that education contributes to the growth of national income by improving the skills and productive capacities of the labor force.

Formal education is seen as a vital investment that guarantees individuals lifelong earnings for the enjoyment of a better standard of living. Appropriate and adequate education can, among other things, help to develop entrepreneurial talents, improve the decision-making process, and improve health. Studies have also shown that education fulfills basic human needs for acquiring knowledge, attitudes, values, and skills upon which a better life can be built. The ability to learn helps individuals adapt to social and cultural change. The educated individual has enhanced potential for participation in social and political activities. The role of education is critical in developing countries because all developmental programs and projects depend on the learned abilities of skilled workers to manage capital, administration, and technology. Unfortunately, the critical role of education as an instrument for sustainable development has not been fully realized in sub-Saharan Africa.

At the 1995 African–African American Summit in Dakar, Senegal, African heads of state, government leaders, and delegates discussed the educational crisis that exists today at the primary and secondary schools, as well as university and professional levels in sub-Saharan Africa. Due to rapid population growth, economic stagnation, and declining public expenditures on education, the majority of sub-Saharan African countries now face a shortage of trained teachers, declining funds for education, deteriorating teaching conditions at all levels, and decaying educational facilities and infrastructures.[5] Evidence of a decline in the quality of education due to overcrowded classrooms, low teachers' salaries, and a shortage of instructional materials and school facilities in most African nations has been documented.[6] And at the Harare Summit, PROSERA — the tripartite agreement between the Organization of African Unity (OAU), the United Nations Educational, Scientific, and Cultural Organization (UNESCO), and others — developed self-help initiatives with expanding schools, skills training, and learning to every summit-cooperating country in sub-Saharan Africa.

One of the major problems in sub-Saharan Africa is illiteracy. In a modern economy, basic education is a key factor for human survival. Unfortunately, some 890 million people are illiterate in the world today, and their number could exceed one billion by the year 2000.[7] The majority of Africa's poor have little or no formal education or skills to provide themselves with a livelihood. Children from poor homes usually drop out of school because their parents cannot afford to pay for their schoolbooks and uniforms, much less the school and activity fees, thus perpetuating the vicious cycle of illiteracy, under-employment, unemployment, and poverty. Furthermore, the existing traditional schools in Africa are elitist: they provide limited access to skills training in carpentry, plumbing, construction, electricity, auto mechanics, welding, fence making, and other microenterprise skills.

In most African countries, access to quality education is beyond the financial reach of the majority of poor parents and their children. Be-cause the government is the only significant support for the recurrent and capital costs of African education, the quality of education has deteriorated in the last two decades. Also, due to the economic cri-sis, most African governments are spending less and less money on education. The World Bank reports that sub-Saharan African gov-ernments spent less than \$0.60 annually per primary school pupil.[8] As a result of low expenditures on education, essential educational materials such as textbooks, visual aids, chalkboards, furniture, and toilets are either in short supply or absent altogether, especially in rural schools. The illiteracy rate among women is higher than men in most African countries. Unfortunately, illiteracy has more adverse effects on women than men in terms of the connections between poverty and a high fertility rate, a high infant mortality rate, poor health status of the family, poor income to meet basic needs, and irregular school at-tendance by children.[9] Studies have shown that households headed by uneducated women are significantly poorer than those headed by women with a college education. In a 1988 survey of 134 women con-ducted in low-income areas in Dar es Salaam, Tanzania, A. Tibaijuka found that only 7 of the 134 women had "professional" jobs. Of the women interviewed, 58 percent said that "they had been forced to reduce the number of meals from three to two per day in their house-holds and 61% indicated a reduction in protein-rich foods."[10] These women were absolutely poor because they were illiterate and had no means of support.

The biggest problem confronting African universities is a lack of adequate funding. In most African universities, 85 percent of fund-ing is provided by the government, compared to 57 percent in the United States and Britain. As a result of underfunding for higher edu-cation, most African institutions of higher learning face overcrowded academic and service facilities, deteriorating buildings and equipment,

critical shortages of funds for library acquisitions and laboratory supplies, a lack of support for research, low salaries for faculty, and
deteriorating morale.

Therefore, it is critical that attention be focused on primary,
secondary, and university educational systems that are relevant to
sustainable development in sub-Saharan Africa. Otherwise, there is a
distinct possibility that the average African will be materially worse off
in the near future than he or she is now. Sub-Saharan African nations
need international support for educational reforms and capacity-
building support for formal education and policy analysis. In an effort
to assist in the alleviation of the educational crisis, the Sullivan Plan
has identified different areas of need to upgrade and uplift African
educational systems.

Planned Strategies

During this period, the Sullivan Plan will explore several ways to
at least reduce the illiteracy rate in sub-Saharan Africa through the
establishment of learning centers, the Teachers for Africa (TFA)
program, the Schools for Africa Program, the Books for Africa Program, and the Long-Distance Learning Program. Emphasis will also
be placed on the expansion of vocational training centers. At the
primary- and secondary-school levels, this plan, through the TFA program, will encourage more teacher volunteers throughout the world to
teach in Africa. At the university level, special consideration will be
given to the expansion of research, teaching, and upgrading the skills
of the professionals; the expansion of library holdings; the provision of
laboratory equipment; and the creation of exchange programs.

Teachers for Africa Program

IFESH has successfully implemented the TFA program for five years
in many African countries including Benin, Ghana, Gabon, Gambia,
Nigeria, Côte d'Ivoire, Kenya, Ethiopia, and Zimbabwe. This program
has proven to be the most successful program for training teachers and improving the academic skills of students in sub-Saharan
Africa. It was designed to place qualified and experienced American
teacher volunteers (e.g., school administrators and college professors) in formal and informal educational institutions in sub-Saharan
African countries for one academic year to help improve these nations' educational systems. Teachers have been assigned to a variety of

educational institutions, including elementary and secondary schools, colleges and universities, technical training institutes, and government ministries. During their tenure, teachers perform various functions in their host institutions including developing improved methods for devising school curricula and syllabi revision, teacher training seminars, workshops on improving teaching methodologies, training sessions for school inspectors and master teachers, computer literacy programs, HIV/AIDS prevention education, collaborative workshops, and pedagogy training and policy revision. Teachers also perform extracurricular activities for their school in their free time, including raising funds for textbooks and school supplies, participating in school committees, organizing cultural field trips, guest lecturing at neighboring universities, and upgrading school libraries. Surveys of the alumni and current participants show that a significant number of men, women, and children are being affected outside of the classroom. Since the TFA program began in the fall of 1992, over a million men, women, and children in Africa have been affected (both directly and indirectly) by the presence of IFESH teachers in rural and urban areas in Africa.

The Sullivan Plan will replicate the TFA program in many parts of Africa to alleviate the educational crisis. This plan will be built on the experiences and resources that have been acquired from the existing IFESH programs. During the next fifteen years, the Sullivan Plan will recruit and place ten thousand credentialed teachers, education administrators, and university professors from all over the world, including Europe, North America, and Africa to help alleviate problems of teacher shortages and the larger educational crisis in Africa with the goal to improve the teaching skills of five hundred thousand teachers in African nations. In all, ten thousand schools, over the next ten years will be built. Experienced educators who are retired or on sabbatical will work to improve the educational systems in sub-Saharan African countries that have requested assistance. Some educators will be in the classrooms filling vacancies within the school system, assisting local teachers in improving their pedagogy, updating course contents, and improving work plans. Educational administrators will also provide technical assistance in the areas of office management, administration, proposal development, curriculum development, enhancing and updating course content, and resource mobilization. University professors will teach and fill specific vacancies that exist in the university system. The technical assistance extended by the teachers in educational and specialized disciplines will help strengthen the indigenous population's internal capacity for self-sufficiency and economic growth.

IFESH will work in collaboration with the African ministries of education by conducting needs assessments at the national and local level, identifying placements for teachers, developing program models, recruiting participants, coordinating the selection process, organizing orientation programs for the participants, reviewing the progress of the participants, visiting work sites, and maintaining a harmonious working relationship with all constituencies. The country representative in each participating country will coordinate logistical arrangements for the teachers and all the participants. He or she will be responsible for organizing in-country orientations, in-country transportation, and securing housing, visas, work permits, and other required necessities.

Promotion of Women's Education

Women play a critical role in sustainable development. Women constitute about one-fourth of the labor force in the industrialized world, and in sub-Saharan Africa, women produce, process, and market more than two-thirds of food and cash crops. Women also have the primary responsibility for the care of children, and especially in developing countries, many poor households are headed by women. In spite of the significant role that women play in development, many women, particularly in Africa, still lack access to education, vocational training, health education, and sufficient support to enhance their contributions to socioeconomic and political development. In almost all regions of Africa, for example, the primary-school enrollment rate for girls still lags behind that of boys. In addition, women often encounter barriers against entering the labor market because of poor health, high fertility rate, and cultural traditions. To improve family welfare, reduce poverty, and enhance women's earning potential, we must encourage the active participation of women in productive resources and the labor market.

Because of the critical role that women can play in the promotion of economic development, part of the overall goal of the Sullivan Plan is to assist women in several ways. First, efforts will be made to encourage the participation of African women in all the projects specified in this plan so as to enhance their productive capabilities. The Sullivan

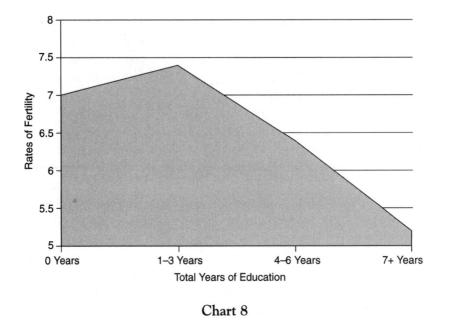

Total Years of Mothers' Education in Relation to Rate of fertility

Chart 8

Plan will seek financial support in terms of grants and loans to improve women's health and educational status. Much emphasis will be placed on women's education in this plan. As illustrated in chart 8, studies have shown the relationship between mothers' education and their rate of fertility. Mothers with one to three years of education have higher fertility rates than mothers with at least seven years of education. This implies that the more years of education a woman has, the less children she is likely to have. This plan will therefore encourage the education of women in sub-Saharan Africa. In addition to improving the quality of education in Africa, the Sullivan Plan will encourage the development of school curricula that encourage the recruiting and training of more female teachers, will establish more community-based schools, and will also schedule flexible classes to allow illiterate women to attend literacy classes.

Support of Sub-Saharan Africa Program (SOS)

In addition to educational training support to the disadvantaged schools in sub-Saharan Africa, the plan will encourage massive support throughout the United States for sub-Saharan Africa, especially among African Americans. With the expansion of the successful Support of Sub-Saharan Africa (SOS) campaign among African Americans and friends of Africa in the United States, millions of books and educational supplies for African schools have already been donated and shipped to schools in several African countries including Nigeria, Ethiopia, Liberia, Kenya, Benin, and Gabon. The Sullivan Plan will encourage the United States government and some private and public American institutions, along with those from other nations of the world, to get involved in this SOS campaign to help with the elevation and expansion of education for African children.

Schools for Africa Program

The Schools for Africa Program, which is now being implemented in many African countries by IFESH, will also be replicated in many other African countries. The Schools for Africa Program has already taken off in Sierra Leone, Zimbabwe, and South Africa, where schools have been constructed as part of the project to build one thousand schools for Africa. The schools are being built at a minimum cost from generous donors. This plan will encourage the building of thousands of two-classroom elementary schools in remote rural areas where there are not enough schools for the poor African children to attend. Millions of teaching supplies and, in the future, millions more will be sent to help the schools and children of all summit-cooperating nations.

At a higher education level, a number of well-equipped institutions of higher learning, such as colleges and universities, will be constructed in countries where there is no higher institution of learning, such as Gambia. The plan will also help to strengthen higher educational systems where education is facing a financial crisis. Some African universities, which have suffered deterioration due to this financial crisis, will be renovated and equipped with educational and learning facilities. This type of project has already started in Nigeria, where IFESH is working in collaboration with the World Bank to renovate six polytechnic schools in Nigeria.

Promotion of Educational Linkages
between the HBCUs and African Universities

In this plan, efforts will be made to create links between African universities and the historically black colleges and universities (HBCUs) in the United States. Studies have shown that the curricula of many HBCUs have been most suitable to the needs of African nations, particularly in agriculture. Many of these HBCUs in the United States will be encouraged to affiliate with some African universities during this plan. In the next fifteen years, the Sullivan Plan will call for partnerships with United States educational institutions that have educational institutions in Africa, making it possible for the development and improvement of African institutions to the highest levels with special emphasis on advanced teacher education. According to this plan, HBCUs will be placed in partnership with African institutions, along with the fullest involvement of other public and private colleges, universities, and medical institutions from the United States. This massive effort of partnerships in education should be supported by bilateral and multilateral organizations, along with the former colonial nations.

Scholarship and Faculty Exchange Program

Also, the plan will make efforts to encourage the establishment of regional community colleges in sub-Saharan Africa, most of which will be affiliated with HBCUs which have common specialties. The community colleges will be serving several local and rural communities in African countries. This program will also facilitate the exchange of teachers and students in both directions, encourage research programs between American and African universities, and introduce refresher training courses into the HBCUs for African university professors. Academic-year scholarships will also be provided to American scholars to study in African universities. Some Africans will also be assisted financially through scholarships to attend HBCUs for both degree pursuits and nondegree and short-term training programs for practical skills improvement. Funds will be provided to promote in-service teacher training. Joint projects between universities and the private sector for research and development of information technology and telecommunications will also be encouraged.

Books for Africa Program

Due to the acute shortage of educational materials afflicting most schools in sub-Saharan Africa, the Books for Africa Program will be strengthened to make more educational materials available to students on the continent. In this program, basic necessities such as books, pencils, desks, maps, and charts will be provided to African schools through donations. The program has already started in which tons of relevant textbooks, maps, and dictionaries have been shipped to Nigeria, Kenya, Ethiopia, and Benin. In the future, tens of millions of teaching supplies will be sent to help the schools and children of Africa.

Health

Statement of the Problem

Lack of an adequate and effective provision of primary health-care systems for the poor is a major problem in sub-Saharan Africa. Due to chronic malnutrition, caused by insufficient consumption of nutritious foods, Africa has the highest infant mortality rate in the world. According to UNICEF reports, the mortality rate among children under five years old in Sweden is less than 10 per 1,000 births, while in sub-Saharan Africa the figures range from 110 in Zimbabwe and Kenya to an appalling 300 per 1,000 in Angola, Mali, Sierra Leone, Chad, Ethiopia, Guinea, and Malawi.[11] The infant mortality rate is considerably higher among poorer households. Staple foods like beans, maize, and cassava are the daily diets for the poor. The absolute poor do not often include meat in their diets; eggs and milk are beyond the financial reach of many poor households, making their diets protein deficient.[12]

Another important element for maintaining good health, according to Christiaan Grootaert, is access to safe drinking water. But unfortunately, the degradation of fresh water resources is posing an increasing threat to the developmental process, particularly in the developing countries. Increased urban population and toxic waste dumps are polluting water and making water resources scarcer. Other various sources of groundwater pollution include landfills, toxic waste-injection disposal systems, and underground storage tanks for chemicals and petroleum.

In sub-Saharan Africa, for example, contaminated drinking water and poor sanitation contribute to infections and parasitic diseases that account for more than 62 percent of all deaths, twelve times the level in industrial countries. Polluted waters also cause roundworm infection with schistosomiasis especially in children. In Nigeria, for example, 640,000 cases of Guinea worm disease were reported in 1989. This number declined to 282,000 in 1991 as a result of improved water supply.[13] Onchocerciasis, usually referred to as river blindness, is a riverborne virus that causes permanent blindness in human beings. The disease is very common in the riparian communities of southwest Nigeria and the Volta basin in West Africa. Unfortunately, studies indicate that in 1988 only about 1 in 5 persons in Côte d'Ivoire had access to tap water from house connections or outdoor pipes.[14] The average walk for water in some villages is five miles each way. Because of poor nutrition and the lack of safe drinking water during their early years, children from poor homes are highly susceptible to common infectious diseases such as measles, kwashiorkor, guinea worms, malaria, bronchitis, and pneumonia.[15] Infant malnutrition and mortality rates are worse among absolute poor households with uneducated and unskilled mothers. In most of rural Africa where primary health care is lacking or inadequate, indigent young people at their prime age die or suffer from protracted illness due to preventable diseases. A sick head of a household with no access to medical care may prolong his or her inability to be productive and thus hinder his or her capability to support the family. A lack or shortage of primary health-care facilities, particularly in rural and urban areas, has increased death rates resulting from epidemic HIV/AIDS, which has continued to undermine the life and workforce of many African countries, especially among the low-income group. Studies indicate that two-thirds of all HIV/AIDS cases are believed to be located in sub-Saharan Africa (see chart 9). According to a WHO report on Africa, in early 1993 some 7.5 million adults were infected by HIV in cities, and 30 percent to 50 percent of beds in major hospitals were occupied by AIDS patients.[16] Of every 10,000 African women of childbearing age, 2,500, or one-fourth, are infected with HIV; this compares to 140 in North America, 70 in Western Europe, and 30 per 10,000 in Asia (see chart 10).[17] In fact, AIDS is now considered the number one killer of youth and adults in Uganda. Alerting the world about the devastating effects of AIDS in his country, President Museveni of Uganda has predicted

Global Cumulative AIDS (Adults and Children) Estimate Total (late 1996): 20 million

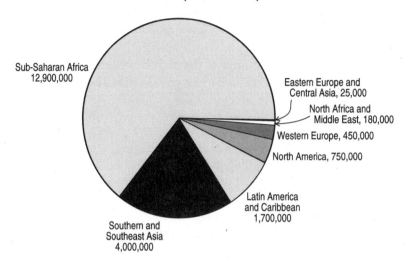

Chart 9

Estimated Cumulative HIV Infections in Women by Early 1994

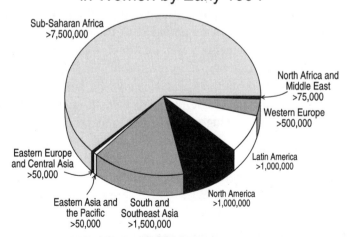

Chart 10

that AIDS will reduce Uganda's population, which is now seventeen million, to twenty million, instead of thirty-seven million, by the year 2015.[18] Unfortunately, World Bank statistics show a ratio of 1 physician to 300,000 people in sub-Saharan Africa, which means that, in their lifetime, many poor Africans will never have the opportunity to see a physician. Prostitution is the major cause of the spread of AIDS, and absolute poverty is the root cause of female prostitution in sub-Saharan Africa.

Planned Strategies

Based on the recommendations of the Health Commission of the African–African American Summit that convened in Atlanta, Georgia, from July 14 through July 16, 1994, which were approved at the Third African–African American Summit in Dakar, Senegal, in May 1995 and again in 1997 at the Harare Summit, the Sullivan Plan will focus on the use of appropriate health education for preventive, curative, and rehabilitative health-care services. Greater efforts will be given to the progress made in the control or elimination of endemic diseases in sub-Saharan Africa. This plan will be executed by African and African American experts, as well as by friends of Africa. The following programs will take priority.

Promotion of Maternal/Child Care and Health Education

The Sullivan Plan's major implementation strategy will focus on health education, which will be provided to the poor. The plan will give priority to the implementation of health-care programs for mothers and children, helping with the prevention, but also treatment, of the health problems of mothers and women who have no access to public health-care facilities. The plan will help to improve the quality of life for children through a reduction and prevention of child sickness and death. Mothers will be counseled in basic preventative health behaviors that save children's lives, including immunization, oral dehydration therapy, nutrition/growth monitoring, child spacing, and maternal health. The plan will also encourage low-risk pregnancy programs that will integrate pregnancy monitoring, effective pathological coverage, and deliveries assisted by qualified staff. Women will be trained in hygiene and family planning education. Also, women will be trained in different methods to improve the health of young children and their mothers by reducing morbidity and mortality due to malnutrition, diarrhea and dehydration, and immunizable diseases.

Also, emphasis will be placed on the retention of literacy skills by developing a curriculum geared toward the local setting and by having such professionals as health-care practitioners and extension workers include learning reinforcement techniques in their work with the rural population. The Sullivan Plan will make every effort to help organizations and communities who are disadvantaged, residents in rural and urban areas, women, and the marginally poor who are generally bypassed by the existing government and nongovernment initiatives.

Mobilization of Medical Support for Sub-Saharan Africa

To combat these endemic but preventable diseases such as malaria, HIV/AIDS, malnutrition, river blindness, diarrhea, maternal, and other diseases in sub-Saharan Africa, there will be a massive call on the private sectors in the medical industry, such as the pharmaceutical industries in the United States and other industrialized countries, to establish and provide clinics, hospitals, health outposts, drugs, medical equipment and personnel, and other health institutions in Africa. Medical schools, health training centers, medical doctors, nurses, and everybody in the allied health industry in the industrialized countries will be mobilized to get involved in the alleviation of health problems in sub-Saharan Africa. Donor groups, corporations, and individuals will be encouraged to work with nongovernmental organizations (NGOs) to contain epidemic diseases in sub-Saharan Africa. Some African health institutions will be affiliated with some American universities. For example, public health training at the Institute for Health and Development of Cheikh Anta Diop University in Senegal has begun and is connected to two American universities: Tulane University in New Orleans, Louisiana, and the School of Medicine of Morehouse, Atlanta, have already been exchanging professors, students, and programs. Building on this existing experience, the Sullivan Plan will create and reinforce the exchange of experiences and the joint preparation and implementation of an education and research program to encourage the exchange of pedagogical materials of students and professors. This will also encourage support from the American and African and other educators for the dissemination of scientific information among and between African and American medical institutions.

River Blindness Containment Program

Since 1989, IFESH has been implementing river blindness projects in Africa. The foundation has implemented a river blindness project at the University of Ibadan in conjunction with the government of Nigeria with a grant from Merck & Company and the foundation's Debt for Development Program. The project involves rapid community diagnosis of onchocerciasis, establishing ivermectin distribution centers at village sites, and preventative health education. Health-education classes have been established in six villages of Ibadan, and an ivermectin distribution schedule has been developed by the university, which extends beyond the immediate project area and is expected to reach two hundred thousand persons over a three-year period.

HIV/AIDS Containment Program

A pilot program aimed at the containment of HIV/AIDS has already been planned for several African countries by IFESH in conjunction with officials from WHO and the Centers for Disease Control and Prevention in Washington, D.C. The Sullivan Plan will build on this project to contain the spread of HIV/AIDS in African countries. The plan will combine multilateral, bilateral, and debt conversion programs for the control of HIV/AIDS in sub-Saharan Africa.

To combat the spread of HIV/AIDS in Africa, the Sullivan Plan will take a multidimensional approach. The plan will equip communities to develop and implement AIDS prevention and control projects, using the existing social networks of infrastructures, strengthen the capacity of existing self-help and community infrastructures, and facilitate initiatives to care for people living with HIV/AIDS and their families.

The ultimate goal of the plan is the prevention of new HIV infections among the African population. Therefore, promoting safer sexual behaviors among community members will be the focus of the priority interventions. The plan will encourage the limitation of the number of sexual partners, the consistent and correct use of condoms by those who engage in sexual relations that carry the risk of HIV, and delaying the onset of sexual intercourse by young people who have not yet experienced sexual intercourse. Given that certain segments of the population are too poor to buy the supply of condoms they need, the plan will also support the strengthening of the free distribution system to meet their needs.

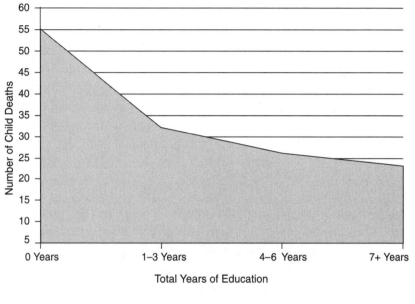

Total Years of Mothers' Education and Deaths of Children under Five Years

Chart 11

The plan will also mobilize the communities, country by country, to actively participate in the campaign against the spread of the deadly disease. The idea is to make people understand the ways in which the disease can be spread and prevented. To accomplish this strategy, the plan will encourage the strategy of working through existing social networks and institutions such as community leaders, indigenous organizations, schools, and churches to brief them on the importance of the AIDS epidemic so as to get their support in the development of programs for its control and prevention.

Skills Training Program for Women

Studies have shown the relationships between the level of mothers' education and the infant mortality rate. Mothers with at least seven years of education have a high probability of reducing the number of child deaths from 60 to about 25 per thousand (see chart 11).

To achieve this goal of reducing the infant mortality rate, women's education through literacy tied to health education will be encouraged in the rural areas. Women will be trained in income-generating skills to support their families. In other words, in an effort to help with capacity building in sub-Saharan Africa, the plan will encourage the development of microenterprises for women. Under this program, local grassroots people, particularly women, will be trained to operate small businesses that are suitable for the local environment. The program will emphasize business plan development, project management, production, marketing, technical skills, accounting, and reinvestment.

Family Planning Program

A family planning program will be another cornerstone of the Sullivan Plan during this implementation period. In collaboration with African governments, developmental organizations from America, and other experts, the plan will develop programs for the control of sexually transmitted and waterborne diseases in sub-Saharan Africa. These programs will be implemented with the participation of the beneficiaries from the program, particularly the indigenous people. This approach will facilitate understanding the sociocultural factors that cannot be obscured in an operation based on the concept of partnership. Most importantly, the implementation of health-care services will work with the traditional medicine, wherever possible, which has proved very beneficial to the indigenous people for so many decades in sub-Saharan Africa.

Provision of Safe Drinking Water

The provision of safe drinking water is crucial not only to the prevention of waterborne diseases but also for human survival and economic development. As such, the Sullivan Plan will focus on how to improve water needs in sub-Saharan Africa. The plan will explore how appropriate water technologies can be used to provide water resources for both domestic and industrial uses through low-cost techniques, water distribution, and conservation. The plan will utilize part of the debt conversion proceeds to dig wells in local communities where there is no access to clean drinking water. International donors will be encouraged to provide water to the needy. IFESH has already started such projects in many African countries, particularly in Nigeria.

In collaboration with the World Bank, about fifty thousand wells are being dug in northern Nigeria for irrigational and agricultural projects. The projects will not only provide adequate water for domestic uses and irrigation but will also help to contain the spread of the Saharan desert into the northern part of Nigeria.

Population

Statement of the Problem

The most serious single problem confronting the human race today is the rapid increase in the size and growth of the human population. In many cities, the effects of rapid population growth can be seen or felt in the overcrowded schools, overcongested highways and roads, the conversion of more land to freeways and buildings, the pollution of air and water, the disappearance of forests and vegetation, starvation in developing countries, a scarcity of housing, an increasing rate of unemployment, and rural-urban migration. The world population is now about 6 billion, and it is still increasing by 100 million people a year. It is projected that in the next four decades, sub-Saharan Africa's population may rise from 600 million to 1.5 billion, Asia's from 3.1 billion to 5.1 billion, and Latin America's from 450 million to 750 million.[19] It has also been projected that by the year 2000, there will be over twenty-one cities in the world with more than 100 million inhabitants, with about three-quarters of them located in the developing countries. As a result of rapid population growth, infrastructural facilities, land, and resource management systems may be unable to adapt fast enough to prevent overuse and land degradation. The governments, especially in the poor countries, may not be able to keep up with the infrastructural and basic human needs of a rapidly growing population.

Many people in sub-Saharan Africa have persistently suffered from starvation as a result of a rapid growth in population. High population density can lead to deforestation, depletion of water resources, overgrazing of grassland, soil erosion, and the loss of natural habitat. As a result of the population increase, there has been much devastation of land due to overuse and animal grazing on the limited natural vegetation, causing people and livestock to move northward and southward. It has been admitted that the domestic livestock population in the Sudanese province of the Kodofan region on the Sahara fringe in North Africa has quadrupled between 1957 and 1980. This type of intensity and pressure in semidesert vegetation often results in the destruction of plant cover and exposes the base soil to serious wind erosion, which gives more opportunity for the Sahara desert to expand. As a result of rapid population growth, the United Nations Food and Agriculture Organization (FAO) reported that about 80 percent of Africa's pasture and range areas show signs of damage due to excessive cutting of trees for firewood and failure to replace them. More than 250,000 acres of farmland in West Africa are lost to desert each year. If this trend of desert expansion continues unchecked, it is clear that by the year 2100, the present Republic of Sudan in North Africa might be rendered uninhabitable for human beings as a result of plant and soil destruction.

Several factors contribute to rapid population growth, particularly in the developing countries. These include improved health conditions, which are lowering death rates, the attitudes of some minority groups in many countries, who denounce the use of family planning as genocide against their ethnic groups, and some opposition from certain religious groups denouncing birth-control methods as sinful to God. In sub-Saharan Africa, the average number of children per woman is 6.5, compared to less than 4 in industrialized countries. In some African societies, for example, couples tend to have a preference for male children, and for this reason, some women may not stop having children until they have a satisfactory number of male children. Having male children in some African societies is considered to be very important because men are believed to have the responsibility of carrying forward the family traditions, while women have more responsibilities to their husbands' families. Polygamy is another factor that influences men to have many children. Also, because of the high rate of infant mortality, some traditional women tend to maintain high fertility rates because fertility enhances both female and male status in many African societies. Infertility can be socially and economically devastating to some African women. This is because most women use their children as their social security as they grow older and become unable to provide for themselves. In spite of the problems arising from the rapid population growth, there are still some people who do not agree that overpopulation is the main cause of environmental degradation and poverty in developing countries. The real problem, they claim, is the lack of proper management of global resources, not the number of people.

If something is not effectively done to curtail the rising population in the next fifteen years, there will be devastating consequences, such as an increase in land fragmentation resulting in lower agricultural productivity in developing countries. Overpopulation may lead to overutilization of agricultural and grazing land, which will in turn lead to the migration of cattle and people to other parts of the region. Overpopulation on a limitedly arable land may lead to high unemployment rates, more frequent famines, and abject poverty in sub-Saharan Africa.

Planned Strategies

Establishment of Vocational Training Institutions for Women

Education is the most effective weapon for reducing rapid population growth. In fact, improving education for women is the most important long-term environmental policy for reducing rapid population growth and environmental degradation in the developing world. Formal or informal education systems, if used very effectively, can promote later marriage and lower fertility rates among educated women (see chart 8, above p. 252). Studies have shown that a secondary-school education can reduce, on average, from 7 to 3 the number of children a woman is likely to have in the developing countries. Investment in female education can also increase the income of the poor household through employment opportunities. Educated women will be more likely to have access to family planning services than uneducated women. Better educated women have more chances of raising healthy and educated children than the uneducated. Scholarship programs for women will encourage women enrollment in schools.

Family Planning Program

This plan will encourage women's education in schools and colleges. Literacy classes tied to health, such as family planning and skills training in income-generating activities, will be introduced. The Schools for Africa Program will be expanded to accommodate more female schoolchildren. Health-education centers will be provided to teach family planning. Experts and educators from the United States will be encouraged to work with women on lowering fertility, child spacing, and proper health care. Seminars and workshops will be organized to discuss issues related to women.

Organizing Regional Conferences and Seminars on Population Control

Regular regional conferences and international seminars will be set up as part of a strategy to create an awareness among African people, especially women, about the dangers of rapid population growth. Women will play a prominent role in the seminars and workshops of such conferences. Experts on population issues, including prominent scholars, activists, politicians, religious leaders, and many other leading personalities, will be invited to share their views on how to curtail rapid population growth in Africa. The plan will also work through existing facilities and infrastructures such as community leaders, churches, indigenous organizations, local NGOs, and governmental institutions for the promotion of the campaigns against overpopulation.

Agriculture

Statement of the Problem

Based upon recent studies, the agricultural sector still remains the most important sector in the African economy. In spite of its low productivity, agriculture still employs over 70 percent of the population in sub-Saharan Africa. Besides Nigeria, Congo, and Gabon, which are the major oil-exporting sub-Saharan African countries, the majority of the foreign exchange earned by many sub-Saharan African countries is derived from agricultural related exports. Yet, due to several environmental problems such as deforestation, desertification, soil degradation, the loss of biodiversity, and an increasing scarcity of water resources, recurrent hunger and famine continue to threaten millions of Africans today.

Low agricultural productivity contributes to the problem of hunger, malnutrition, and unemployment in Africa. The agricultural output per worker in many African countries is less than 10 percent of that of most industrialized countries. In Africa, failure to utilize resources such as human labor and arable land is the immediate cause of structural poverty. The outdated, traditional shifting-cultivation and subsistence methods of growing food are still widely practiced by many African farmers. These methods are employed without the use of modern agricultural tools, soil-enriching products, or pest- and weed-control products, and there is no adequate scientific research to improve seed varieties. The lack of scientific research to improve agricultural technology for small-scale farmers and the lack of technically trained personnel and facilities to assist farmers contribute to low agricultural productivity. These problems have resulted in severe food shortages and in hunger.[20]

During the Commission on Agriculture planning meeting of the African–African American Summit in Kampala, Uganda, from November 3 through November 4, 1994, the commission members, who were among the best-known professionals and experts in agriculture and related fields, were dismayed at the dismal performance that the agricultural sector in Africa has experienced in recent years. The experts agree that there is a total absence of infrastructural facilities, such as roads, storage facilities, and processing plants, to support the demand for a strong agricultural program. Per capita food production has decreased in sub-Saharan Africa. Owing to a lack of financial resources, not enough emphasis has been placed upon research, transportation, or policy development, leaving most sub-Saharan African countries with programs that do not meet the acceptable living conditions of most people. The challenges facing agriculture in sub-Saharan Africa can be summarized as follows:

- inadequate management of their natural resources and insufficient safeguards in the food production environment;

- inappropriate and insufficient production of adapted and cost-effective technologies;

- the lack of basic rural infrastructures to support modern agriculture;

- the virtual nonexistence of postharvest technologies to curtail crop losses and food wastage;

- limited market opportunities to promote interregional trade and international trade links;

- insufficient agricultural support services to back up agro-financial institutions, farmers' associations, and agricultural input delivery system;

- inadequate technical and socioeconomic human capacities for generating needed technologies and making necessary innovations and discoveries to enhance food productivity.

Planned Strategies

Sub-Saharan Africa has the capability not only to feed itself but in future years to become the breadbasket for the world. It is the summit's plan, looking ahead in the next fifteen years, to multiply by at least fivefold the food production in sub-Saharan Africa and to make sub-Saharan Africa a major competitor with and food exporter for other parts of the world.

Promotion of Agribusiness in Africa

The Sullivan Plan will encourage and mobilize multinational institutions, private businesses, universities with good records in agricultural training programs, NGOs with developmental programs in agriculture, and individuals from America and other parts of the world to improve the agribusiness potential in Africa through the implementation of the following objectives:

- support of agricultural research and appropriate technology;
- establishment of agro-financial institutions and businesses in agricultural delivery systems;
- improvement of food processing and packaging;
- improvement of food transport, animal husbandry, fish farming, etc.;
- introduction of appropriate technological development and natural resource management;
- provision of training facilities to farmers.

Education and Research Development

The Sullivan Plan believes that if the living conditions of most African people are to improve, greater emphasis must be placed on education and research development to increase farm productivity, food security, and water management. Therefore, during the implementation period, the plan will develop agricultural training programs to assist in increasing farm productivity, village income, and community living standards. The plan will promote and encourage local self-help and self-reliance, assist in long-term self-sustaining agricultural development, develop and implement demonstration projects utilizing local resources, train local farmers on how to improve farm productivity, and cooperate with local governments' agricultural development efforts in participating countries.

Promotion of Agro-Financial Institutions

Realizing the importance of capital investment in agriculture, the Sullivan Plan will encourage the establishment of African agro-financial institutions and businesses in agriculture for delivery systems and to empower and motivate local farmers in increasing agricultural productivity. These institutions will be encouraged to provide financial support in term of credits and tools to the farmers so as to enable them to increase their productivity.

During this twenty-year plan, massive developmental efforts in agriculture will be initiated and mobilized to improve agricultural productivity in sub-Saharan Africa. The Sullivan Plan will make every effort to develop partnerships with the African governments to fully encourage the private sector to support research and technological development in sub-Saharan Africa.

Introduction of Appropriate Technology

One of the frequent solutions to the joint food-labor constraint has been the introduction of mechanical implements to increase output per unit of labor. These implements vary from simple hand-powered devices to sophisticated engine machinery. To achieve sustainable agricultural development, greater emphasis will be placed on the development of appropriate technology that people can operate, fix, and maintain by themselves. Studies have shown that capital-intensive technology based largely on imported inputs in agriculture is not suitable for the African environment. For example, although tractors have generally proven well adapted to large-scale, Western-style commercial farming, their role in African small-holder agriculture is inappropriate. The use of tractors in many parts of Africa can bring many problems, including the high capital costs of the equipment and herbicides, the high overhead involved in maintaining and servicing the underutilized machinery, the administrative problems in sharing a limited number of machines among a large number of diverse users, and the technical difficulties of using tractors under certain topographical and soil conditions.

Multinational corporations who have appropriate technologies will be encouraged to continue to provide continuous technical support to indigenous agricultural research, agricultural tools, equipment, and seed production. This Plan will encourage the use of plows, oxen, weeders, and carts to increase labor productivity. The investment cost for a pair of oxen and a plow is much lower than for a tractor. Such technologies, science, and research will be utilized to contain the expansion of drought, desertification, and deforestation in most part of sub-Saharan Africa. The use of such appropriate technologies will be encouraged in order to find permanent solutions to the scarcity of clean water for domestic and industrial uses.

But these business plans for the highest technology must also be developed now for African countries and implemented and followed as soon as practicably possible in order for African countries to become fully competitive with other nations of the world in the twenty-first century.

Adoption of New Agricultural Policies

The plan cannot be successful unless the governments of the participating countries are involved in its planning and implementation. The Sullivan Plan will encourage the governments of the participating sub-Saharan African countries to modify their existing agricultural policies in removing trade barriers within and between African states and with the industrialized countries.

Agricultural Skills Training Program

The Sullivan Plan will work with African governments to encourage, through developmental programs, the diversification of African agricultural products in relation to the existing processing plants for agricultural foodstuffs via the creation of breeding farms, the establishment of farm-product trading centers, the preservation of the forests, and the establishment of fishing industries.

In collaboration with other agricultural institutions, the Sullivan Plan will promote technical and socioeconomic human-resource capacities at all levels, including training of farmers and particularly women farmers who are responsible for more than 80 percent of food production in many sub-Saharan countries. Also included in this plan are activities such as a commodity exchange program, the training of farmers in agricultural techniques, health education, farmer-to-farmer initiatives, computerized genetic education, and genetics for food productivity.

The Sullivan Plan also envisions a farmer-to-farmer program that will bring together five hundred farmers from the United States and other nations, mostly African Americans, with five hundred farmers from Africa to improve farming capacities and capabilities throughout sub-Saharan Africa, leading to the development of tens of thousands of improved farms — small and large — throughout the region using the latest and best technical and agricultural resources: seed, fertilizer, equipment, and the most modern know-how, as well as the appropriate use of traditional methods

In all, the Sullivan Plan intends a renaissance in African agriculture to help feed the population that will grow to more than one billion by the year 2010 and two billion by the year 2030. Every use and resource to be made available to assist African agricultural development and growth will be sought from international agencies and organizations, such as the United Nations, the World Health Organization, the Food and Agriculture Organization, the World Bank, and the International Monetary Fund, and from developed countries of the world, especially the United States. Beginning in 1999 a Farmers for Africa program will be launched from the United States that will engage the participation of one thousand farmers from Africa and the United States from 1999 to the year 2010. The Farmers for Africa program will be assisted with training from major universities and colleges in the United States engaged in agricultural training and education, with particular participation of historically black institutions in America, and will make extensive use of training institutions dealing with agriculture established in Africa in order to assist with expansion and help with modern technical capabilities for farming. The Farmers for Africa program foresees an exchange process bringing African farmers to America and other developed countries for practical studies and assistance and partnerships with American farmers, especially African American, and farmers from America spending a month to six weeks in Africa with African farmers to help train farmers in Africa with technical and practical skills for the enhancement and development of farming in Africa.

The Sullivan Plan for agriculture in sub-Saharan Africa calls for by the year 2010 tens of thousands of farms — individual, village, and commercial — in numbers and sizes equal to those already being developed in many developing countries with support of the United States, Europe, Asia, the United Nations, the World Bank, and other supporting world agencies and organizations. It is intended in the next decade that African farming will be developed to assure adequate food supply in developing African countries during the coming period of extraordinary population growth.

Business and Industries

Statement of the Problem

Since the beginning of human history, bartering, trading, business, and work have been the basis of human development and advancement, from the days of the accumulation of stones for wealth and the trading of fish and animals for food. Without trade and business, no people can survive. Without business development on a grandiose scale, the nations of sub-Saharan Africa cannot compete in the future with the rest of the world. Since the first meeting in Abidjan, Côte d'Ivoire, of the African–African American Summit in 1991, a major focus of the summit has been on the development and creation of businesses in various African countries. Economic development is at the forefront of all summit activities.

Africa is a land of opportunity. An entire continent is waiting to be developed. There is business to be done and money to be made for both Africa and America. There are cities to be expanded and built, a need for roads, electrification, telecommunication systems, irrigation, banking, food production, factories, schools, hospitals, environmental programs, tourism, and unlimited investment opportunities, all leading to the creation of untold numbers of new businesses and jobs for Africa, America, and elsewhere. Prospects are now especially bright, with technical and other assistance from the new South Africa. America, by helping Africa to become strong and competitive, will help itself with new jobs, more trade, more business, a greater availability of natural resources for industrial and military needs, and a closer tie to a valuable and pivotal geographic region in a volatile, dangerous, and politically unsettled world. In the future, America will need Africa as a friend. As unbelievable as it may seem, Africa can be as important to American business as Europe, the Middle East, and South America.

More and more African nations, once saddled by colonialism, some by debt burden, and some by heavy dictatorial and selfish rule, are supporting open- and free-market principles and the promotion of democracy, human rights, and democratic values; this is the time for America to show its economic and moral strength to help with the development of a struggling continent that is striving to rise and move ahead. Assistance to Africa for education, businesses, jobs, human development, and democracy is a challenge for America that must not pass.

Country	Market	Market Capitalization	# of Listed Companies
1. Botswana	Stockbrokers Botswana Ltd.	$336 million	9 (1993)
2. Egypt	Cairo Stock Exchange	$1.8 million	573 (1990)
3. Côte d'Ivoire	Abidjan Stock Exchange	$567 million	23 (1991)
4. Ghana	Ghana Stock Exchange	$68.8 million	12 (1992)
5. Kenya	Nairobi Stock Exchange	$647 million	53 (1993)
6. Mauritius	Stock Exchange of Mauritius	$294 million	80 (1988)
7. Morocco	Morocco Stock	$1.5 billion	87 (1991)
8. Nigeria	Nigerian Stock Exchange	$1.2 billion	145 (1993)
9. South Africa	Johannesburg Stock Exchange	$171 billion	728 (1993)
10. Swaziland	Swaziland Stockbrokers	$39 million	6 (1992)
11. Tunisia	Tunis Stock Exchange	NA	25 (1994)
12. Uganda	Uganda Stock Exchange	NA	NA
13. Zimbabwe	Zimbabwe Stock Exchange	$820 million	60 (1993)

Chart 12

African economies are dependent economies. Their economies are primarily agricultural with a focus on the export of raw materials to the developed countries. Some of them depend on the export of mineral resources for about 80 percent of their national revenues. However, as a result of unfavorable terms of trade with the industrialized countries, African economies have remained unstable in the postindependence period. The prices for African commodities remain unstable in the world market.

The implementation of the Structural Adjustment Program (SAP) in African countries has not alleviated poverty and suffering among the poor. In many African countries, the implementation of the SAP has had devastating effects on the poor people. The SAP has drastically devalued African currencies, increased the inflation rate, worsened the standard of living, caused a high rate of unemployment through retrenchment, and lowered the quality of education.

The absence of capital markets in most African countries, coupled with limited indigenous professional security brokers at the management level, is a major barrier to economic development in Africa. For example, only thirteen of the fifty-four countries in Africa have active capital markets (see chart 12). Without capital markets accompanied by a high level of African professional brokers, consultants, managers, and directors to organize and coordinate markets, these countries cannot benefit from the foreign investments necessary to move their economies forward. Furthermore, the tremendous potential for intra-African trade is being wasted because the markets are neither coordinated nor organized.

Planned Strategies

During the implementation period, the Sullivan Plan will develop strategies to encourage social development, capital investment, the expansion of the banking system's capacity, the creation of market economies, and the revitalization of human resources to ensure effective, indigenous, and sustainable development.

Creation of Jobs

What has to be realized by the United States and other countries is that the economic developmental growth and the growth of sub-Saharan Africa will accrue to the benefit not only of Africa but of all the participating developing countries. It is our plan in the next fifteen years through the efforts of the African–African American summits to help with the development of businesses of all kinds at all levels throughout the sub-Saharan region. The Sullivan Plan will encourage the creation of two million new industrial, manufacturing, and agricultural jobs for Africans in sub-Saharan Africa. During this implementation period, two hundred thousand additional new jobs will be created and developed in America and other nations in support of sub-Saharan African business initiatives and development.

Promotion of Business Opportunities

One of the first priorities of the plan is to create an enabling environment that will encourage an expansion of investments in sub-Saharan Africa to stimulate economic growth throughout the region. The plan will encourage African Americans and other friends of Africa through the African–African American summits to expand their investments and commercial transactions in Africa from other parts of the world and to consider seeking new businesses and industrialization opportunities on the continent, especially through joint ventures. To accomplish this, African governments will be encouraged to initiate conducive and appropriate economic policies and regulations governing tariffs, import and export policies, adequate infrastructures, technology transfer, and exchange rate policies so as to encourage new investments into their economies. These policies will offer new incentives that will facilitate an appropriate environment for new business opportunities for joint ventures, particularly for African Americans to invest in sub-Saharan Africa. Regional cooperative trade among African countries such as ECOWAS, ECA, SADC, and ADB will be encouraged.

Introduction of New Financial Adjustments

The Sullivan Plan will help induce African countries to implement new financial adjustment programs. Because the existing structural adjustment program has not worked to the advantage of the common people in sub-Saharan Africa, the plan will work aggressively towards the elimination of the bilateral, multilateral, and commercial debt of African countries. To improve banking and financial institutions in the next fifteen years in sub-Saharan Africa, the Sullivan Plan will replicate the successful African Bankers Training Program, which has already trained about 250 African midlevel bankers from nine African countries in the last three years. These trained bankers are now back to their countries helping to improve the financial institutions. This experience has convinced IFESH that a systematic approach is needed to assist banks in sub-Saharan Africa to strengthen the financial and management skills of their professional staff. The African Bankers Training Program is a banking and management short-term course for midlevel African bankers and financial professionals in Africa.

The course will be targeted to reach midlevel bankers who have the potential to move to senior management positions. The course will be taught in the United States over a period of approximately five weeks. During the training, the participants will be introduced to the U.S. banking system and other components of the course, including accounting, auditing, budgeting, credit and risk analysis, fundamentals of management and supervision, strengthening leadership skills, and case studies based on current issues within the banking community in Africa. In addition to lectures, case studies and role playing will be used to allow participants to utilize the concepts and processes discussed in the course.

During the training period, IFESH will engage the services of major financial institutions with banking experience in Africa to conduct the classroom portions of this course. All logistical arrangements for this program will be coordinated by IFESH, including recruitment, notification of selections, travel arrangements, contracting faculty, site selection, and lodging.

Promotion of Capital Markets

Business development will not succeed unless it is backed up by a viable, functioning financial system. In order for sub-Saharan African countries to benefit from foreign investments, the Sullivan Plan will encourage the development of active securities, capital market, and brokerage management-training programs. The establishment of training programs in the stock exchange will be encouraged in selected sub-Saharan African countries for hundreds of professional, indigenous African personnel in the finance sector, capital market, and stock exchange profession. As a short-term training program, it will provide technical, practical, and regulatory knowledge in the arenas of raising capital; understanding brokerage operations, international securities, and equity instruments; accounting and auditing; rural finance; and methods of trading securities. In the program, participants will also be introduced to the theoretical and practical aspects of capital and equity markets and stock exchanges, the need for regulatory oversight and how it functions, the need for free markets, and methods for attracting foreign investment. The training program will encourage indigenous African enterprises over the next fifteen years.

Promotion of Tourism

Realizing the role of tourism as a powerful element in development, the Sullivan Plan will encourage and mobilize African-American people and friends of Africa in the tourism business to promote Africa by organizing workshops and seminars to inform the American public and communities about the wealth and business opportunities in sub-Saharan Africa. This can be promoted through radio stations and televisions. Priorities will be given to Africans and African Americans who are already established in tourist businesses such as air and marine transport, hotel management, tourism, and the promotion of tourism.

Provision of Loans and Grants

Finally, grants will be provided to encourage income-generating community-based developmental projects in many rural African countries. The grants will be provided as seed money to generate small-scale income-generating businesses. The results of this initiative are expected to reduce absolute poverty among disadvantaged women, school dropouts, illiterates, and other poor people. Since 1984, IFESH has awarded more than one hundred grants for community-based developmental projects in sub-Saharan Africa. The grants have improved living conditions in most of rural Africa. The Sullivan Plan will continue with this successful experience.

Self-Help Investment Plan

One of the cornerstones of the Sullivan Plan is to encourage self-help investment projects that will be organized by the people themselves in individual communities throughout African villages and American cities and towns. The purpose of this plan is to help the economically disadvantaged community-based organizations to cultivate the habit of long-term savings and investment as well as business ownership.

Each local community-based organization will be encouraged to set its own investment objectives based on its community's characteristics, needs, and opportunities. Investment priority will be in basic needs such as income-generating ventures, small businesses, housing, food production, and other moderate income-yielding activities.

The Sullivan Plan will also develop a feeling for ownership at the community level. This will be done through personal savings and loans from local organizations, along with new investment plans involving tens of thousands of new investors for Africa.

Governance and Democracy

Statement of the Problem

There is a growing realization that economic reforms cannot be achieved without a much greater degree of decentralization and democratization in the political process. In most sub-Saharan African countries a high level of political instability and social alienation has impaired developmental efforts.

The political reforms being implemented in some African countries, especially with the development of multiparty systems of government, the extension of press freedom, and respect for human rights enforcement of the rule of law are commendable. In spite of the new political reforms being witnessed in many sub-Saharan African countries, political instability is still a major obstacle to development on the continent. There are many civil wars going on in many African countries including Angola, Sudan, Burundi, Rwanda, Somalia, Liberia, Sierra Leone, and Niger, where millions of lives have been lost and many developmental projects destroyed. There are boundary disputes between Nigeria and Cameroon. Nigeria is currently experiencing a very dangerous internal political turmoil among its more than four hundred ethnic groups. Some African countries are still ruled by the military institutions. Human rights abuses and lack of press freedom are still common in many sub-Saharan African countries. In many countries, trade unions are either driven underground, or their members are incarcerated.

The political liberalization spreading to sub-Saharan Africa in the last few years is encouraging, but fragile. Political liberalization must include massive economic support to sustain it. There is no guarantee that democratic societies will survive and eventually flourish without support for initiatives that address the pervasive poverty, lack of education, unemployment, and violence that afflict these nations in sub-Saharan Africa. A nation that respects and protects the rights of its own citizens to be educated and self-reliant is much more likely to develop peace and prosperity. In this regard all companies in African nations will be expected to follow the Global Sullivan Principles for equal opportunity, right of association, education, health, protection of the environment, and political justice and to work for the advancement of the culture of peace.

Planned Strategies

To make this Plan work effectively, unity and solidarity among sub-Saharan African countries are essential. Problems of the nations are so interrelated and similar that cooperation among the countries and leaders is imperative for effective and long-term, durable results.

Promotion of Political Reforms through the African–African American Summits

The ability of the African–African American summits to assemble large numbers of Africans, African Americans, and leaders of other countries presents a unique and classic opportunity for sub-Saharan African nations to participate in summit activities to plan and work together for the benefit of the African continent along with their friends and supporters, especially African Americans. The summit relies on the large-scale involvement and support of African Americans for the first time since slavery, helping with the needs of African societies, playing a vital role as direct supporters of their African motherland, and becoming a much-needed political catalyst in the United States to ensure greater attention and assistance from the United States government for Africa. Also a large-scale collective investment plan for Africa, involving thousands, will be launched.

Promotion of Regional Cooperation

The issue of political reform is very sensitive in Africa. The democratization process will take time to yield positive results. However, the Sullivan Plan will work at a high-level political profile with African leaders to introduce more political reforms. African leaders and governments will be encouraged to introduce more press freedom and free association and to stop human rights abuses.

In addition, future plans envision a new concord between sub-Saharan Africa and North Africa in a new alliance: an educational, technical, trade, and business alliance as is being seen today in Asia, Europe, and the Americas. Toward this end, historical, sectional, religious, and cultural barriers must be broken down, and a new spirit of unity and solidarity must be developed among all peoples of the African continent. The great and extensive capabilities of North Africa can help with formidable and enlightened technical assistance to a newly developing sub-Saharan Africa, with mutual benefits to the south and the north via trade, jobs, and increasing economic strength for both parts of what is presently a culturally and economically divided North and sub-Saharan Africa. The plan also encourages the use of the resources of America and other developed countries and other organizations, such as the United Nations and the Organization of African Unity, to help with conflict resolutions in sub-Saharan Africa, supporting the leadership of Africans.

Black Diaspora

Black people are spread all over the world. They are in South America, the Caribbean, North America, Australia, Asia, Europe, and

Africa. They must all assist in the development of Africa. All peoples need a base to advance. Africa is the base for people of African descent working for the development of Africa as well as for uplifting themselves.

African Americans in particular have economic leverage to help Africa. For example, the cumulative annual income for African Americans is more than the total annual income of Africans in all of sub-Saharan Africa. Therefore, African Americans have the economic power and technical expertise to help Africa. I strongly believe that the presence of blacks in the diaspora can be turned around to fulfill a purpose from God. Three decades ago, this view was expressed at the conclusion of my book *Build Brother Build*:

> When I plan for the future, my thoughts turn eventually to Africa. Somehow, I believe, slavery will be turned to the advantage of our future. The day will come when the continent from which my forefathers came will blossom into a paradise. I have a feeling that my ultimate freedom and my ultimate security are tied to the development of Africa. Of course, I have no intention of forsaking America, for America is my home and I have helped to build her and shape her. But like the Jews and others who came to make this country what it is, I need an anchor in the past, a place my children can proudly call their ancestral home. My citizenship is here, but a part of my spirit is in Africa, also.
>
> I envision a bridge from America to Africa over which one day my children and my black brothers and black sisters will move freely from one side to the other and back again. The Bible said, "The day will come when Ethiopia shall stretch forth her hands again," and I know that day is coming, though I shall not live to see it. The time is not far off when black technicians, artisans and craftsmen by the thousands and tens of thousands will visit a flourishing Africa, helping to mold that continent into a new greatness glorious to see.[21]

Dual citizenship first began in the Greek world to enable the people to keep hold of their original base. My interest in Africa is not a back-to-Africa idea, but the utilization of what we have. It is my hope and prayer that in future years thousands and tens of thousands will become dual citizens of different African countries in the next century. In the next twenty years, I strongly believe that Africa will become strong economically and politically. The brain drain, that is, the generations of sons and daughters who were forced into slavery, will come back to develop Africa. They will come in large numbers, bringing with them their expertise and developmental programs such as job creation, education, skills training, agriculture, science and technology, resource development, conflict prevention, trade, and investment.

I am pleased with the new trends toward positive development in Africa in the last decade, and it is time we stop perceiving Africa as a dark continent or a theater of violence. Many observers see the 1990s as a decade of democracy in Africa. Some of the positive events that are taking place in Africa convince me that there is hope for Africa and that her time has come to be reckoned with in the international community. Since 1990, and especially in the post-cold-war era, a wind of democracy has been blowing across the continent by which many African leaders have come to power through ballot box instead of coup d'état. In fact, in more than thirty African countries, democratic political systems have emerged, which have opened up economic and political opportunities for the development of the African people. On the economic front, the economic reforms being implemented by several African countries and encouraged by many international donors have not only made most African leaders accountable to their people, but such reforms have made international assistance conditional on good governance through open elections and the tolerance of opposition parties. Another area of improvement in Africa is peace and stability. Civil wars and armed conflicts that ravaged and devastated Mozambique, Liberia, Ethiopia, Angola, Rwanda, Somalia, Eritrea, and Sierra Leone during the 1980s and '90s are past, and these regions are once again beginning to experience peace and economic growth. Lastly, Africa is still very rich in mineral resources, including crude oil deposits, and especially human resources. The blacks in the diaspora should be encouraged by the current movements toward peace and development in Africa. The blacks in the diaspora, especially in the United States, should be encouraged to invest in Africa.

Efforts are underway in one hundred cities in the United States, in Caribbean nations, in Europe, and in South America to establish summit follow-up committees in the black diaspora to ensure the growing support and collaboration among the African heritage in assisting with the advancement of sub-Saharan Africa in education, health, business, women's programs, youth programs, and collaboration among youth in the diaspora. Also in the United States, the development of political empowerment to support sub-Saharan Africa must be promoted, as it must throughout the world diaspora. Assistance will be encouraged at city, state, congressional, and presidential levels to assist African countries in peace development and economic growth packages. The main objective of this collaboration among black diaspora countries is to develop global private and public support for sub-Saharan Africa as well as wide-scale assistance to sub-Saharan Africa by African Americans, in particular with respect to education, health, extensive investment, economic aid, and other human development assistance.

The Sullivan Plan must be seen only as a beginning, not as an end, to sub-Saharan African development and must be changed, depending on future and unforeseen needs necessary for the social, economic, cultural, and political advancement of sub-Saharan Africa.

All efforts should be made in tandem, with the fullest cooperation possible, with objectives and goals of the Organization of African Unity — which remains the most viable, African-led organization on the continent committed to African unity, development, and peace — and with continuing and special cooperation with the objectives of the United Nations, especially in development, human rights, and peace, which must be a reliable ally to Africa in all future developments regarding the Sullivan Plan.

Notes

1. Beverly A. Davies, *Preparing Black Children for School and Life: Guide for Parents and Educators* (Rochester, N.Y.: B. A. Davis and T. M. Associates, 1995), 17.

2. See Eric R. Wolf, *Europe and the People without History* (Los Angeles: University of California Press, 1982), 195–231.

3. Peter O. Paretti and Tweetie T. Wilson, "Unfavorable Outcomes of the Identity Crisis among African-American Adolescents Influenced by Enforced Acculturation," *Social Behavior and Personality* 23, no. 2 (1995): 171–76. See also Winthrop D. Jordan, *White over Black: American Attitudes toward the Negro, 1550–1812* (Chapel Hill: University of North Carolina Press, 1968), 3–34; George M. Fredrickson, *The Black Image in the White Mind: The Debate on Afro-American Character and Destiny, 1817–1914* (New York, Harper & Row, 1971), 1–42.

4. David T. Wellman, *Portraits of White Racism*, 2d ed. (New York: Cambridge University Press, 1993), 1.

5. World Bank, *Sub-Saharan Africa: From Crisis to Sustainable Growth: A Long Term Perspective Study* (Washington, D.C.: World Bank, 1989), 22.

6. See World Bank, *Education in Sub-Saharan Africa: Policies for Adjustment, Revitalization, and Expansion* (New York: Oxford University Press, 1989), 1–22.

7. World Bank, *World Development Report 1990: Poverty* (New York: Oxford University Press, 1990), 1.

8. World Bank, *Sub-Saharan Africa*, 22.

9. World Bank, *A New Agenda for Women's Health and Nutrition* (Washington, D.C.: World Bank, 1994), 22–27.

10. A. Tibaijuka, "The Impact of Structural Adjustment Program on Women: The Case of Tanzania's Economic Recovery Programme" (paper commissioned for the Commonwealth Expert Group on Women and Structural Adjustment, Dar es Salaam, Tanzania, 1988), 14.

11. Anthony O'Connor, *Poverty in Africa: A Geographical Approach* (London: Belhaven Press, 1991), 17.

12. *West Africa* (27 June–3 July 1994): 136.

13. World Bank, *Development in Practice: Better Health in Africa: Experience and Lessons Learned* (Washington, D.C.: World Bank, 1994), 31.

14. Christiaan Grootaert, "Poverty and Basic Needs Fulfillment in Africa during Structural Change: Evidence from Côte d'Ivoire," *World Development* 22, no. 10 (1994): 1530.

15. David A. Levitsky, "Malnutrition and Brains," *Development Digest* 16, no. 2 (1978): 3–9.

16. See Gwendolyn Calvert Baker, "Day of the African Child: June 16, 1995," *New York Amsterdam News* 86, no. 24 (17 June 1995): 1–2.

17. International Institute for Rural Reconstruction (IIRR), "AIDS in Africa," *International Institute of Rural Reconstruction Fact Sheet* (New York: IIRR, 1994).

18. *Africa Recover* (June 1991).

19. World Bank, *World Development Report 1992: Development and the Environment* (New York: World Bank, 1992), 7.

20. Jan Morris, *Extension Alternatives in Tropical Africa*, Overseas Development Institute, Agricultural Administration Unit, Occasional Paper 7 (Boulder: Westview Press, 1991); see also Bill Rau, *From Feast to Famine: Official Cures and Grassroots Remedies to Africa's Food Crisis* (London: Zed Books, 1991).

21. Leon H. Sullivan, *Build Brother Build* (Philadelphia: Macrae Smith Company, 1969), 178.

Appendix D

Summary of the Self-Help Investment Program (SHIP)

Concepts of SHIP

It is our view that the future development of SHIPs in cities and towns throughout the United States will become a major factor in inner-city and small-town revitalization and development. The Self-Help Investment Program (SHIP) is an investment corporation that will be organized in each of many cities and rural areas throughout the United States according to the Self-Help Investment Plan devised by the Reverend Leon Sullivan. The purpose of the plan is to help with community development and jobs to encourage a habit of long-term savings and investment and ownership from within economically disadvantaged communities, thereby serving the needs of the community and the nation. To the extent that SHIPs choose to invest in ventures involving Africa, that continent's needs will also be served.

Local SHIPs will be formed with advice and guidance from a national SHIP Support Committee. Each local SHIP will set its own investments in housing and small-business development. SHIPs will invest only in sound investment projects that are highly likely to realize a profit and to repay the SHIP's capital.

Captains and executive committee members of each local SHIP will be required to sign compliance agreements and to comply with state laws and guidelines to help ensure credibility, integrity, and the protection of investors.

Each member of a local SHIP must invest at least $1,000, but no more than $5,000, as a long-term commitment. Each investor must be a full-time resident of the state in which the SHIP is incorporated and must have a total household income of at least $30,000 annually.

The development of SHIP began in January 1994 in Philadelphia.

Friends of SHIP Fund

Parallel to this effort to organize local SHIPs, Reverend Sullivan also plans a Friends of SHIP Fund by which foundations, pension plans, and financially secure private investors who wish to assist the SHIP effort can participate while receiving returns on their investment. Friends of SHIP Funds would be organized locally to provide matching capital for one or more SHIPs operating in a particular city, region, or state. A Friends of SHIP Fund would also be organized on a national level to provide capital for particular types of investment anywhere in the United States or Africa. Friends of SHIP investors would specify in advance the locale and types of investments for which their funds would be used.

Investment capital provided by Friends of SHIP could be on an equity or debt basis. Banks and other financial institutions making loans to SHIP projects or directly to the SHIPs themselves would probably prefer that Friends of SHIP capital be provided as equity, or at least subordinated to the banks' own loans, since in the event of default loans are in a preferred position to equity if there are any assets to be disbursed. Injecting Friends of SHIP capital as equity, whether as a separate class of common or as preferred, would provide greater overall leverage for SHIPs since this method would lower the debt-equity ratios of the investment projects, but with a greater risk for the Friends of SHIP capital. Some prospective Friends of SHIP investors have stated a willingness, however, to be the last to be repaid, after the community SHIP investors.

Friends of SHIP investors, once the programs are fully in place, would hopefully receive approximately a 6 percent return on investment (either dividends or interest), deferred if necessary until after community investors have received their dividends. The public relations benefit of staying current in paying the 6 percent return to the Friends of SHIP investors would probably outweigh the small economic benefit of retaining the 6 percent in the Friends of SHIP Fund for reinvestment.

Attempting to use a single Friends of SHIP Fund to meet the needs and wishes of all potential friends of SHIP investors would probably create insurmountable legal problems, so a national and several local Friends of SHIP Funds would need to be created. It is anticipated that the national Friends of SHIP Fund may act in concert with one or more local Friends of SHIP Funds to finance a particular project secured from company pension funds, equity and municipal funds, churches, and individual investors.

A major local bank in the city of each SHIP would serve as trustee to administer the local Friends of SHIP Fund, ideally at no charge. A major regional or national trustee bank would administer the national Friends of SHIP Fund. The trustee banks would disburse investment capital only upon the recommendation of the Friends of SHIP Investment Committees. These committees would make all investment decisions for the Friends of SHIP Funds, following the dictates of each fund's charter (e.g., investments only within a particular state or only in housing, etc.). Each Investment Committee would comprise, at a minimum, a representative of the trustee bank and a representative of the Friends of SHIP investors.

Individual SHIP Member Stock Ownership Portfolios

SHIPs will also be encouraged to invest in blue-chip stocks listed on a major stock exchange. For example, a particular SHIP might decide to limit this portion of its investment portfolio to the companies in the Dow Jones index of thirty major companies.

Separate and apart from SHIP and Friends of SHIP efforts, the program also urges community residents to develop a feeling for ownership in American enterprise at the blue-chip level, for both educational and financial benefit and to become a voice in corporate America. Every member of a SHIP is encouraged to develop a personal stock portfolio covering major publicly traded companies by owning two, three, or more shares of a major company. Stock certificates printed with the investor's name would be sent directly to the investor.

Since stockbrokers generally prefer to handle a minimum of one hundred shares at a time, with large percentage commissions on odd-lot orders, special arrangements would have to be made with one or more brokerage firms such as Dreyfus and Merrill Lynch. In all likelihood, buy and sell orders would have to be routed to a single trading desk with a toll-free number. If the broker is willing to take phone calls from individual SHIP members and verify the names from a list provided by the SHIPs, that would be preferable. If not, the SHIP treasurers may have to collect orders monthly for forwarding directly to the broker or to some centralized intermediary. Perhaps SHIP members' buy and sell orders for their personal stock portfolios could be pooled with the SHIP's buy and sell orders. As an alternative, a similar arrangement might be negotiated with the blue-chip companies directly since the public relations value of this plan might be worth more to, say, IBM or General Motors than to an investment firm. This plan is not meant to discourage other blue-chip investments or the use of other stockbrokers; in fact, this will be encouraged as the individual investor becomes more comfortable with investing.

SHIP groups in 1998 were already underway and being developed in a number of cities — Philadelphia, Pa.; Providence, R.I.; New York, N.Y.; Detroit, Mich.; Saginaw, Mich.; Flint, Mich.; Toledo, Ohio; Milwaukee, Wis.; Baltimore, Md.; and Phoenix, Ariz. — to be expanded to one hundred cities and towns by 2000 with a goal of $250 million in new business and investments and development by 2005 and $1 billion by 2015.

COMPLIANCE AGREEMENT
between the
SHIP CAPTAIN
and the
NATIONAL COMMITTEE

I, _____ , agree to serve as the Captain of the Self-Help Investment Plan of _____ (hereinafter referred to as SHIP). As the SHIP Captain, I warrant the following are true and correct:

1. I will administer the SHIP according to the SHIP Operating Agreement and By-Laws. I will abide by the mandates of those agreements and in the event I find myself unable to do so, I will immediately communicate that fact to the SHIP Executive Committee and the National Committee.

2. I will be loyal solely to the interests of the SHIP investors.

3. I will be impartial regarding any conflicting or diverse interests of SHIP investors. In the event of a conflict of interest on my part, I agree to communicate that to the SHIP Executive Committee and the National Committee and will excuse myself from taking part in such a decision.

4. I will avoid conflicts and promise to engage in no "self-dealing" at any time.

5. I will control and preserve all SHIP documents and will dispose of only unproductive property.

6. I will identify assets of the SHIP as such and will insure the distinct separation of SHIP assets from any other assets.

7. I will enforce all claims of merit regarding SHIP assets or property against all others.

8. I will defend actions of merit regarding SHIP property.

9. I will not delegate my responsibilities regarding the SHIP. I agree to perform all acts required of me myself, and if I am unable to do so, I will appoint others approved by the SHIP Executive Committee and will supervise their performance.

10. I will exercise prudent care at all times regarding SHIP activities.

11. I will apply reasonable interpretation of all language as it pertains to the SHIP.

12. I will inform the SHIP members of investments, regardless of the nature of such activity.

13. I will provide periodic full accounting reports according to the recommendations or request of the National Committee.

14. I will report all receipts, disbursements, assets, deposits, and withdrawals on any and all SHIP accounts to the National Committee immediately upon their request to inspect any of the above.

15. I agree to exercise "good faith" and due diligence at all times.

I understand that if at any time my commitment to the performance of any of the provisions set forth above is not met, I may be asked by the SHIP Executive Committee or the National Committee to resign my duties as SHIP Captain.

_____

SHIP Captain

_____

The National SHIP Committee

Self-Help Investment Program (SHIP)
List of Interested Cities as of 1998

ALABAMA
Hillsboro
Hobson City
Hurtsboro
Lisman
Montgomery
North Courtland
Tuskegee

ARIZONA
Phoenix

ARKANSAS
Little Rock
Madison
Reed

CALIFORNIA
Los Angeles
Sacramento
San Diego
San Francisco
San Mateo

CONNECTICUT
New Haven
New London

FLORIDA
Daytona Beach
Eatonville
Fort Lauderdale
Greatneck
Miami
Quincy
South Bay

GEORGIA
Atlanta
College Park
Decatur
Doraville
East Point
Fairburn
Lithonia
Marietta
Riverdale
Roswell
Sneyma
Stone Mountain

ILLINOIS
Chicago
East St. Louis
Harvey
Robbins
Rockford
Springfield
Sun River Terrace

KENTUCKY
Covington
Lexington

LOUISIANA
Bastrop
Chaneyville
Chataignier
Cullen
Felton
New Orleans
Opelousas
Richwood

MARYLAND
  Baltimore
  Beltsville
  Bowie
  Columbia
  Fairmount Heights
  Forestville
  Issue
  Seat Pleasant
  Silver Spring
  Upper Marlboro

MICHIGAN
  Benton Harbor
  Detroit
  Flint
  Muskegon Heights
  Pontiac
  Saginaw
  Vandalia

MISSISSIPPI
  Arcola
  Hollandale
  Holy Springs
  Mayersville
  Rosedale
  Tuchula

MISSOURI
  Hayti
  Kansas City
  Sikeston
  Velda City

NEW JERSEY
  Camden
  Gibbonsboro
  Newark

NEW YORK
  Brooklyn
  Hempstead
  New York City

NORTH CAROLINA
  Charlotte
  Elm City
  Wilson

OHIO
  Cincinnati
  Columbus
  Fairfield
  Forest Park
  Springfield
  Toledo
  Urbancrest

OKLAHOMA
  Langston
  Oklahoma City
  Tatums

OREGON
  Portland

PENNSYLVANIA
  Chester
  Erie
  Harrisburg
  Philadelphia
  Pittsburgh

RHODE ISLAND
  Providence

SOUTH CAROLINA
  Anderson
  Atlantic Beach
  Columbia

Denmark
Ridgeville
Santee
Waterloo

TEXAS
Dallas
Houston
Paris
San Antonio

VIRGINIA
Alexandria
Dumfries
Lorton
McLean

Reston
Richmond
Vienna

WASHINGTON
Seattle
Yakima

WEST VIRGINIA
Charleston
Huntington
Fairmont

WISCONSIN
Milwaukee
Racine

Appendix E

Opportunities Industrialization Centers of America (Active and Developing)

ALABAMA
Montgomery

ARIZONA
Phoenix

ARKANSAS
Sparkman

CALIFORNIA
Los Angeles
Menlo Park
San Bernardino
San Fernando Valley

CONNECTICUT
Bridgeport
New Britain
New Haven
New London
Waterbury

FLORIDA
Ft. Lauderdale
Immokalee
Miami
St. Petersburg

GEORGIA
Atlanta

ILLINOIS
Chicago
Rockford

IOWA
Sioux City
Waterloo

LOUISIANA
New Orleans
Richwood

MARYLAND
Annapolis
Baltimore

MICHIGAN
Pontiac
Saginaw

MINNESOTA
Anishinabe
Bemidji
St. Paul

MISSOURI
St. Louis

MONTANA
Great Falls

NEBRASKA
Omaha

NEW JERSEY
Camden
Elizabeth
Paterson

NEW YORK
North Amityville
Syracuse

NORTH CAROLINA
Elizabeth City
Greenville
Kinston
Rocky Mount
Wilson

OHIO
Dayton
Springfield

OKLAHOMA
Oklahoma City

OREGON
Portland

PENNSYLVANIA
Carlisle
Harrisburg
Lancaster
McKeesport
Norristown
Philadelphia
West Chester

SOUTH CAROLINA
Columbia

SOUTH DAKOTA
Pine Ridge
Rapid City

TENNESSEE
Nashville

TEXAS
Austin
Corpus Christi
Dallas
Rio Grande Valley
San Antonio

UTAH
Salt Lake City

VIRGINIA
Richmond
Winchester

WASHINGTON
Yakima Valley

WASHINGTON, D.C.

WEST VIRGINIA
Charleston
Fairmont
Huntington

WISCONSIN
Beloit
Keshena
Milwaukee
Oneida
Racine

For further information concerning OIC, IFESH,
the African–African American Summit, and the SHIP program,
please write to:

Sullivan Programs
5040 E. Shea Boulevard
Suite 260
Phoenix, AZ 85254-4610

Index